David Hume: Moral and Political Theorist

David Hume:

Moral and Political Theorist

Russell Hardin

OXFORD
UNIVERSITY PRESS

OXFORD
UNIVERSITY PRESS

Great Clarendon Street, Oxford OX2 6DP

Oxford University Press is a department of the University of Oxford.
It furthers the University's objective of excellence in research, scholarship,
and education by publishing worldwide in

Oxford New York

Auckland Cape Town Dar es Salaam Hong Kong Karachi
Kuala Lumpur Madrid Melbourne Mexico City Nairobi
New Delhi Shanghai Taipei Toronto

With offices in

Argentina Austria Brazil Chile Czech Republic France Greece
Guatemala Hungary Italy Japan Poland Portugal Singapore
South Korea Switzerland Thailand Turkey Ukraine Vietnam

Oxford is a registered trademark of Oxford University Press
in the UK and in certain other countries

Published in the United States
by Oxford University Press Inc., New York

British Library Cataloguing in Publication Data
Data available

Library of Congress Cataloging in Publication Data
Data available

Typeset by Laserwords Private Limited, Chennai, India
Printed in Great Britain
on acid-free paper by
Biddles Ltd., King's Lynn, Norfolk

ISBN 978-0-19-923256-7

10 9 8 7 6 5 4 3 2 1

For Patrick Suppes
Humean by nature, sorely missed friend on a distant coast

Preface

When we read any theorist, and perhaps especially when a philosopher reads another philosopher, we often tend to take a strong critical stance and to pick the theorist apart. I have taken the view here that Hume's work should be considered from within. That is to say, if I find something that seems contrary or inconsistent, I struggle to give Hume the benefit of the doubt and to suppose I might actually be wrong. I have tried to have as nearly Hume's sensibility as I might be capable of, so that I attempt to read him without corrections that I think he would not have wanted to make and could have argued against. This often calls for generosity of interpretation. Fortunately, I find Hume's philosophical views and what I will call his social science very congenial, so that my generosity is not severely tested by the attempt to read Hume's arguments as I think he would read them.

Much of what he says is in a vocabulary that is not fully ours, and this for two reasons. First, Hume has such original and lively ideas that he often has to coin a vocabulary to cover them. He then does what theorists perhaps most often do: he borrows from the vernacular. But he gives the vernacular terms a precision and specificity that they do not have in the vernacular and probably have never had. His vernacular words cover some of his most important terms: sympathy, artificial, utility, convention.

Second, much of the vocabulary grows out of philosophical jargon of the century leading up to Hume. Hume adopts some of this jargon but often with a big twist, as in his use of the notion of virtue and the virtues. Some of the jargon is embedded in social and religious views that many of us do not merely not share, we cannot even, in Hume's term, feel sympathy for those who once held such views. To read the philosophers who set the table for Hume would require even more generosity than I mean to offer to Hume, more generosity than most of us could muster while reading views that are often objectionable and even outrageous with, for example, claims that some awful prejudice is in fact the product of reason.

There is another, perhaps even harder obstacle to reading Hume with any ease. His moral psychology and his social science are highly original and are a couple of centuries ahead of their time in that almost no one grasped many of his theoretical claims until recent decades. I address his basic psychological and strategic theories in chapters 2 and 3, respectively.

For almost all of the arguments here, I attempt to give license from Hume by citing where he specifically says what I claim is his view. One can readily bias any case by omitting passages that go against one's interpretation. And one cannot readily show that the general tenor of some part of the work is what one says it is. I trust that if I have omitted important contrary passages or if I have misread the tenor of Hume's work, I will be corrected. Someone writing fifty years ago on Hume's political thought could not have been so confident of being corrected. Political theorists should be glad of the growing attention to Hume and to its concomitant chance of criticism.

There is only one context in which I do not take Hume's statements as part of his theory, and that is when the statements are, by his own critical judgment, what he calls panegyric or, when they are longer, sallies of panegyric. I think it clear that he does not mean these statements of praise of substantive moral principles or of actions that have seemingly moral consequences to be part of his theory. Having the emotivist views in such panegyrics is predictable from his theory, and he has approbations of many things, just as his psychological theory says people must have. It would be odd if he held himself above his own social scientific theory, and he does not. But his approbations are not part of the content of a theory of morality.

Finally, two bibliographic notes. First, citations to Hume's two major works on morals follow the current practices of *Hume Studies*. Citations to the *Treatise of Human Nature* are in text and follow the format: (T3.2.2.9, SBN 489), where 3 is book 3; 2 is part 2; 2 is section 2; 9 is the paragraph number within section 2 as given in the version of the *Treatise* edited by Norton and Norton for the Clarendon Critical Edition of the works of Hume; and SBN 489 is the page number in the edition of Selby-Bigge and Nidditch, which was long the standard for work on Hume. Citations to the *Enquiry Concerning the Principles of Morals* are of the form (EPM2.3, SBN 177), where 2 is section 2; 3 is the paragraph number in the edition edited by Beauchamp; and again SBN 177 is the page number in the edition of Selby-Bigge and Nidditch. Citations to the *Enquiry Concerning Human Understanding* (EHU) follow a similar format. The somewhat random numbering of some paragraphs in SBN is not noted in the citations. All other works are cited in brief form in footnotes and more fully in the list of references. Citations to other traditional works that appear in many editions often follow roughly in the format of these works of Hume.

Second, I have cited many of Hume's shorter essays. About half of these essays are on political topics. The topics are quite varied and they do not present a systematic account of politics. Several are on economic topics, primarily about free trade and open markets, and several of these are acute and insightful in their economic principles. The longest of the essays is a historiographical discussion of the populousness of ancient nations; it displays Hume's empirical method at its best. The remainder of the essays are on literary and diverse other topics not especially relevant to the present book.

Acknowledgements

I wish to thank several classes over twenty years—at Chicago, New York University, and Stanford—for opportunity to explore Hume's and others' arguments toward an eventual plan to write such a book as this. I especially thank participants in my Stanford seminar on Hume during spring quarter 2003. Debates in that seminar were superb and I regretted the end of term that ended the discussions. I also thank the University of Bayreuth for sponsoring five lectures on Hume under the broad canopy of the annual Wittgenstein Lectures. I especially thank Rainer Hegselmann for inviting me to give those lectures and then for being one of the world's greatest hosts for a full week of lecturing, eating, and hiking. His colleagues and students made the week of lecturing and meeting with discussion colloquiums challenging and exciting. I am daunted at the thought of listening, as many of them did, to one person speaking for upwards of twelve hours in a single week.

For energetic research assistance, I thank Paul-Aarons Ngomo, Andrea Pozas-Loyo, and Huan Wang at New York University and Mariel Ettinger at Stanford; from an earlier time I also thank Paul Bullen at Chicago for his assistance. I admire the resourcefulness, intensity, and commitment of all these wonderful people. They have all creatively got themselves into the project and have found things I should have known to ask for but did not.

I also thank Mark Philp for suggesting that I write a book on Hume, and Timothy Barton and Peter Momtchiloff at Oxford University Press for encouraging the project. They cannot have expected it to take so long. For extensive critical readings, I thank Andrea Belag, Charles Griswold, Michael Kates, Mark Philp, Paul-Aarons Ngomo, and three anonymous referees for Oxford. And I thank Kate Williams and Nadiah Al-Ammar for editorial work.

Finally, I thank Pat Suppes for the seminars we taught together at Stanford, including one on Hume and John Rawls, and for many lively and extensive lunch conversations. It is especially pleasing to dedicate this book to him as the most nearly Humean person I know.

Although I have borrowed snippets of argument from prior published papers, sometimes no doubt unconsciously, I have not used much of any of them directly except for about half of one in scattered places in the book: 'Rational Choice Political Philosophy,' in Irwin L. Morris, Joe Oppenheimer, and Karol Soltan, editors, *Politics from Anarchy to Democracy* (Stanford: Stanford University

Press, 2007). I thank the editors and the publisher for permission to use that material here. Chapter 5 was originally presented at the Branco Weiss Laboratory for New Ideas in Economics and the Social Sciences, Central European University, Budapest, Hungary, 22 May 2003. Earlier variants of chapters 1, 3, 5, and 6 were presented as the Wittgenstein Lectures for 2003, at the University of Bayreuth, 16–20 June 2003.

Contents

Detailed Contents

1

Hume's place in history

[The] distinction of vice and virtue is not founded merely on the relations of objects, nor is perceiv'd by reason.[1]

In a vocabulary of the first half of the eighteenth century, David Hume presents a theory of politics and government that still roughly fits with the intellectual developments of the late twentieth and the current century. Many commentators remark on how extraordinary Hume was to write and publish the *Treatise of Human Nature*, one of the stellar works of philosophy, before he had reached the age of 30. After an accounting of Hume's dates, John Rawls remarks, 'These astounding facts leave one speechless.'[2] One is reminded of Tom Lehrer's quip that it was sobering to note that, 'when Mozart was my age, he'd been dead for two years. It's people like that who make you realize how little you've accomplished.' Had Hume died at age 30, he would still have been one of the greatest of philosophers. It is Hume's analytical theory that enables him to grasp so much; and that theory has virtually mathematical clarity.[3] Unfortunately, the analytical clarity is in Hume's head and in his ordering of topics and examples for discussion, not always in a display of the principles that drive his insights.

Knud Haakonssen says that Hume was hardly read as a political theorist until the 1960s and finally the 1970s.[4] Haakonssen's only exceptions to this were Hume's being a supposedly Tory apologist for certain of his remarks in the *History of England*. But in 1793 William Godwin cites Hume's 'principle which has been so generally recognized, "that government is founded in opinion." '[5] He must therefore have been in some discussion in the 1790s. It is now increasingly common to present the British tradition of political philosophy

---

[1] T3.1.1.27, SBN 470.   [2] Rawls, *Lectures on the History of Moral Philosophy*, 21.
[3] Great mathematics, unlike great philosophy, is often done by the very young. Perhaps it is Hume's youthful grasp of a quasi mathematical formulation of his problem that led him to such a remarkable philosophical achievement.
[4] Haakonssen, 'Hume's Political Theory,' 211.
[5] Godwin, *Enquiry Concerning Political Justice*, book 1, chapter 6, p. 148.

as going from Thomas Hobbes (1588−1679) to John Locke (1632−1704) to Hume (1711−76) to John Stuart Mill (1806−73). Locke is a misfit in many ways and the direct line skips a generation to go from Hobbes to Hume (see chapter 9).[6]

On his Tory leanings, one might also note Hume's remarks on the vacuity of the idea of the social contract, a position that further seems to affirm (wrongly) his Tory anti-Whig status, because early Whigs, true to Locke, define their position as contractarian and consensual.

Authors in the eras of Hume and Hobbes notoriously often do not cite the authors with whom they agree or disagree, and Hume makes only minor references to Hobbes, but the rudiments of his political theory are mostly those of Hobbes. Of course, he thinks Hobbes is misguided in many ways, primarily in his social science, and he corrects his detailed views while keeping the rudiments in place. That this is true can be seen in many parallels between Hobbes and Hume, many of which I will note. My purpose is not to elucidate Hobbes, however, but only to make better sense of the sources of Hume's views. Mill continues their commonsense approach to the world, although in some ways Hume seems to come after Mill, so innovative is his theory. One could argue that the central unifying feature of the arguments of Hobbes, Hume, and Mill is Hume's dictum that we cannot derive an ought from an is or their naturalism and focus on the kind of creatures we are. Hobbes and Hume begin the tradition—which Pierre Manent and many others criticize[7]—of not letting value judgments into their analyses, which they see as scientific. These issues are closely related and both are discussed below.

My views on these issues and on the interpretation of Hume's political philosophy are not universally shared.[8] Indeed, as one Hume scholar notes, 'Given that readers of Hume almost invariably praise the clarity and precision

---

[6] If this book were a treatment of Hume's epistemology, with its focus on book 1 of the *Treatise*, we would find that Hume acknowledges the great importance of Locke in the background. Much of what Hume argues responds to, accepts, or builds on Locke's *An Essay Concerning Human Understanding*. Because the focus here is on Hume's political philosophy, we can acknowledge the great importance of Hobbes's arguments, which seem to be at play very often in the more important foundational claims of Hume. Indeed, we can see Hume as cleaning up Hobbes's account in *Leviathan* by introducing his moral psychology and better social scientific understandings. In keeping with his era and maybe even exceeding its norms, Hume commonly does not cite the authors with whom he deals, and he seldom cites Hobbes. The parallels between their theories, however, are substantial and Hobbes therefore seems to be in the background much of the time as Hume writes. I will bring him to the foreground, partly to show Hume's debt to him and partly to make Hume's own positions clearer.

[7] Manent, 'Aurel Kolnai: A Political Philosopher Confronts the Scourge of Our Epoch.'

[8] For example, one might compare my views to those of Nicholas Capaldi. See Capaldi, *David Hume*, chap. 7, and 'The Dogmatic Slumber of Hume Scholarship.'

of his writing style, it seems odd that they carry from his works nonetheless such hopelessly conflicting interpretations of exactly what he is trying to say.'[9] In large part, of course, the problem lies with Hume, whose writings are far too extensive to expect them to be entirely consistent. In part, it lies with the change in intellectual climate and vocabulary from Hume's time to ours. And in perhaps the largest part it lies with the deep difficulties of the issues themselves and with the novelty of Hume's resolutions of them. In particular, his sentences are commonly so felicitous as to distract us into thinking their message is clear—and simple—while we fail to keep the complex overall claims in view.

Writing in the 1930s, Michael Oakeshott judges *Leviathan* to be 'the greatest, perhaps the sole, masterpiece of political philosophy written in the English language.'[10] It is a strange oversight, perhaps provoked by the greater breadth of Hume's *Treatise* but more likely merely a symptom of the times, to leave its Book 3 out of the category of masterpiece of political philosophy. It is a great contribution to the theory of social order. For Hobbes, that would make it a fundamentally great work of political philosophy, as it should also for Oakeshott.

In this book I primarily address Hume's political theory, although Hume's work belies a common view that modern philosophers tend to separate moral and political philosophy. Hume makes them part of a single coherent account.[11] The chief difference between the two is the scale of the interactions at issue and, therefore, the forms of the resolution of the problems we face at the dyadic or small scale and those we face at the large or societal scale. In his political philosophy, Hume has greatest affinities with Hobbes, whose assumptions are similar but more restricted; comparisons to Hobbes will help to elucidate Hume's views in several contexts by showing how sophisticated additions to Hobbes's understanding yield a far more compelling theory of politics.

Although they are in a field (social philosophy or social science) that is not fully hived off from philosophy, Hobbes and Hume are proto social scientists who foremost wish to understand the empirical world. They are not empiricist in the manner of Francis Bacon or Tycho Brahe, collecting a mass of facts and

[9] Dendle, 'A Note on Hume's Letter to Gilbert Elliot.' Warner Wick, my late colleague at the University of Chicago, said he far preferred to teach Aristotle and Kant over Plato and Hume. The latter two, he said, write so well that readers too quickly think they understand everything. The former two are conspicuously hard to read and no one mistakes their arguments as being transparent.

[10] Oakeshott, 'Introduction to *Leviathan*,' 3.

[11] The criticism is oddly wrong for utilitarianism, but those who criticize moral theories often seem to exclude utilitarianism from the field. Theirs is an auto-criticism.

then inferring conclusions from them.[12] But they solidly ground their theories and explanations in the real world. They are also not Cartesian, assuming that they have all the relevant knowledge in their heads to deduce central principles; they dislike, even detest, pure speculation.[13] But they are driven by theory, or deduction from a few given objective principles, and are therefore early moderns in their approach to science.[14]

In his effort to make 'public interest and utility' the central force that unifies our explanations of human society and personal behavior, Hume sees his project as more nearly a relative of Newton's. He needs mastery of empirical facts across a broad range of activities as well as of a unifying principle. The subtitle of his *Treatise* is 'An Attempt to introduce the experimental Method of Reasoning into Moral Subjects.' He looks for general principles, saying, if 'any principle has been found to have a great force and energy in one instance [we can] ascribe to it a like energy in all similar instances. This indeed is NEWTON's chief rule of philosophizing' (EPM3.48, SBN 204). He finds such general principles as that all men 'are equally desirous of happiness' (EPM6.15, SBN 239).

Clearly Hume does not do anything that would typically be called an experiment today, but he considers real issues, not made up, weird examples.[15] He says we 'must glean up our experiments in this science from a cautious observation of human life, and take them as they appear in the common course of the world, by men's behaviour in company, in affairs, and in their pleasures.'[16] In his political philosophy, he draws comparisons across real societies. He tests his claims by fitting them to alternative conditions, as when, for example, he considers what are the circumstances under which principles of justice as order would be useful and those under which they would be pointless or would be overridden by other considerations (chapter 6). He says, 'We have happily attain'd experiments in the artificial virtues, where the tendency of qualities to the good of society, is the *sole* cause of our approbation, without

---

[12] Hobbes worked for Bacon but was more influenced by his reading of Euclid and by his later meeting with Galileo (Macpherson, 'Introduction: Hobbes, Analyst of Power and Peace,' 16–19).

[13] With what might seem some confusion, Hobbes sees his project as Euclidian but also as about individuals' impulses to motion, as in Galileo's physics (Macpherson, 'Introduction: Hobbes, Analyst of Power and Peace,' 17–19). Hobbes apparently reviled the 'new or experimental philosophy' of his time (Oakeshott, 'Introduction to *Leviathan*,' 20).

[14] There are those who disagree with this assessment of the one or the other. For example, Oakeshott thinks Hobbes is a rationalist in that 'the inspiration of his philosophy is the intention to be guided by reason and to reject all other guides...' Hobbes seems to be ambiguous on this issue but, as Oakeshott says, we should not expect an order and coherence in his thoughts that is foreign to any seventeenth-century writer. 'Introduction to *Leviathan*,' 24–7, 68.

[15] Stroud (*Hume*, 223) says that Hume's method is not genuinely experimental.

[16] Hume, *Treatise*, 'Introduction,' xix.

any suspicion of the concurrence of another principle. From thence we learn the force of that principle' (T3.3.1.10, SBN 578). Hume's Newtonian move is to reach conclusions 'deduced from the phenomena.'[17] He does not argue a priori but via contingent causal reasoning. Perhaps his main assertion is that his account of morality will not be the hollow, purely 'reasoned' nonsense of theological and rationalist moral theory.[18]

In comparison to Hobbes, Hume has the larger program in social and moral philosophy. In that realm Hobbes focuses almost entirely on politics. Hume wishes to understand not only politics but also our views on morality from which many of our approbations of politics and government must generalize. One challenge to readers of Hume is to see how his account of our moral beliefs, or the psychology of morals, at the informal level of interacting with each other generalizes into an account of how these beliefs structure the institutions that govern us when we go very far beyond informal small-number interactions.

Hobbes is primarily important today for his political philosophy and some of his other work is largely forgotten. Hume is important across the theory of mind and epistemology and all of moral and political philosophy. The concern with epistemology (especially psychological epistemology, or how people know what they know or why they believe what they believe) is important in both Hobbes and Hume. Both of them write in a period that has yet to experience many very important intellectual developments, especially in economics and the social sciences more generally. Indeed, when they wrote, there were no social science disciplines, which were de facto merely part of philosophy. Physics had broken away from philosophy about the time of Galileo among physicists and astronomers, although not for another century or more for the Roman church. Still, Hobbes wrote on physics and Adam Smith wrote on astronomy.

After discussing Hume's naturalism, I will address the role of the is–ought argument in his moral theory. That argument is that theorists commonly move from is-statements to ought-statements without justification; and that move often seems to leave the implication that the normative ought-claims are merely objective observations. Because Hume specifically argues against them and is sometimes engaged in showing how his account refutes them, I will briefly take up two schools of moral theory—rationalist and intuitionist

---

[17] Noxon, *Hume's Philosophical Development*, 39.

[18] Hobbes is also concerned with real-world conditions, but he is much less experimental in Hume's sense not merely because he is concerned only with the conditions of the Great Britain of his time but also because some of his principles seem to be purely speculative or a priori rather than empirically grounded.

ethics—here to set the background for Hume's theory. They are also addressed more fully in chapter 8, along with other major schools that Hume explicitly or implicitly argues against. I suppose I would be pleased if readers think this is overkill for these two schools.

I will bring Hobbes's arguments into comparison with Hume's throughout this book where relevant. Locke will also come up on occasion, but here I wish explicitly to address the misfit of Locke's political theory with those of Hobbes and, especially, Hume. Hume is almost as harsh in his criticisms of Locke as he is of religious views, and it is instructive to see why. Then I will take up Hume's use of virtue theory, some of which—the account of artificial virtues (chapter 2)—is relatively novel and probably even objectionable to traditional virtue theorists. I argue that Hume used the language and paraphernalia of virtue theory primarily because it was the going language of his time and he had to use it if he was to join the ongoing debates.

Naturalism

Perhaps the strongest tie between Hobbes and Hume is their focus on naturalistic accounts of politics and human values. They do not present normative theories of the right or the good; rather, they present what they think are scientific analyses of how people think and behave. If they seem to give recommendations, these are usually in the form not of normative claims but of correcting mistakes in means-ends reasoning while taking for granted that people have certain general ends. For example, Hobbes supposes that no one has ever previously understood the actual nature of the problem people face in achieving social order for their own benefit.[19] Hobbes hopes that his work will enable people to do better means-ends analyses and thereby finally to see just how destructive are certain of their behaviors and just how important is having a powerful state to govern them.[20] Hume has similar ambitions, worrying that his 'train of reasoning may be too subtle for the vulgar' (T3.2.9.4, SBN 553) but craving attention to his work and ideas.

---

[19] Hobbes, *Leviathan* 20.19 [107]. References to Hobbes's *Leviathan* will be cited in this format: chapter number, followed by paragraph number in Curley's edition of *Leviathan*, followed by the pagination of the original edition in brackets.

[20] In an apt metaphor, Hobbes attributes part of the success of his understanding to the slow process of historical learning from experience, as we learn over the centuries how to build better, more lasting houses. 'So, long time after men have begun to constitute commonwealths, imperfect and apt to relapse into disorder, there may principles of reason be found out by industrious meditation, to make their constitution (except by external violence) everlasting' (*Leviathan* 30.5 [176]).

Both are normative theorists only in the very limited sense of explaining what would get us to better states of affairs, in the sense of those states' being de facto in our interest or better for us by our own lights. Hume is, however, more consistent and systematic in his anti-normative stance. Hume occasionally slips into what he calls 'panegyric' and advocates particular moral beliefs or actions. On one occasion, he virtually apologizes for the slip even while slyly defending it: 'But I forget, that it is not my present business to recommend generosity and benevolence, or to paint, in their true colours, all the genuine charms of the social virtues. These, indeed, sufficiently engage every heart, on the first apprehension of them; and it is difficult to abstain from some sally of panegyric, as often as they occur in discourse or reasoning.' He says his object here is more the speculative than the practical part of morals, but still he goes on with his panegyric, praising the virtues of 'beneficence and humanity, friendship and gratitude, natural affection and public spirit, or whatever proceeds from a tender sympathy with others, and a generous concern for our kind and species' (EPM2.5, SBN 177–8). In a letter to Francis Hutcheson, who had criticized Hume's lack of warmth for the virtues in the manuscript of book 3 of the *Treatise*, Hume replies that 'Any warm Sentiments of Morals, I am afraid, wou'd have the Air of Declamation amidst abstract reasonings, & wou'd be esteemed contrary to good Taste.'[21] According to his own psychological theory, his praises here are merely his own personal feelings—therefore he calls them panegyric and worries about their air of declamation. That he writes so forcefully against the elder Hutcheson's views suggests just how forcefully he means what he says. He explains such approbation psychologically and in so doing he meets his own strictures against inferring an ought from an is. On his account, we can only explain moral feelings or judgments but cannot establish the truth of any moral principles.

The break of the physical sciences from philosophy took the form primarily of actually looking at the real world. Perhaps even more important, it took the form of *supposing that one might actually be wrong about something*—an idea that was anathema to the church and to many Aristotelians and traditional virtue theorists.[22] Galileo did experiments that refuted views of Aristotle that were utterly unempirical, such as his a priori claim that heavier objects fall faster

---

[21] *The Letters of David Hume*, ed. Grieg, 1.33. See further Moore, 'Hume and Hutcheson,' 24–5. In the opening salvos of the *Treatise*, book 3, Hume also declares himself hostile to declamations (T3.1.1.3, SBN 456).

[22] Schneewind says of some schools of virtue theory that direct perceptions of the virtuous person are the source of knowledge. Hence, if two people disagree, one must be not merely wrong but morally defective. This fact must discourage moral debate that might subject one's views to revision and oneself to damnation (Schneewind, 'The Misfortunes of Virtue,' 62).

than lighter ones. Why? Because it's obvious, isn't it? So why bother to look. Unfortunately, as obvious as it seems, it happens to be false.

Throughout this book, I assume that *Hume's project is the science of moral judgments as a psychological phenomenon*, as will be more fully spelled out with Hume's psychology in chapter 2. Hume's naturalism makes sense if his enterprise is about why we have our moral views, not if his enterprise is about what our substantive moral views should be. If explanation rather than declamation is his project, then efforts to read demonstrations of the truth of substantive moral views into his *Treatise* are misguided. Such readings are warranted by his own panegyric claims, but these are his psychology, not his theory, speaking. Psychology is a natural phenomenon, and therefore scientifically analyzable. In a parallel claim, Hume says it is time for philosophers to get out of the business of analyzing theological claims, which mere reason is unfit to handle. Reason should be 'sensible of her temerity, when she pries into these sublime mysteries; and leaving a scene so full of obscurities and perplexities, return, with suitable modesty, to her true and proper province, the examination of common life.'[23]

Is and Ought

The break of the social sciences from philosophy has been much less sharp than the break of physics and astronomy, and it is arguably not yet complete. It is sometimes asserted that the difference is the difficulty of using the experimental method in the social sciences, and no doubt that is a problem, although astronomy has advanced without experiments at its impossibly grand scale, and the alchemists performed countless experiments without much understanding before Galileo. Even without experiments, predictions can be made and tested.[24]

More fundamental reasons are that the social sciences are often about values, hence about value theory, and they are intentionalist. Hume famously asserts that we cannot establish the truth of a value from empirical facts—we cannot deduce an ought from an is (T3.1.1.27, SBN 469). Not everyone in moral and social philosophy today agrees with Hume on this fundamental point, but even those of us who do agree with him regularly slip into violating his dictum.

[23] EHU 8.36, SBN 103.

[24] For example, some astronomers believe that the star Rho Cassiopeiae, at about 10,000 light years from earth, is the star in our galaxy that is likely to be the next supernova when it runs out of fuel and explodes (*Scientific American*, April 2003, p. 12).

Intentionality is a problem if I try to put myself in the position I am trying to analyze, because "'tis evident this reflection and premeditation would so disturb the operation of my natural principles, as must render it impossible to form any just conclusion from the phaenomenon.'[25]

Consider an important thesis in contemporary political philosophy that seemingly violates Hume's dictum. H. L. A. Hart and Rawls assert that free-riding on the provision of a collective good is morally wrong. Hart says that, if others are cooperating for mutual benefit and I benefit from their cooperation, then I have an obligation to do my share. In his words, 'when a number of persons conduct any joint enterprise according to rules and thus restrict their liberty, those who have submitted to these restrictions have a right to a similar submission from those who have benefited by their submission.'[26] Rawls cites this argument favorably with the strong conclusion that 'We are not to gain from the cooperative labors of others without doing our fair share.'[27] Having a right in the sense that Hart and Rawls want here is not a legal but a fundamentally normative issue. Yet Hart and Rawls reach this strong normative conclusion from nothing more than a factual description of a certain kind of action. From the action, an is, they deduce a right, an ought. One could try to pack some normative principle into the tale that implicitly motivates Hart and Rawls in their quest for a right here. It is hard to imagine what that principle would be other than some variant of the immediate principle that not to contribute to a collective good from which one benefits is wrong.

Robert Nozick dismisses the Hart claim, as would anyone who thinks with Hume that we cannot deduce an ought from an is.[28] Nozick notes that Hart's position would entail the possibility that others could impose an obligation on me merely by their acting cooperatively to provide some good from which I also benefit. They need not obligate me intentionally but merely by the way. In this very peculiar argument, my obligations then turn not on what I do but on what others do. Their acting in their *self-interested* way to provide themselves collectively with some benefit makes me *morally* obligated. This is one of the more remarkably contrived arguments in contemporary philosophy, and Nozick's complaint against it is compelling.

---

[25] Hume, *Treatise*, 'Introduction,' xix.   [26] Hart, 'Are There Any Natural Rights?' 185.

[27] Rawls, *A Theory of Justice*, 96 and 301. Rawls also uses this argument more than a decade earlier in 'Justice As Fairness,' 60. Rawls goes on to adapt this principle to defend principles of justice: when a person avails himself of the institutional set-up, its rules then apply to him and the duty of justice holds (*A Theory of Justice*, 302). This is not a legitimate move. If I live in this society and am harmed in some way, then of course I might have an interest in calling on the institutions of justice to correct the harm. But that is a matter of virtual necessity, not a matter of genuinely accepting the rightness of those institutions, which may be awful.

[28] Nozick, *Anarchy, the State, and Utopia*, 90–5.

One might conclude that free-riding in some instance is wrong, but this cannot follow merely from the fact that it is free-riding, as Hart and Rawls wrongly presume. Incidentally, Hart uses this argument to establish a political obligation to obey the law, although he later disavowed this claim.[29] Rawls thinks on the contrary that citizens, because they have accepted no obligation to the state, have none.[30] (Officials who have sworn an oath of fealty do have obligations to the state.) It seems that Rawls is inconsistent with himself to hold both these views, and Hart is right to have rejected his earlier view. By enjoying the benefits of some group's collective efforts, I do not eo ipso accept an obligation to help in its provision.

Hume's is–ought paragraph (T3.1.1.27, SBN 469–70) seems to have been an afterthought, perhaps added very late in the printing of book 3 of his *Treatise*.[31] Among others, J. L. Mackie thinks the is–ought problem is overstated by Hume and also not very important for his other arguments; he cites John Searle's claim that to say I promise just does mean to accept the obligation to keep the promise within reason—it is a speech act.[32] The fact that I have said 'I promise' entails a moral obligation. One can suppose that many other acts and kinds of act could similarly entail such an obligation. For example, in *Resurrection*, Leo Tolstoy has Missy think of Nekhlyudov that after 'all that has happened' it would be very bad if he did not marry her. 'She could not have said anything very definite, and yet she knew beyond doubt that he had not only raised her hopes but had almost given her a promise. It had not been done by any definite words—only looks, smiles, hints, silences—but still she regarded him as hers, and to lose him would be very hard.'[33] Nekhlyudov was falling ever deeper into religious commitments and, although he might have agreed with Missy's view that he had implicitly become engaged to her, still he could not give up his Christian commitments to be a proper husband in the society Missy wanted for them.

What is the force of the claims of Searle and Missy? They clearly seem to have in mind more than merely actions. They attribute an intention to the acting party, moreover an intention that seems designed to provoke action of some kind. If Nekhlyudov does promise a future to Missy, he seems to have

[29] Hart not only disavowed his view but also thought Rawls should not have borrowed it. I was with him in the Seminary Co–op Bookstore in Chicago, where the collection of his essays was on a display table (Hart, *Essays in Jurisprudence and Philosophy*). I asked why he had left out 'Are there Any Natural Rights?' and he said he had come to disagree with what everyone took away from it as the central argument. He said he either had not seen Nozick's criticism of the argument or had forgotten it, but he agreed with it as I rendered it to him.

[30] Rawls, *A Theory of Justice*, 97–8.   [31] Stroud, *Hume*, 187.

[32] Mackie, *Hume's Moral Theory*, 61–3; Searle, 'How to Derive "Ought" from "Is." '

[33] Tolstoy, *Resurrection*, 136.

an intention to mobilize her to do something that he wants her to do.[34] This gives the whole interaction the character of an exchange. Most moral theories would make this a moral problem. But they do so because of his intention that mobilizes beneficial action from another so that she will now be worse off if he does not perform. One might say that this is not merely an action and that the inference of an ought here is grounded in intention and not merely in action.

Hume, however, rejects this route to moralizing the promise. Nekhlyudov's intention is merely another fact, and it does not bring morality in its train (T3.1.1.24, SBN 467). We might find a way to elicit an approbation from the fact that his promise causes actions by Missy. What in the law of some societies would make such a promise a potentially binding commitment eventually, although not necessarily immediately, is Missy's acting on the promise and incurring a reliance interest in its being fulfilled; she makes investments in the promised future. What psychologically moralizes promising is such considerations—the utility loss to Missy of relying on the promise—and not claims that to promise logically means to fulfill.

It is okay to think, for example, of murder as a moral notion—murder is a moralized and legalized term for certain instances of killing. As Hume says, 'it is impossible for men so much as to murder each other without statutes, and maxims, and an idea of justice and honour' (EPM4.20, SBN 210–11). Indeed, without these, there is no category of murder. But we still have to decide whether some action is murder, and that decision will be our own disapprobation or sentiment of blame, not an objective part of the action we are judging.

With his strictures on inferring an ought from an is Hume is not merely engaging in linguistic play. An even more important point, however, is that in his discussion of such an inference Hume is making a psychological claim, not a claim within moral theory. Again, in the *Treatise* he does not expound a moral theory; rather, he wishes to explain the moral views that people tend to have. He is struck by the way people reason in such matters. In essence, people seem to suppose that they can simply see morality as they might see actions. But morality is not there to be seen, it has none of the qualities of the visible or physically recognizable. It is not blue or shapely or dense. When you observe an action, you do not observe morality. Nevertheless it is part of the psychology of many people, including moral theorists, to suppose that morality is objective, and to suppose metaphorically that they know it when they see it. For example, Locke seems to think that natural laws of justice and

---

[34] Promising is strategically more multifaceted than this; see further discussion in chapter 3.

property are as much engraved in the brain as is logic.[35] Hume strenuously rejects any such claim. In this, he is a forerunner of twentieth-century logical positivists.[36]

The addition of the is–ought paragraph as an afterthought says little about its importance. It is not so much the idea as the phrasing that is an afterthought. Hume writes as though he fully relies on this psychological point throughout his discussions; but he may only have thought of a particularly perspicuous way of saying it after having finished book 3 (for other failings in finding catchy phrases, see below). It seems to be difficult for many of his readers to believe how rigorously he means his objection to is–ought reasoning, just as, and in part because, it is difficult to believe the full force of his naturalism, to believe that his program is about objective claims in psychology rather than objective claims in morality.

Rawls argues that Hume's is–ought discussion is not about what is often called Hume's law, which is the claim that we cannot derive values from facts. Rawls offers a psychological reading of the passage. We use 'ought' and 'ought not' in connection with judgments of praise and blame. These judgments express a sentiment of blame from contemplating a matter of fact. But the sentiment is not connected to the matter of fact except through psychology, so there is no inference of ought from is.[37] This reading is compatible with Hume's law if we add the consideration that there is no objective fact of morality. This claim seems to be what G. E. Moore deals with in his naturalistic fallacy.[38]

Hobbes seems to hold the same view. He writes that 'these words of good, evil, and contemptible are ever used with relation to the person that useth them, there being nothing simply and absolutely so, nor any common rule of good and evil to be taken from the nature of the objects themselves.'[39] This view may be the reason he does not do moral philosophy per se.

---

[35] Aiken ('Introduction,' xv) says that Locke still works, 'in his ethics and social philosophy, within the framework of the medieval tradition.' In his epistemology and physical science he broke from that tradition, but he left it to Hume to secure a similar break in the science of man.

[36] Stroud (*Hume*, 219) thinks it a mistake to associate Hume closely with the logical positivists.

[37] Rawls, *Lectures on the History of Moral Philosophy*, 82–3.

[38] Moore, *Principia Ethica*, 62. Moore says it is a common mistake about 'good' for philosophers to suppose it is identifiable from natural properties. He says, 'it is a fact, that Ethics aims at discovering what are those other properties belonging to all things which are good. But far too many philosophers have thought that when they named those other properties they were actually defining good; that these properties, in fact, were simply not "other," but absolutely and entirely the same with goodness. This view I propose to call the "naturalistic fallacy" and of it I shall now endeavor to dispose.' His disposal is not convincing, possibly because the idea is tortured and unclear.

[39] Hobbes, *Leviathan* 6.7 [24]. Here Hobbes is primarily criticizing moral claims as essentially self-regarding: 'Whatsoever is the object of any man's appetite or desire; that is which he for his part calleth good; and the object of his hate, and aversion, evil; and of his contempt, vile and inconsiderable.'

Some writers who impute factual judgments to Hume when he speaks of moral actions generally claim something very different from any argument against his view that moral judgments are not matters of fact, they cannot be shown true or false. They take factual judgments such as that you do believe X to be a criticism of Hume's complaint against moving from is to ought. The reinterpreters rightly say that Hume does make factual statements concerning *judgments* of 'ought.' When he does, however, these statements are essentially functional. They have the form, 'you ought to X *if* you want to make people happy,' with emphasis on '*if*'. For example, Hume says a reason for being virtuous is that it pleases others as well as oneself.[40] This does not entail that it is therefore right or good, morally, for you to do X. He does not make claims such as that, if you want to be moral, do X. That would be a conditional, functional claim, but it would require that there be a truth content to the morality of doing X.

Nicholas Sturgeon suggests that the is- and ought-statements to which Hume refers are both statements of facts, just that the facts are in different categories. The is-statements refer to objective facts in the world whose truth can be investigated by reason. The ought-statements refer to our moral sentiments, which have their own truth.[41] This view seems to entail that we somehow have a large catalog of moral views in our heads and that the relevant one of these is evoked when we see some action that our sentiments say is immoral. This suggests that somehow these are moral intuitions. I think, as noted below, that Hume is quite hostile to the idea of moral intuitionism and that he cannot suppose that ought-statements are statements of facts. I argue in Chapter 2 that when we see another acting from a virtue we respond very generally to the good effects the virtue has on them and others, not to the rightness or goodness per se of exactly that virtue.

Don Garret provides many instances of factual claims by Hume. For example, 'To say that [as Hume does say], from the constitution of one's nature, one has a feeling or sentiment of blame from the contemplation of an action or character, is certainly to affirm a definite matter of fact.'[42] This is true, but that fact is about one's feelings; acknowledging that this is a fact claim does not imply that there is any moral truth content in this factual judgment unless one adds something like Sturgeon's view. To make this as clear as possible, suppose we are told by Hareward, one of Walter Scott's soldiers, that to be called a liar is 'the same as a blow, and a blow degrades him into a slave and a beast of

---

[40] Owen, *Hume's Reason*, 11.
[41] Sturgeon, 'Moral Skepticism and Moral Naturalism in Hume's *Treatise*,' 8–9.
[42] Garrett, *Cognition and Commitment in Hume's Philosophy*, 190.

burden, if endured without retaliation.' Therefore, Hareward knows he must duel his insulter to the death.[43]

Here we have a string of facts about a moral belief. Nowhere in that string is a moral fact other than in the prejudices of the boorish Hareward. Hareward has his sentiments; you have yours. Most likely, yours say Hareward's are wrong. That you and he have these sentiments is a fact, but the contents of your sentiments or Hareward's are not inherently morally true. If you want to say one of them is morally true, you have to say the other is false. Somehow, you will then have to demonstrate or explain why that one is false. If it were a fact about the objective world (whether it is hotter than usual today, for example), we have ways of settling the case. For you and Hareward, we have no idea how to settle the case—unless we are intuitionists who rudely assert we just do know which of you is wrong.

Sturgeon's view seems to be licensed by Hume, who says, 'Nothing can be more real, or concern us more, than our own sentiments of pleasure and uneasiness; and if these be favourable to virtue, and unfavourable to vice, no more can be requisite to the regulation of our conduct and behaviour' (T3.1.1.26, SBN 468–9). As with esthetic beauty, taste, and sensations, 'Our approbation is imply'd in the immediate pleasure they convey to us' (T3.1.2.3, SBN 471). All of this is, however, strictly personal and it is not generalizable. In a given case there will be variant sentiments and responses. For Sturgeon's category of ought-knowledge, we therefore need intersubjective rules for how to settle disagreements about our putative facts. Surviving such tests is what it means to say something is an objective fact of the world. This is a difference between science and faith, between evolution and 'creation science,' for example. The one is subjected to tests to settle variant claims, the other is not—indeed, is not even subjectible to such tests. It is hard to imagine just what we must do to settle a disagreement that some sentiment is a non-objective fact. The very category is not merely dubious, it is somehow weird.

Finally, note that at the end of the is–ought passage Hume refers to 'all the vulgar systems of morality' (T3.1.1.27, SBN 470). Here he almost certainly means the morality of ordinary people, which is the meaning of vulgar in a non-judgmental sense. Such people cannot plausibly have in mind the elegant, artful view of Sturgeon or many other of those philosophers who attempt to interpret this passage. It is ordinary persons who most readily slip into supposing that what they take to be true is also moral, indeed, is *therefore* moral. It is also they who slide most readily from is to ought. It is difficult to square

---

[43] Scott, *Count Robert of Paris*, chap. 2; quoted by Kiernan, *The Duel in European History*, 237.

this concluding note with the more esoteric readings of Hume's injunction in this passage.

Rationalist Ethics

The title of the opening section of the *Treatise*, book 3, is: 'Moral Distinctions not deriv'd from Reason.' This is Hume's speech act of laying down the gauntlet. Hume's naturalism stands against the theories of most philosophers in his time, and arguably also of our time. Hume and his contemporaries see his project as a refutation or at least as an attempt at refuting rationalist moral philosophy. Rationalists in Hume's time mostly present theological accounts of morality. Somehow, a god implants moral knowledge in our minds or instructs us via reason that, properly put to work, must yield moral truths. The Earl of Shaftesbury, for example, argues the former view—that god implanted in us a moral sense.[44] Samuel Clarke argues the second position that clear reason, a gift from the deity, must lead us to moral truths.[45] His is a theory of rational intuitionism, including universal benevolence as its main principle.

Most rationalist theorists suppose that we can determine what are the best ends for humans, so that reason—or what is commonly called practical reason—can be applied to our ends to refine them. Rawls says repeatedly that Hume lacks a conception of practical reason.[46] It is not merely that he lacks such a conception but rather that he rejects any such idea. There are no objective moral truths, including no truths about what is *the* best life for us. Best lives differ according to circumstances and Hume would reject the Socratic claim that the best life must be the examined life. He happens to do philosophy and to examine life, but that is because he enjoys doing philosophy (T1.4.7.12, SBN 271). He would not for a moment recommend such activity to many people—although he would like for more people to read moral philosophy so that his books might not be dead-born from the press.[47] Reason can help me live well but only through its instrumental role of helping me choose the actions that will fulfill the demands of my passions. It cannot be used to determine how I should live or what is my good.

[44] Shaftesbury, *Characteristics of Men, Manners, Opinions, Times*.
[45] Clarke, *A Discourse concerning the Unchangeable Obligations of Natural Religion, and the Truth and Certainty of the Christian Revelation*.
[46] Rawls, *Lectures on the History of Moral Philosophy*, 38, 50, 69, 84, 96–8.
[47] Hume, 'My Own Life,' xxxiv.

Rawls offers this syllogism for Hume's rejection of reason as a guide to the content of morality:

Reason alone cannot move us to action;

Knowledge of morality can move us to action;

Therefore: Moral distinctions are not discerned by reason.[48]

Note that it is misleading or even wrong here to use the term 'knowledge.' We do not have moral knowledge except in the sense that we might claim to know what someone holds to be moral or what our approbations are when we see or learn that someone has acted in a certain way. Hume's anti-rationalist arguments about the content of morality mean 'that moral distinctions do not report any objective features at all: moral goodness or rightness is not any quality or any relation to be found in or among objective situations or actions, and no purely intellectual or cognitive procedure can issue in a moral judgment.'[49] Therefore there can be no moral knowledge. Or can we plausibly suppose that we have 'original, innate ideas of praetors and chancellors and juries?' (EPM3.43, SBN 202).

The Hobbesian state of nature and the ideal of a golden age are philosophical fictions; but they are useful for reasoning to show that justice makes no sense in those states; hence justice cannot be a prior or universal principle; and hence it cannot be deducible from pure reason (T3.2.2.14, SBN 493). Our condition in the world includes our own selfishness and limited generosity plus scarcity of the things we desire (16, SBN 494). If we change these conditions, justice and the idea of property make no sense. Hence 'it is only from selfishness and confin'd generosity of men, along with the scanty provision nature has made for his wants, that justice derives its origin' (18, SBN 495). As a moral principle justice is entirely contingent, it is not a priori or purely rational. Hence, (1) regard for public interest is not our first motivation to be just, (2) justice is not a notion derived from pure reason, and (3) justice is an artificial virtue that is a human convention (20, SBN 496). (See further discussion of the 'circumstances of justice,' chapter 6.)

Intuitionist Ethics

A near relative of rationalist ethics is the family of theories that hold that moral principles are embedded in the brain, as color seems to be, so that we simply

---

[48] Rawls, *Lectures on the History of Moral Philosophy*, 79.

[49] Mackie, *Hume's Moral Theory*, 2.

know what is right or wrong in various contexts. The variety of such theories is daunting—it rivals the number, perhaps exceeds the number, of theorists who hold such views. The pile of intuitionist claims is like Franz Kafka's rejected writings. That pile has grown so large that by its very mass it now pulls every new writing to itself.[50] Philosophers in Hume's time commonly suppose that a deity put these ideas in our brains. If so, that was one radically confused deity. Later philosophers often have no explanation for how they got there, but despite wild disagreement about the content of morality, they seem to have overweening confidence that *their* intuitions are true.

Hume specifically addresses those who assume that we have substantive moral knowledge, not merely abstract moral principles. Hume's strictures on intuitionist morality would not block, for example, Kantian ethics. Kant starts from a single principle, the categorical imperative: to adopt only those (substantive) moral principles that one could will to be universal laws. He does all of this purely rationally, so that Hume would have rejected his project almost in toto, but only because of its rationalism. This primary principle, however, could plausibly fit with many standard theories, including Hume's empiricist, anti-rationalist theory and utilitarianism. Speaking of justice, he says that "'tis only upon the supposition, that others are to imitate my example, that I can be induc'd to embrace that virtue; since nothing but this combination [all of us following the same principle] can render justice advantageous, or afford me any motives to conform my self to its rules' (T3.2.2.22, SBN 498). Hume would, of course, start from how the principles affect utility in determining whether we could sensibly will them to be universal laws, and even then he would restrict the universality of any principle to a small universe of humans under certain conditions. But it is mutual advantage that fits especially well with the categorical imperative.

H. A. Prichard, one of the most influential intuitionists of the twentieth century, reduces the intuitionist program to its elemental core of anti-Humean silliness. He says that, if ever we do not immediately know whether we should do A in circumstance B, 'the remedy lies not in any process of general thinking, but in getting face to face with a particular instance of the situation B, and then directly appreciating the obligation to originate A in that situation.' So how does the mind perform this task? We let 'our moral capacities of thinking do their work.'[51] One may be forgiven for lacking the Victorian public schoolboy mentality of the great exhorters, such as Cecil Rhodes—whose scholars are enjoined to fight the good fight—and Prichard's later generation, that allows

---

[50] Kafka, *Tagebücher*, 17 Dec, 1910, p. 21.
[51] Prichard, 'Does Moral Philosophy Rest on a Mistake?' 17.

one to make such vacuous statements in a mode of deep thought. One imagines Prichard's squinting hard and squeezing his temples to aid in seeing the situation clearly enough and to force correct moral judgments into lively combat.

Anton Chekhov parodies this view in his story, 'The Duel.' The deacon asks, 'Have the philosophers invented the moral law which is innate in every man, or did God create it together with the body?' The zoologist answers, 'I don't know. But that law is so universal among all people and all ages that I fancy we ought to recognize it as organically connected with man. It is not invented, but exists and will exist.'[52] No doubt, as ostensibly a man of science, he had surveyed all people and all ages to establish his claim. The charm of the zoologist is that he has no idea that he is a fatuous fool as he holds forth on anything and everything with arrant confidence.

Kant would have detested such claims as those of Prichard and Chekhov's zoologist. He shares Hume's view that in morals we want a systematic science of morals—although he wants a science of objective or substantive morals while Hume wants a science of our moral beliefs. 'To appeal to common sense,' Kant writes, 'this is one of the subtle discoveries of modern times, by means of which the most superficial ranter can safely enter the lists with the most thorough thinker, and hold his own.'[53] Prichard could not have held his own against either Kant or Hume (that is no great criticism—theirs is a high standard that most of us would shy from).

In the context of claiming that, as in any other empirical science, we must begin with a few principles to which we can fit the great variety of phenomena we wish to explain, Hume nearly ridicules intuitionist claims to know the relevant set of deontological claims about all our duties: 'For as the number of our duties is, in a manner, infinite, 'tis impossible that our original instincts should extend to each of them, and from our very first infancy impress on the human mind all that multitude of precepts, which are contain'd in the compleatest system of ethics ... 'Tis necessary, therefore, to abridge these primary impulses, and find some more general principles, upon which all our notions or morals are founded' (T3.1.2.6, SBN 473). Hume's own few principles are pleasure and pain or, in summary, utility—'the chief actuating principle of the human mind' (T3.3.1.2, SBN 574). He also, of course, needs to elicit many other empirical facts about our conditions, so that his conclusions are contingent on the state of the world as well as on our psychology. But even these things he hopes to reduce to fairly general principles from which the rest follows.

---

[52] Chekhov, 'The Duel,' 130.   [53] Kant, *Prolegomena to Any Future Metaphysics*, 6.

It would be fair to retort to Hume and Kant that they too rely on intuitions. But theirs are very broad general intuitions that could be characterized, in Kant's case for example, as formal rather than substantive. Hume arguably has intuitions about utility and our pleasure in it, although he would say that these supposed intuitions are merely empirical observations about what actual people typically value and want. In the end therefore he might side with Kant in defending certain formal intuitions while definitively rejecting all substantive moral intuitions. From his psychological perspective, he might also suppose that moral theorists should be the last group of thinkers to claim any confidence in their moral intuitions, because they more or less pollute their thoughts with extensive moral debates that must finally color any intuitions they might think they have.[54] Of course, it is ordinary people, perhaps far more than most moral philosophers, who most strongly believe in the necessary truth of their own idiosyncratic moral intuitions.

Briefly note that a contemporary response to these problems is Rawls's assertion that, as philosophers, we move back and forth between moral intuitions and actual analyses of their implications in the world. 'Reflective equilibrium' is his misleading label for the state we reach after doing this repeatedly until—never?—we have no further revisions to make in our theory. Rawls attributes the argument for this process, but evidently not the term, to Nelson Goodman, who writes: 'A rule is amended if it yields an inference we are unwilling to accept; an inference is rejected if it violates a rule we are unwilling to amend.'[55] Goodman is concerned to understand the problem of induction in the physical world, the problem some of whose aspects are the subject of Hume's treatment of epistemology (*Treatise*, book 1, and EHU). The induction at issue is in the development of our scientific views in, of course, empirical realms having to do with 'matters of fact.'[56] For Goodman we constantly check our theories against factual observations of some kind.

In Rawls's variant of this method, we are basically checking our theoretical intuitions (about what constitutes distributive justice) against our intuitions about the goodness of the state of the world. *Testing intuitions against other intuitions is not a compelling way to defend our theoretical claims.* There is, for obvious Humean reasons, no objective reality that is distributive justice whose truth or validity we might be approaching through experimental or other observations. A physicist starts with some empirical claims and some theoretical claims. There are no empirical claims to be made about distributive justice other than claims that, if our theory requires X, then a certain society

---

[54] See further, Hardin, *Morality within the Limits of Reason*, 189.
[55] Goodman, *Fact, Fiction, and Forecast*, 64.   [56] Ibid. 59.

either does or does not achieve X, or achieves it to a greater or lesser degree. Such assessments are not ways to test or correct our theory and are not part of a process of reflective equilibrium. Rawls's theory is therefore intuitionist. Two of his intuitions are relatively abstract: that egalitarianism is good and that mutual advantage is good. All the rest of them are substantive and are as questionable as any intuitions of Prichard and others discussed above. The Kantian Rawls should reject them and the strangely intuitionist principle of reflective equilibrium.

Virtue Theory

Hume puts his claims in the vocabulary of virtue theory.[57] He does so because that was the going theory and vocabulary of his time. Because he radically alters the nature of virtue theory, it is arguably more important that the vocabulary of the virtues was the dominant way of discussing morality than that he was actually moved by any standard virtue theory.[58] Hume redefines virtues as characters that please us (EPM6–8, SBN 233–67). 'It is the nature,' he says, 'and, indeed, the definition of virtue, that it is a quality of mind agreeable to or approved of by every one, who considers or contemplates it' (EPM8 n50, SBN 261 n1). As Hobbes makes natural law functional,[59] so too Hume makes the virtues functional (as Aristotle generally did).[60] They are functional, however, for utility; they are essentially utilitarian and they have no moral standing in their own right. This view makes nonsense of those virtue theories in which the virtues are good in themselves (as in religious virtue theories).

It would be a mistake, however, to see Hobbes as continuing the natural law tradition or to see Hume as contributing to the tradition of virtue theory.

---

[57] The list of these is very long. See Baier's elegant catalog, *A Progress of Sentiments*, 198–219.

[58] Schneewind ('The Misfortunes of Virtue,' 50) supposes that Hume adopted the vocabulary of artificial versus natural duties to try to show that a theory making virtue rather than law the central concept of ethics can give a better account of the perfect–imperfect distinction of the natural lawyers. However, Hobbes already a century earlier uses the term artificial roughly in Hume's sense. We have made an 'artificial man, which we call a commonwealth' (*Leviathan* 21.5 [108]).

[59] Hobbes argued from natural law because that was the going theory of law in his time. But Hobbes uses natural law arguments very differently not to say what is a priori right at all times but only *what would be right—because useful—if it were the positive law*. This makes natural law functional or sociological. We determine what is the natural law in some context by the result it would have if applied—not by a priori deduction, intuition, or revelation.

[60] One might argue that for Aristotle the connection between, say, the virtue of a leader and the goodness of the leader's actions as leader is conceptual, rather than causal. It would then be wrong to say that the connection is functional.

To some extent they wreck these traditions, although, at least symbolically, Bernard Mandeville was the arch-wrecker of traditional, religious virtue theory with his provocative subtitle, 'private vices, publick benefits' and his clever demonstration of the case for the beneficial economic effects of greed.[61] Hume also wrecked such (monkish) virtue theory, which he clearly despised, by pointing out that, for example, pride can be a beneficial character, not a vice, when it stimulates us to perform well because we take pride in our efforts. Hume notes, with his usual subtlety, that 'whether the passion of self-interest be esteem'd vicious or virtuous, 'tis all a case; since itself alone restrains it: So that if it be virtuous, men become social by their virtue; if vicious, their vice has the same effect' (T3.2.2.13, SBN 492).[62]

Hume praises Mandeville's view (without naming him): 'Luxury, or a refinement on the pleasures and conveniencies of life, had long been supposed the source of every corruption in government, and the immediate cause of faction, sedition, civil wars, and the total loss of liberty. It was, therefore, universally regarded as a vice, and was an object of declamation to all satyrists, and severe moralists. Those, who prove, or attempt to prove, that such refinements rather tend to the encrease of industry, civility, and arts, regulate anew our *moral* as well as *political* sentiments, and represent, as laudable or innocent, what had formerly been regarded as pernicious and blameable' (EPM2.21, SBN 181).

Hume argues that pride is a virtue because it follows from our recognition of our own good actions and it stimulates such actions, which are likely to benefit others as much as ourselves (T2.1.7.8, SBN 297). This makes pride at least partially functional and utilitarian. It also cuts strongly against what Hume disparagingly calls the 'monkish virtues' of religious virtue theorists, for whom pride is a sin. Here, Hume's move is similar to that of Mandeville, for whom greed is a virtue because it stimulates production of what people want. Hume, Mandeville, and others making such moves vitiate one traditional strain of virtue theory, that strain which focuses on virtues as morally good for the individual who has them. That strain of theory includes greed, pride, ambition, and other characters as vices. Hume and Mandeville recognize that these strongly human characters are in fact often beneficial. They are also psychologically inescapable. On this psychological issue, Hobbes argues that

---

[61] Mandeville, *The Fable of the Bees: Private Vices, Publick Benefits.*

[62] Hume was familiar with Mandeville and, in a criticism of Mandeville's praise of vice (especially greed, which leads to productivity), he seems to contradict his own comments here (Hume, 'Of Refinement in the Arts,' 280). For more consistent views, see EPM App. 1.13–16, SBN 291–3. This passage yet again poses—especially against any claims for reason—our psychology of sentiments as the ground of approbation (disapprobation) of the morality (immorality) of any action or character.

to make such passions as lust a sin or crime is 'to make sin of being a man,' because such passions are 'adherent to the nature ... of man.'[63]

The core elements of virtue theory are the character and dispositions of the virtuous (or vicious) person.[64] For Aristotle, agents individually as well as the community they compose benefit from virtue. In some strains of virtue theory, the value of virtuous habits lies in the fact that they lead to the correct action in the sense of producing utility. Hence virtues are functional (Hume is with this tradition). Moreover, virtuous people will tend to contribute to the common good. There are varied traditions, descending from Greek, Roman, Catholic, and Protestant writers. Cardinal virtues for the ancients are prudence, temperance, fortitude, and justice. Christian writers focus instead on duties, and group these under duties we owe to god, to ourselves, and to our neighbor. Hume strongly dislikes the self-abnegating 'monkish' virtues of Catholic and Protestant religious moralists; he thinks they are vices. He compares the self-destructive virtues of Pascal to the virtues of Diogenes. 'The austerities of the GREEK were in order to inure himself to hardships, and prevent his ever suffering: Those of the FRENCHMAN were embraced merely for their own sake, and in order to suffer as much as possible' (EPM Dial. 55, SBN 342).

If, however, private vices benefit the public, it is hard to think them wrong. Mandeville was especially concerned to show the public benefits of greed, which leads people to be productive and competitive so that they provide us with a panoply of goods that we would never have without their greed. But greed was traditionally the worst of the Catholic vices and was countered by charity, the greatest of the virtues. Smith makes greed a central part of the explanation of economic productivity and prosperity. In one of his most often quoted formulas, it is 'not from the benevolence of the butcher, the brewer, or the baker, that we expect our dinner, but from their regard to their own interest.'[65]

In making greed a virtue, Mandeville implicitly uses a later trick of Hume's. He supposes that, given the conditions in which we live in our world, we are better served by greed than by altruism in the general economy that enables us to live well. Actions per se do not have a moral valence independently of the context in which they are taken and the effects that they have. Hume supposes that, if food and all other things we need for our health, comfort, and enjoyment were plentifully available without effort on our part, then we would have no reason for conceiving of property, and there would be no law of

---

[63] Hobbes, *Leviathan* 27.1 [151].   [64] See further, Schneewind, 'The Misfortunes of Virtue.'
[65] Smith, *The Wealth of Nations*, 1.2.2, 26–7.

property and no principle of justice (EPM3.2–3, SBN 183–4). In these moves to redefine virtues and natural laws, Hume—like Hobbes and Mandeville—is a naturalistic political sociologist. They do not rationally assume or deduce moral principles; they find practical principles that fit us and our conditions, although Hume is more rigorous than Hobbes in abiding by his naturalism.

Many of those who think Hume's program is to argue for a particular moral theory with moral content—and not merely a psychological account of why we have the moral views we have—argue that he is a moral virtue theorist.[66] He insists that the approbation we feel toward certain virtues derives not from the virtues themselves but from their tendency to benefit people and even society (T3.3.1.10, SBN 578). Except in his panegyric moments, he does not go further to say that the virtues are therefore good or even that our acting to benefit others and society is good. It merely evokes approbation. Those moments, however, give warrant to the claims of many scholars that Hume has a substantive moral theory.

Concluding Remarks

In this chapter I have surveyed several theoretical stances that Hume takes. These are not theories so much as they are positions on how to theorize and on the hollowness of various ways others have gone (and still go in many cases). In the chapters that follow I will lay out Hume's political theory analytically rather than topically. Hence, my account will mingle arguments from throughout Hume's works and will not order them in the way he does when he presents them. Hume's purpose is to develop the case for moral and political theory in many substantive contexts. My purpose is to do what he therefore does not do, which is to make the general theoretical positions clear by making them drive the discussion.

The main task of this book is specifically to explicate Hume's political theory. Because it is methodologically whole with his moral theory, however, we can extrapolate from the moral to the political theory. The background for the political theory is therefore the analysis of moral beliefs (chapter 2) and the strategic structures of the problems that we face in achieving social order (chapters 3 and 4). The beliefs can be generalized from assessment of fellow individuals to collectivities and institutions. And the strategic structures can be generalized from the small scale of individual morality to the large scale

---

[66] Others hold that he is a utilitarian or a rule–utilitarian.

of social order. We can divide the political theory into, first, Hume's general explanation of the state (chapter 5) and, second, his account of how it works once in place in his analysis, for example, of law and justice (chapter 6). In both cases, the primary background understanding is the force of convention in maintaining order. Convention stands behind the power of the state and behind the virtually automatic self-enforcement of social order and obedience to law among the populace.

Hume's arguments for the latter are astonishingly advanced over any ideas before him. He cuts through the view of many, especially theological, thinkers that we can be brought to order only by, in today's language, commitment to common values; and he demolishes the Hobbesian view that we can be kept in order only through the imposition of draconian force. Neither of these widely held views is correct. When we are massively coordinated by relevant conventions, we acquiesce in the power of government and thereby empower it.[67] This seemingly circular reasoning has offended some thinkers who have commented on Hume, but it is valid causal reasoning, as will be seen in detail in the discussion of convention and functional explanation (chapter 4).

Finally, note that Hume has much in common with his forerunner, Hobbes, but also with his friend and follower Adam Smith. Indeed, some of Smith's most important insights are already stated by Hume who, indeed, in one of his last letters to Smith, chides him for clouding the theory of price with things other than supply and demand (for example, the rent of farms as part of the cost of the produce).[68] Unfortunately, however, Hume lacks Smith's gift for phrasing. For example, his term for the division of labor is 'the partition of employments' (T3.2.2.3, SBN 485; T3.2.4.1, SBN 514). It did not catch on.[69] He remarks that the economy, driven by our individual self-love, is a system that, 'comprehending the interest of each individual, is of course advantageous to the public; tho' it be not intended for that purpose by the inventors' (T3.2.6.6, SBN 529). Smith writes acutely of the invisible hand and the unintended consequences that our self-seeking has for the general welfare.

Hume saw the influence of unintended consequences of explainable regularities of action in many contexts. The import of such insights is to undercut the commonplace supposition that understanding the results of human action requires accounts from intentions. Explanation from convention and functional

---

[67] Hardin, *Liberalism, Constitutionalism, and Democracy*, chap. 4.

[68] Letter of 1 Apr. 1776, *The Letters of David Hume*, ed. Grieg, 2. 311–12. The letter is written to praise Smith's newly published *Wealth of Nations*.

[69] Indeed, not even Hume's careful, fastidious editors include the term in their indexes of important and not so important ideas (see Norton and Norton, Beauchamp, Selby-Bigge, and Nidditch indexes for EPM and T).

explanation make far more powerful sense of our social world than would any intentionalist or value-based account of why we have the institutions and practices we have. This scientific fact undercuts many criticisms of Hume's failure to explain outcomes as somehow fitted to his utilitarian views.[70]

Hume's literary failings—the tendency to express things somewhat plainly and without memorably catchy phrasing unless he is deliberately challenging his readers with his more outlandish sounding claims (for example: reason is only the slave of the passions (T2.3.3.4, SBN 415))—probably lost for Hume the opportunity to be seen in some ways as the innovator he was, certainly in economic theory but even more fundamentally as a theorist of social order. His often powerful arguments are seen as merely conservative commitments to the status quo,[71] when in fact they are explanations of the status quo and even of social evolution toward a different world (Donald Livingston gives a rich survey of responses to Hume's supposed conservatism).[72] It is ironic that the philosopher and theorist who, more than any other before the twentieth century, insisted on a separation between judgments of facts and claims of value should be misread as the purveyor of conservative values rather than as the scientific explainer of social order.

In Hume's own view, the *Treatise* was a specifically literary failure. He thought it suffered from youthful excess. It suffered far more from the extraordinary subtlety of its argument and of the lack of a language in which even to express many of his ideas. We have had the relevant language for some decades now, and we still do not do justice to Hume's arguments. Many of the best of his ideas were more or less entirely missed by his readers until very recently. Advances in the social sciences have now surpassed many of those ideas without ever being influenced by them.

Barry Stroud says that, if Hume's 'contributions are to be judged as part of the empirical science of man, if he is properly seen as what would now be called a "social scientist," then his "results" will appear ludicrously inadequate, and there will be no reason to take him seriously.'[73] Stroud supposes Hume was maybe important historically for his insistence on the scientific study of human nature, but not otherwise. This is an astonishing claim. As a political theorist, Hume was not otherwise very important historically for the sad reason that he was not read seriously and deeply enough. But he is more relevant today than Stroud grants. His strategic categories of moral and political problems are still advanced beyond almost anything else in moral and political theory. Although

---

[70] See for example, Hiskes, 'Has Hume a Theory of Social Justice,' 74–5
[71] See for example, Wolin, 'Hume and Conservatism.'
[72] Livingston, *Hume's Philosophy of Common Life*, 306–42.   [73] Stroud, *Hume*, 223.

strategic analysis, now usually in the form of game theory, has gone on to become a field of mathematics, a major part of economic theory, and a standard definer of psychological experiments, it has not often been so richly applied to the description of central issues in social order as it was by Hume, and most theorists writing today could learn substantially from him. In this book, I hope to establish the force of this claim, not for the benefit of Hume or his reputation, but for the benefit of all of us who struggle to understand social order.

Hume is a proto game theorist, or at least a very clear-headed strategic thinker. Hobbes is very clear about a specific set of strategic interactions, but Hume seems to grasp the whole panoply of possible strategic interactions much more fully. I will lay out his strategic account of the problems that moral and political theory must address in chapter 3. That account naturally joins moral and political philosophy in one theory, because moral and political problems differ strategically primarily because they differ in scale, that is, in the number of participants acting in some way together.

It is ironic that Hume has chiefly been read for his epistemology. This has primarily been seen as skeptical. Norman Kemp Smith argues that 'its main governing principle is the thorough subordination ... of reason to the feelings and instincts.' Kemp Smith endeavors 'to show how it was by way of his Hutchesonian approach to the problems of morals, that [Hume] came to formulate the "logic" ... of his theory of knowledge.'[74] This eminently plausible claim fits Kemp Smith's view that book 3 of the *Treatise* was written before books 1 and 2. On this account, once Hume comes to understand the psychology of moral beliefs, he sees that his analysis can be taken further to encompass all beliefs and not only moral beliefs. He sees that the form of the explanation of moral beliefs, which themselves are not objective facts, can be applied to belief in facts about the objective world. It is the naturalism of these accounts that distinguishes Hume. *His fundamental move is to recognize that our moral beliefs are just natural phenomena, to be explained as are any other natural phenomena.* Explanation does not make the beliefs right. It is perhaps because he sees the abuses of moral claims by various authorities that Hume comes to advocate a skeptical attitude generally.[75] He comes to the generalization that, "Tis impossible upon any system to defend either our understanding or senses; and we but expose them farther when we endeavour to justify them in that manner' (T1.4.2.57, SBN 218). I apply this claim to moral and political philosophy in the remainder of this book.

---

[74] Kemp Smith, *The Philosophy of David Hume*, 84–5.   [75] Ibid. 129–31.

2

Moral Psychology

As men's faces smile with those who smile, so they weep with those who weep—Horace, quoted by Hume[1]

Many scholars have held that Hume's moral theory must be taken as a scientific theory of our moral beliefs, not a normative theory of the content of morality.[2] More recently, several scholars have argued persuasively that he presents a moral theory, with virtually objective content.[3] Unfortunately, there are textual warrants for both views. I think that the warrants for the earlier view are stronger than those for the later view, not least because they are more systematic (that is to say, they are stated at the level of his system of explaining our ethical views) and less directed at specific actions or judgments of them. When he makes specific claims that some behavior or character is truly virtuous or vicious, he sometimes qualifies the claims by attributing them to his own psychological urge for panegyric. That is just his own psychology, not true morality, speaking. I will therefore suppose that he is, as he says forcefully and repeatedly, concerned to present a scientific theory of our moral beliefs—not of the content of morality in principle but of our beliefs in fact and why we believe those things.[4] Those beliefs are partly conventional and

---

[1] Quoted in Latin in EPM5.18 n1, SBN 220 n.

[2] Consider two among many claims. Hume 'has taken a sheerly naturalistic view of morals' (Kemp Smith, *The Philosophy of David Hume*, 563). 'Hume's ethics is a twofold psychological enquiry into human nature ... These enquiries are not the same as those which philosophers undertake in what are now called Normative Ethics and Meta-Ethics' (Penelhum, *Hume*, 131).

[3] 'Hume is a moral realist who believes that virtue and vice have objective status' (Norton, *David Hume: Common-Sense Moralist, Sceptical Metaphysician*, chap. 3; this book gives an elegant defense of its subtitle). Hume accepts 'the reality and significance of moral distinctions and the common list of what constitutes right conduct and what constitutes wrong conduct' (Capaldi, *David Hume*, 151).

[4] There is one important passage in which Hume makes moral claims somewhat insistently at a general level. In the first, opening, section of EPM, Hume even presents a morality variant of his circumstances of justice, noting that if we were very different creatures, we would not be bothered with morality. He ends several pages of praise for certain virtues with the charge that it is time to reject every system of ethics that 'is not founded on fact and observation' (EPM1.9, SBN 175). The last twist is the dagger in the heart of the claims of the previous pages. Fact and observation are the foundations of Hume's psychology of morals, not of the immutable content of morality.

therefore subject to what might now be called social construction or, in John Mackie's felicitous phrase, they are a matter of inventing right and wrong.[5]

I will suppose that Hume's account does not tell us what is right or wrong, good or bad. It explains moral views; it does not justify them or even argue for them beyond fitting them to the actual psychology of people. Hume has no moral theory, only a theory of the psychology of our moral views. A purely psychological theory cannot be satisfactory for anyone who seeks 'true' moral positions. In Hume's view, however, true is not a term that can apply to moral beliefs. You may say it is right or wrong to do X or that it would be good or bad to cause Y, but those claims are only expressions of your views or approbations, they are not proofs of or inferences from the truth of the content of your views. When people make such claims, they typically are saying that the approved action is beneficial to someone, even that it serves utility. This is not moral utilitarianism but only psychological utilitarianism; we just do approve actions that benefit ourselves and, less strongly, others.

Hume's argument that there is no truth of moral content is in two parts, each of which occupies a lot of space in various discussions in the *Treatise*. The first argument is that reason has the limited function of helping us decide truth or falsity about factual claims. The second is that moral approbation or disapprobation is not a response of reason, and is therefore not a response that has any truth value. 'Reason is the discovery of truth or falsehood' and 'it cannot be the source of the distinction betwixt moral good and evil' (T3.1.1.9–10, SBN 458). This is the meaning of the title of the very first section of book 3: 'Moral distinctions not deriv'd from reason.'

In these arguments, Hume lays aside the classical view that reason is in control and that it defines our ends and masters our passions. He also lays aside any theological underpinning for morality and thereby rejects a major element of the moral theories of most of his contemporaries. He gives a strictly naturalist account, just as a Darwinian might do. The Darwinian might back up from our passions to explain how they evolved. Hume is content to let them be the starting points of his explanations of our moral views 'without any further proof' (EPM App. 2.5 fn 60 and 5.17 fn19, SBN 298 fn1 and 219–220 fn1). His project is therefore virtually unique in the history of moral philosophy up until his time. It rightly can be called a social scientific enquiry and that enquiry does not go beyond explanation. Hume does not, as Herbert Spencer seems to do, conclude that the sentiments that have evolved in us are therefore right or good. They just are. Indeed, they just are us. If other sentiments had evolved (either genetically or socially), we and our moral views would be different.

---

[5] Mackie, *Inventing Right and Wrong*.

In addition to rejecting theological views, as noted in chapter 1 Hume rejects rationalist views that we can somehow deduce what is right or wrong, good or bad, from first principles of some kind (EPM App. 1.5–10, SBN 287–9). Reason is inadequate for discovering or defining morality. If it is not objective, then it cannot be demonstrated by reason, as physics can be. Moral judgment is not objective; it is subjective, it is in us, not in the circumstances or actions on which we pass judgments. To find it, we must look into our own breasts (T3.1.1.26, SBN 468–9).

Our circumstances partially determine what is appealing to us. For example, if we lived in a world of plenty with easy grasp of whatever we might want, as perhaps the dwellers of some South Sea islands once did, we would have little or no concern with justice and property. Rawls's theory of justice is bound in time and place, although perhaps a moderately large part of human time and space on earth, as much as a few centuries in the industrial states of the North Atlantic but, as he rightly says, his is only 'A' theory of justice, not 'the' theory of justice. In Hume's view, there cannot be 'the' theory of justice.

Put together these two considerations—contingencies of human nature and contingencies of the conditions in which we live—and we have to agree with Hume that "tis only from the selfishness and confin'd generosity of men, along with the scanty provision nature has made for his wants, that justice derives its origin' (T3.2.2.18, SBN 495). There is no moral truth and there can therefore be no deduction or intuition of moral truths. In the vocabulary of logical positivism, morality, moral principles, and moral claims of any kind have no truth value. Morality does not and cannot come from reason. Indeed, a rationalist view implies that human nature is irrelevant to our concern with morality. This is a view that sounds deeply perverse when stated baldly. It is ironic, therefore, that the rationalist view seems to have a strong hold not merely on philosophical ethics but also on popular thought.[6] Hume thinks a philosopher must accept his or her nature for what it is, with all its instincts.[7]

Against any rationalist view, Hume famously says, 'Reason is, and ought only to be the slave of the passions, and can never pretend to any other office than to serve and obey them' (T2.3.3.4, SBN 415). He surely knows that this claim is provocative. He immediately recognizes that it is 'somewhat extraordinary,' and he goes on to defend it at some length. Reason cannot direct our actions except indirectly by giving us insight into causal relations that suggest our passions would be better fulfilled by one action than by another. Reason can be a useful slave in that it may help us assess and choose among means to ends, but it can recommend nothing to us about what should be

---

[6] Penelhum, 'Hume's Moral Psychology,' 125.   [7] Ibid. 144.

our ends, only about our means. With causal reasoning, however, Hume can give the beginnings of an account of why people hold to impossible rationalist views of morality. Lest we doubt his view, he drives it home with a series of assertions about reason's lack of motivating power, beginning with the deliberately provocative claim that "Tis not contrary to reason for me to prefer the destruction of the whole world to the scratching of my finger' (T2.3.3.6, SBN 416).

Utility Pleases

In the *Enquiry Concerning the Principles of Morals* (section 5, SBN 212–33), Hume introduces the claim that utility pleases. The view is not new, but the vocabulary has changed. In the *Treatise*, he argues that the chief actuating principle of the human mind is pleasure or pain (T3.3.1.2, SBN 574). These are basic facts, not to be explained: 'Ask a man *why he uses exercise*; he will answer, *because he desires to keep his health*. If you then enquire, *why he desires health*, he will readily reply, *because sickness is painful*. If you push your enquiries further, and desire a reason *why he hates pain*, it is impossible he can ever give any. This is an ultimate end, and is never referred to any other object' (EPM App. 1.18, SBN 293). He further remarks that pleasure is a basic desire, not to be explained further. Both pleasure and pain are foundational and have no prior reason or explanation. Today we might think to give an evolutionary explanation, but success in that endeavor would not change or reduce the status of Hume's project, and it might even strengthen Hume's psychological study of our moral beliefs.

It is in human nature to find utility pleasing. This is not a brief for full-blown utilitarianism, which would be to find the utility of everyone pleasing, possibly even as pleasing as one's own utility. We are not like that—it is primarily our own utility that is pleasing. Hence, we are not strictly utilitarian in our motivations although we are moderately utilitarian in our assessments. There are many other claims for utility, both for natural virtues and artificial virtues. Justice, as discussed in chapter 6, is a moral virtue merely because it has a tendency to the good of mankind and, by implication, to the good of each of us so that each of us has reason to approve it (T3.3.1.12, SBN 579). It is only that tendency that earns our approbation (T3.3.6.1, SBN 618). The virtues merit our approbation because they serve utility.

What is then the normative role of utility in Hume's account? One possibility is that, because our nature is what it is, *utility is good for us*. This is a strictly functional claim that does not entail that utility is good per se. Whatever additional claims we might make, at the very least it is pleasing to us.

To see that *our* utility is not good per se, suppose you are one of the creatures Hume describes in his account of the circumstances of justice:

Were there a species of creatures, intermingled with men, which, though rational, were possessed of such inferior strength, both of body and mind, that they were incapable of all resistance, and could never, upon the highest provocation, make us feel the effects of their resentment; the necessary consequence, I think, is that we should be bound, by the laws of humanity, to give gentle usage to these creatures, but should not, properly speaking, lie under any restraint of justice with regard to them, nor could they possess any right or property, exclusive of such arbitrary lords... Whatever we covet, they must instantly resign: Our permission is the only tenure, by which they hold their possessions. (EPM3.18, SBN 190)

Now suppose that you and your fellow creatures are very useful to humans, who typically put you to harsh labor. Whatever else you might think of humans, you are unlikely to think that service of *their* utility is a good thing.

Throughout his accounts, Hume makes utility a good for someone, not a good per se. In a way, this is not a surprise in intellectual history, because he argues from the virtues, and a sensible way to see the virtues is as functional. Qualities of leadership, say, are good for what they can do for us, and not good per se. Hume's morality is morality for humans, not MORALITY writ large. This fact befits his account of the psychology of our moral views. In chapter 1, I attribute Hume's use of virtue theory to the prevailing views of his time. There is an important sense, however, in which virtues are a good way to capture a central element of his moral views. As he says, virtues are means to ends (T3.3.6.2, SBN 619); they are not, like the monkish virtues that he disparages, good in their own right for no purpose (EPM 9.3, SBN 270). He makes related statements often.

At the core of our seemingly moral lives is a sense of approbation or disapprobation of the actions of ourselves or others. Generally, we react positively to actions that are useful to us or to others and negatively to actions that give pain. I react most immediately to pains or pleasures that I experience in reaction to actions of others. But I can also react, through sympathy, to your pains and pleasures. And, in what Bishop Joseph Butler might have called a cool moment, I can react, albeit most likely only calmly, to the presumed pains and pleasures of people distant from me, so that I could favor particular principles for social organization on the ground that they would give pleasure or reduce pain for others, that they would de facto be utilitarian. Hume asserts often that our approbation arises from the utility of various virtues or actions, so that we could say, again, that he is a psychological utilitarian; that is, he supposes that people desire pleasure and usefulness.

Morality Psychologized

For Hume morality is a natural phenomenon arising from human psychology. That is to say that we seem to pass moral judgments on ourselves and others. Rawls says Hume presents 'morality psychologized.'[8] It is simply a fact of human nature that we have relevant psychological, motivational urges. None of this entails anything about the truth of our moral assessments, only that we have them. Terence Penelhum rightly says that Hume is almost Darwinian in his views of human psychology.[9] We could get Hume's psychology from evolutionary development, but Hume does not enquire into why we make moral judgments, why we approve and disapprove various things just because we see pleasure or pain in them. He simply starts from the 'fact' that we do. We must stop somewhere in our quest for prior reasons or causes (EPM5.17 n, SBN 219–220 n).

Rawls's critique here is very important to establish the radical difference between Hume's enterprise and that of Rawls and many other, especially Kantian, contemporary moral and political philosophers, many of whom are rationalists with theories of practical reason—that is to say, with reasoned theories of what is right or good for us. As noted, Rawls argues that Hume lacks an account of practical reason, which should be binding or motivating for us: 'What is distinctive of [Hume's] view is that it seems to be purely psychological and to lack altogether what some writers think of as the ideas of practical reason and of its authority.'[10] That is just right. For Hume, reason provides no motive for action, it has no authority, it only provides causal understandings.[11]

In the alternative moral views of most moral theorists, getting the right or true content of morality is a central concern. This is true of rationalist deductive

    [8] Rawls, *Lectures on the History of Moral Philosophy*, 21.
    [9] Penelhum, 'Hume's Moral Psychology,' 124. It is historically more accurate to say Darwin is Humean.
    [10] Rawls, *Lectures on the History of Moral Philosophy*, 38, 50, 69, 84, 96–8.
    [11] A special value of Rawls's critique is that he is resolutely un-Humean but still usually shows correctly what Hume's views are. His own commitment to practical reason drives him repeatedly to note Hume's lack of any principle of practical reason—almost to the point of our thinking he doth protest too much. He *wants* Hume to have a theory of practical reason, perhaps because he wants Hume on the side of his own project. We all should want Hume on our side, but only if our views coincide with his. He can be a tenacious opponent if our views do not fit with his.

theorists such as Kant; theorists who pose substantively objective moral views by intuition or by work of a deity, who might teasingly have implanted correct moral views in our brains while not implanting relevant motivations; theological moral theorists who hold that the authority of god makes right; or even more or less commonsense theorists who hold that morality is purely conventional but still right. Hume holds that many of our moral views do arise by convention. These views may be psychologically persuasive to us, but this fact does not make them right. Indeed, we might conclude from the very fact of their conventional origin that we could have held alternative moral views so that our actual views cannot be necessarily right.

In Hume's psychological program, our moral views are an empirical matter (EPM1.10, SBN 174–5). As with any other empirical matter, therefore, they are to be explained, and Hume offers us a theory of our psychology that makes sense of our moral views. In understanding his project and most of his conclusions about moral behavior or beliefs, it does not entirely matter whether we agree with his psychological theory. Indeed, it would be surprising if nearly three centuries of further work on such an empirical science had not undercut most of the views of even the sharpest thinkers of the distant past. There has, however, arguably been a deterioration in our understanding of psychology in one important sense. Hume has a systematic theory, his theory of associations (elaborated in *Treatise* book 2, but not here). Contemporary psychology seems to be a vast and vastly varied collection of more or less independent findings and explanations. To this date, it has not reached the status of those sciences in which it is irrelevant to cite past views and to identify the thinkers who proposed those views. In some of the sciences, such matters are of little more than historical curiosity. Unfortunately, in the sciences of human nature, past views are not simply superseded by or incorporated into more comprehensive contemporary views.

The Limited Role of Reason

Hume does not present an account of rational deliberation understood as normative.[12] Rather he says how, psychologically, we do deliberate. In general, however, this final note is far too strong. As Hume says, 'Our Thought is fluctuating, uncertain, fleeting, successive, and compounded; and were we to remove these Circumstances, we absolutely annihilate its Essence, and it wou'd, in such a Case, be an Abuse of Terms to apply to it the Name of Thought or

---

[12] Rawls, *Lectures on the History of Moral Philosophy*, 38.

Reason.'[13] In our moral lives we seldom deliberate at all. We feel and we react psychologically. What we feel is often a sense of approbation or disapprobation without thinking through what we have seen. We impute to people virtues that are not empirically recognizable or visible in any sense. Ought and is mix all too freely in our judgments, as though we could impute a motive to any action we observe. As F. A. Hayek slyly notes, 'Reason was for the rationalist no longer a capacity to recognize the truth when he found it expressed, but a capacity to arrive at truth by deductive reasoning from explicit premises.'[14]

In a particularly strong and compelling statement that could be taken as definitional as well as explanatory, Hume says, 'We do not *infer* a character to be virtuous, because it pleases: But in *feeling* that it pleases after such a particular manner, we in effect *feel* that it is virtuous' (T3.1.2.2.3, SBN 471, emphases added). Feelings are on both sides of this equation and there is no role for reason and inference to mediate between them. This is the core implication of his naturalist stance of trying to explain our moral views. Our views are grounded in feelings all the way and not in reason. Indeed, we might note that our reactions are virtually instantaneous and allow no time for reasoning through what we have observed.

Francis Hutcheson, who stands in the background as Hume writes, forcefully says, there can be 'no *exciting Reason* previous to *Affection*':

We have indeed many confused Harangues on this Subject, telling us, 'We have two Principles of Action, *Reason*, and *Affection*, or *Passion* (i.e. strong Affection): the *former* in common with Angels, the *latter* with Brutes: No Action is wise, or good, or reasonable, to which we are not excited by *Reason*, as distinct from all *Affections*; or, if any such Actions as flow from *Affections* be good, 'tis only by *chance*, or *materially* and not *formally*.' As if indeed *Reason*, or the Knowledge of the Relations of things, could excite to Action when we proposed no *End*, or as if *Ends* could be intended without *Desire or Affection*.[15]

Reason provides no motive for action, it only provides causal understandings. Reason can intrude by showing us that our means will not get us the ends that we seek so that it redirects our actions to better fulfill our passions, not to derail their fulfillment. For example, bare knowledge of our future passions generates present passions that lead us to make at least some provision for the needs that will be aroused by our future passions. Hence, again, reason plays a role only causally. It plays no role in actually defining what is moral or what ends we

---

[13] Hume, *Dialogues Concerning Natural Religion*, part 3 (final paragraph), 180. See also, Suppes, 'Rationality, Habits and Freedom.'

[14] Hayek, 'The Legal and Political Philosophy of David Hume,' 337.

[15] Hutcheson, *Essay with Illustrations*, 139.

should seek. Hence the claim that it is not contrary to reason for me to prefer the destruction of the whole world to the scratching of my finger. 'Since a passion can never, in any sense, be call'd unreasonable, but when founded on a false supposition, or when it chuses means insufficient for the design'd end, 'tis impossible, that reason and passion can ever oppose each other, or dispute for the government of the will and actions' (T2.3.3.7, SBN 416).[16]

These facts must cut against the possibility of a rationalist derivation of immutable right and wrong.[17] Hume says we should 'reject every system of ethics, however subtile or ingenious, which is not founded on fact and observation' (EPM1.10, SBN 175). One can best see just how devastatingly serious he is when he presents the empirical reasons for why justice cannot be a purely reasoned or deduced principle in his discussion of the *empirical, not deducible* circumstances of justice (see Chapter 6). He holds moral theories that are entirely about the substantive content of what is moral or immoral to be vacuous. What can be handled by reason is capable of being true or false (T3.1.1.9–10, SBN 458); morality cannot be handled by reason. More generally, reason cannot motivate at all. What role does reason serve with passion in motivation or action? At most an informational, evidentiary role (T3.1.1.12, SBN 459).

Rationalist deduction requires two conditions that are violated:

1. Understanding cause and effect can only come through experience (T3.1.1.22, SBN 466), it cannot be deduced from pure reason or first principles;
2. Imputing value to a cause cannot be done merely empirically; this is just Hume's objection to inferring morals from facts; for example, incest is not inherently an immoral action. 'The vice entirely escapes you, as long as you consider the object. You never can find it, till you turn your reflection into your own breast, and find a sentiment of disapprobation, which arises in you, towards this action. Here is a matter of fact; but 'tis the object of feeling, not of reason. It lies in yourself, not in the object. So that when you pronounce any action or character to be vicious, you mean nothing, but that from the constitution of your nature you have a feeling or sentiment of blame from the contemplation of it'. (T3.1.1.26, SBN 468–9)

---

[16] We might often think this claim wrong. For example, Violet Trefusis says of Alexa when she is falling for John that a 'civil war broke out between her mind and her senses, cutting off all retreat, replacing her multitudinous activities with one lofty preference for the void' (Trefusis, *Broderie Anglaise*, 26). But Alexa's 'mind' here is merely shorthand for certain of her other desires that would be neglected if she falls for John. It is not reason in any sense that the rationalists would want.

[17] In the 'Advertisement' to book 3 of the *Treatise*, SBN facing p. 455.

Someone who agrees with Hutcheson, Hume, and many others that reason does not motivate other than to correct errors of causal analysis, that there are no ends that reason can select for us, hardly needs discussion. Someone who disagrees with these philosophers and their thesis after reading Hume can likely not be convinced by further argument. One might be tempted to note that these very stances are evidence of the anti-rationalist view. Hayek rightly notes that, although Hume is said to be part of the Scottish Enlightenment, he is hostile to enlightenment claims for the powers of reason.[18] As Sheldon Wolin says, he 'turned against the enlightenment its own weapons.'[19]

Sympathy and Moral Sentiments

Sympathy and moral sentiments are two important terms of art in Hume's moral and political theory. Sympathy is about communication of personal feelings of various kinds.[20] Moral sentiments are judgments or evaluations. Unfortunately, Hume is ambiguous in the ways he uses these and many other important terms, but especially the term sentiments. He sometimes seems clearly to mean emotion or passion, and sometimes judgment or opinion.[21] The first usage seems to run the term into sympathy. He also sometimes makes sympathy more inclusive.[22] I will keep sympathy and moral sentiments separate because the ideas at the core of his discussion are communication and judgment, and these are clearly different and, when Hume uses these latter two terms, he is not ambiguous. He generally associates sympathy with communication and judgment with moral sentiments. Indeed, he often includes sympathy and sentiment in the same passage, and when he does he allows that one of the things we can communicate is our sentiment about the rightness or wrongness of some action. It does not much matter how we use the terms, except that it pays to keep them clearly focused and not to run them together.

Hume first introduces the notion of sympathy early in his discussion of the passions (T2.1.11, SBN 316–24). He needs it there to explain the otherwise odd fact that our virtues, beauty, and riches 'have little influence when not seconded by the opinions and sentiments of others.' This requirement of

---

[18] Hayek, 'The Legal and Political Philosophy of Hume,' 335.

[19] Wolin, 'Hume and Conservatism,' 1001.

[20] Árdal, *Passion and Value in Hume's* Treatise, 152–6. Also see Chapters 3 and 6 more generally.

[21] Jones, *Hume's Sentiments*, 98.

[22] For example, he says that sympathy is the source of moral approbation (T3.2.2.24, SBN 499–500), and again that it 'is the chief source of moral distinctions' (T3.3.6.1, SBN 618). Sentiments should have this role. Most of the time in Hume's usage sympathy is simply communication.

approbation by others is only natural for such things as our good reputation, character, and name, but it is explicable for virtues, beauty, and riches only through the mediating effects of sympathy. Why do we have sympathy? Again, Hume must stop somewhere in explaining motivations, and merely accept human nature as it is in order to investigate our behavior and beliefs. Here he wants a psychological account of judgments from sympathy and of their social role. *We*, however, might be interested in explaining the fact of sympathy (see below).

The third Earl of Shaftesbury, an early advocate of sympathy as the font of most human pleasure, says, 'how many the Pleasures are, *of sharing contentment and delight with others*; of receiving it in Fellowship and Company; and gathering it, in a manner, from the pleas'd and happy States of those around us, from accounts and relations of such Happinesses, from the very Countenances, Gestures, Voices and Sounds, even of Creatures foreign to our Kind, whose Signs of Joy and Contentment we can anyway discern. So insinuating are these Pleasures of Sympathy, and so widely diffus'd thro' our whole Lives, that there is hardly such a thing as Satisfaction or Contentment, of which they make not an essential part.'[23] Hume shares Shaftesbury's evident pleasure in the company of others. Indeed, Henry Aiken supposes that in his doctrine of sympathy, Hume is emphasizing that humans are pre-eminently social beings in the sense that 'whatever others do, their joys and sorrows, loves and hates, have an immediate and continuous impact upon our own sentiments. It is this capacity for reciprocity of feeling which renders possible a common moral life.'[24] For Hume, that capacity, which he calls sympathy, is definitive.

Note that for Shaftesbury, sympathy does not define or explain morality or our moral views. Rather, we have a moral sense that handles all of this, and Shaftesbury's moral sense just knows the good and the right. Hume rejects any such view that moral judgments are somehow planted in our minds, as they would be if they were grounded in a moral sense such as Shaftesbury's. Hume focuses on explaining an important part of our knowledge about others as the result of sympathy. *Sympathy gives me knowledge of others because they are like me in fundamental ways*, so that I can read from their reactions what they feel to a large extent, as Shaftesbury does.

How does sympathy work? This is not a question Hume answers. He merely describes its working and puts the fact of it to use in explaining our moral judgments. He develops the idea in book 2, where it is useful in understanding the passions and how they are communicated from one person to another.

---

[23] Shaftesbury, *Characteristics of Men, Manners, Opinions, Times*, 2. 62.
[24] Aiken, 'Introduction,' xxiii.

There he refers to it as 'the principle of sympathy or communication' (T2.3.6.8, SBN 427). In first introducing the idea, he says, 'No quality of human nature is more remarkable, both in itself and in its consequences, than that propensity we have to sympathize with others, and to receive by communication their inclinations and sentiments, however different from, or even contrary to our own' (T2.1.11.2, SBN 316). He reintroduces the idea in book 3 in discussing the origin of the natural virtues and vices, well after presenting his main political views (T3.3.1.4–18, SBN 575–84).

When we have finished working through the idea and we contemplate how fully and dramatically we can sense what another is thinking or feeling, we too are apt to find it a remarkable human capacity. The fundamental fact that makes all of this possible is our similarity to others and, indeed, it is a stronger phenomenon in dealings with those who are more similar to us. 'All human creatures are related to us by resemblance,' especially in their capacity to feel affliction and sorrow (T2.2.7.2, SBN 369; also see 4, SBN 370).[25] Maybe sympathy is partially hard-wired in us (it may also partially be socially inculcated, at least in its objects, which must differ from one culture to another). Hume cites Horace, in the epigraph for this chapter, as recognizing that we tend to reflect the moods of others.[26] For Hume, this fact of human behavior is a starting point; he does not attempt to explain it but only to characterize it and to put it to use in explaining other things.

Consider briefly Hume's summary of some of the effects of sympathy. Sympathy 'is the chief source of moral distinctions' (T3.3.6.1, SBN 618).[27] This implies, incidentally, that *it is actions toward others that are the concern of morality*, although we may indirectly judge someone by their character and its propensity for the right kind of action. This is, as always, a psychological claim about the way we think about and react to things. The public good is indifferent to us except insofar as sympathy interests us in it (ibid.). Moreover,

---

[25] But contrary to Hume's claim here, when I hear of someone reacting violently to a smear on his supposed honor, I cannot feel their emotions at all. For example, the father of Fadime Sahindal tells a Swedish court that they must sympathize with the depth of the insult he felt when his daughter refused to marry the man her family had chosen for her, an insult so painful that it justified his killing her. I cannot have any Humean sympathy for his action or his feelings. They are outside my ken so thoroughly that they might as well be expressed by a strange creature from another planet. My sense is of horror at him, not of empathy with him. A psychiatric expert said he is 'cognitively underdeveloped and lacking in empathy' (Wikan, 'Deadly Distrust: Honor Killings and Swedish Multiculturalism,' 200). That is probably wrong, at least in Hume's vocabulary. The elder Sahindal has moral sentiments that differ grossly from those of the cosmopolitan Swedish court. The court ruled that he had committed murder. He was inerrantly convinced that he had salvaged his family's honor, that he deserved high praise.

[26] See also Árdal, *Passion and Value in Hume's* Treatise, 57–8.

[27] The two terms, sympathy and sentiments, are somewhat confused here.

Hume goes on to argue that the same must be true finally also of the natural virtues and our approbation of them when we see them in others—so that these are also indirect or functional.[28] Earlier he says that a means to an end can only be agreeable where the end is agreeable; and as the good of society where our own interest or that of our friends is not concerned pleases us only by sympathy, it follows that sympathy is the source of the esteem which we pay to all the artificial virtues (T3.3.1.9, SBN 577).

Rawls thinks that sympathy is the wrong term in our time for what Hume wants here. Rawls refers to 'imparted feeling,' which is passive, so that we are not moved to action by it.[29]This is a feature that we want for Hume's idea here because my sympathy for your pleasures or pains can be purely contemplative and it need not provoke me to any action at all. Rawls's phrase is unlikely to catch on, not least because it is unclear. If I have sympathy *for you*, some feeling you have is imparted *to me*. One almost has to know that this phrase is a substitute for sympathy to get its meaning. We might also wonder just what feeling is imparted to us; surely it is not the literal kind of feeling the other has.

Oddly, Rawls criticizes Hume's term for seeming to imply that I feel your fever when I sympathize with your illness; Stroud makes a similar criticism.[30] This reading is no part of Hume's meaning nor should anyone read him this way. Bill Clinton on the campaign trail said, 'I feel your pain.' He did not say he felt any particular pain, such as shortage of funds to pay medical bills, but only a very general pain. I do not literally have your experience, but I do share the pleasurableness or the painfulness of your experience. For example, suppose I see a child ecstatically enjoying something that I do not even like—say, peanut butter or candy. I do not share the tastes of the child but only the pleasure, and I therefore experience pleasure. Often I could not even know what you taste or experience although I could know that you are experiencing pleasure or pain.

Having sympathy allows us to have knowledge of others beyond ourselves. Sympathy is about knowledge and its communication from one person to another. There is no method of inquiry to discover knowledge of another's mind, but through sympathy we simply gain it, apparently almost directly as though we could read it from facial expressions and ways of expressing things. Rawls is right to suppose that sympathy is not an ideal term here, but it has become a term of philosophical art and we are likely stuck with it. Unfortunately, it is hard to come up with a single term that is both clear

---

[28] As noted earlier, for Hume virtue is a means to an end (T3.3.6.2, SBN 619).
[29] Rawls, *Lectures on the History of Moral Philosophy*, 86–7.   [30] Ibid.; Stroud, *Hume*, 197–8.

and apt, perhaps because the idea behind the term is not part of vernacular understanding or language. The term we would want must convey several things. Hume's sympathy is partial in that it is stronger for those like ourselves. It is emotional rather than reasoned and it can be both very lively and very calm. Finally, however, we might well prefer to continue to use Hume's sympathy as a philosophical term of art. One who reads much of Hume must soon enough make the term include these senses.

It is not clear that we always have direct access to our own emotions. Sometimes we discover what they are from their effect on our behavior or our reactions, or even from the apparent understanding of others who read us better than we do. For example, we notoriously sometimes discover how deeply we love someone only when we might be about to lose the person. Jane Austen is a master of showing examples of such lacks of self-awareness. In *Pride and Prejudice*, she says that Elizabeth 'rather *knew* that she was happy, than *felt* herself to be.'[31] Witold Gombrowicz similarly says that Isabel, 'knowing that when one is in love, one is happy, was happy.'[32] As Hume notes, 'Our predominant motive or intention is, indeed, frequently concealed from ourselves' (EPM App. 2.7, SBN 299).

In *Emma* Austen says of Knightley that he 'had been in love with Emma, and jealous of Frank Churchill, from about the same period, one sentiment having probably enlightened him as to the other.'[33] Earlier, Emma herself has to attempt to infer whether she is falling in love with Churchill from her sudden sense of listlessness when he departs for London.[34] The reader knows well enough that she is not falling for him in any serious way. He is merely lively in sufficiently different ways as to be interesting to her. He is virtually a foreigner to her extremely close and limited community and the appeal of his novelty will pass soon enough. If the reader knows such things, that is because Austen has communicated them, but she has done so only subtly and tangentially so that it is through our sympathy that we receive a communication that is not articulate. Austen's extraordinary gift for such quiet communication lets us flatter ourselves with our own sensibility. We know that Emma will, as did Austen herself, stay in her community and that she likely will, as Austen did not succeed in doing, marry within that community.

Hume's moral sentiments are a matter of moral judgment or opinion; they are among the things we can communicate via sympathy. From sympathy I identify somewhat with your pleasure or pain. From sentiment, I approve or disapprove of some action or state or character. I know the effect of an

---

[31] Austen, *Pride and Prejudice*, chap. 59, 337. [32] Gombrowicz, *Ferdydurke*, 267–8.
[33] Austen, *Emma*, chap. 49, 419. [34] Ibid., chap. 31, 266.

action on another person from sympathy, but I judge from moral sentiment. Our moral sentiments invest what we see with approbation or disapprobation. These sentiments are passions and they are the psychology of moral judgment. In the writings of many philosophers of Hume's time, the moral sentiments are somehow in our heads or emotions, as in the moral sense school of Shaftesbury and others. For Hume they get there through our reaction to things as though they caused us pleasure or pain. When they are coupled with our capacity for sympathy, they lead us to react on behalf of others. It is not hard to see why I might react to your doing something beneficial or harmful to me. Your action affects my interests, and I either like it or dislike it, provoking my sentiments so that I then think well or ill of you, or at least of your action. It is an interesting fact that Hume, who thinks his *Treatise* a failure in reaching the public, relegates much of the discussion of the sentiments to an appendix in the later *Enquiry* (EPM App. 1).

Mirroring

What might stand behind the phenomenon that Hume recognizes and uses to ground his claims for sympathy, but that he does not explain?[35] There are now fMRI (functional magnetic resonance imaging) studies of the brain's reaction to others' sensations that corroborate Horace's and Hume's observed facts and that, in a sense, seem to show the phenomenon of *seeing* another's emotions at work. The fMRI studies do not do much more than Hume already did—they establish that mirroring happens, although they are more definitive than Hume's singular testimony. The part of the brain that perceives a smile is evidently the part that engineers a smile of our own, so that Horace's observation may be a biologically hard-wired fact of our brains. Smiles evoke smiles. The evolution of this feature of our brains might be explained by the benefits of smiling in gaining the good graces of others, especially when we are too young to survive on our own.[36] Smiling may enable humans to enjoy very long periods of infancy, childhood, and adolescence so that we can develop extraordinary abilities that set us apart from other animals.

Hume further notes 'we may remark, that the minds of men are mirrors to one another, not only because they reflect each other's emotions, but

[35] There was no need for him to explain; he could observe the phenomenon and could start from there (EPM5.17 n19, SBN 219–20 n).

[36] There are reputedly recent studies that suggest other connections. Those who yawn when another yawns seem to score higher on empathy tests than those who do not mirror the yawns of others. (Henry Fountain, 'Tarzan, Cheetah and the Contagious Yawn,' *New York Times*, 24 Aug. 2004, F1).

also because those rays of passions, sentiments and opinions may be often reverberated, and may decay away by insensible degrees' (T2.2.5.21, SBN 365; see also T3.3.I.7, SBN 576 and EPM5.18, SBN 179).[37] What in twentieth-century philosophy was the problem of other minds (how can we know another's mind?) is assumed away in limited part by Hume. For this too there may now be neurophysiological evidence from fMRI studies. Sympathy, these studies suggest, is a form of direct, non-verbal communication and the evocation of relevant feelings.

It is psychological mirroring that leads me to like or dislike something that is done to you, by letting me sense what you enjoy or suffer. Contemporary neurophysiological findings seem to strengthen Hume's claims for the moral psychology of mirroring, although the mechanism is not yet clear. Those readers who have had difficulty accepting this part of Hume's argument might soon find it easy to accept. Hume appears to be right on the psychology here. The only question that might remain for some is that of his general claims for morality psychologized. Do we have moral reactions (approbation or disapprobation) to the feelings we get from mirroring? Those would be moral reactions on behalf of another. That is to say, the important and very difficult trick Hume needs to complete his explanatory theory is to evoke *my* sentiments—that is, a moral judgment—in response to actions that affect *your* interests.

From the fMRI data it appears possible that these two phenomena—sympathy and moral sentiments—are at least partially run together in our brains.[38] Hence, Hume's theory is complete but in a way that he apparently did not see. The knowledge and the feeling, the sympathy and the sentiments, may come in a single package. There is no mediating interpretation that our brains have to make. A nearly brand new baby smiles back at our smile. It is implausible to suppose that the baby is interpreting our kindness or good will in its first days of life; it is reacting from an apparently hard-wired capacity. Empathy seems to 'mirror' another person's emotional responses in one's own brain.[39] Happily, 'mirror' is Hume's word and also the terminology of contemporary neurophysiological science (T2.2.5.21, SBN 365). Mimicry, which has long been noted and which is detailed by Darwin, has usually been explained as a two-step process. Our perceptions of, say, a smile stimulate thoughts, which guide our behavioral response: smiling back. Studies of brain activity, as

---

[37] See further, Penelhum, 'Hume's Moral Psychology,' 143.

[38] See also, Árdal, *Passion and Value in Hume's* Treatise, 47 n.

[39] The German psychologist, Theodore Lipps, coined the German term for empathy in 1903, and he described the phenomenon of mirroring (Bower, 'Repeat after Me: Imitation is the Sincerest Form of Perception,' 330).

measured by fMRI brain scans, suggest that the whole reaction is immediate in a single step, not mediated by thought. The part of my brain that recognizes a smile also forces or stimulates my own smile and my own feeling of pleasure.[40] Seeing your smile triggers mine. We are to a degree hard-wired to each other.

At a very young age, Hume seems to have grasped the nature of this phenomenon to a sufficient degree as to make it the foundation of his moral psychology. He does not attempt an explanation of the phenomenon but merely starts from it to explain morality as a matter of fellow feeling. In fact, of course, he had no way to prove his assertion of the nature of this psychological trick other than to elicit our agreement that we too have the experience he describes. The technology of fMRI now seems to give us some entrée to the phenomenon.

Incidentally, mirroring seems to be very weak in those with autism.[41] Hence, David Owen is apparently right in saying that the renowned autistic woman, Temple Grandin, is lacking in Humean sympathy.[42] Her lack is organic. Her reason functions very well so that she is able to see herself as like, in her words, an anthropologist on Mars, where she would have little in common with and no sympathy for others—this is the condition she is in on earth.

Sympathy in the fMRI studies appears to be a form of direct, non-verbal communication and the evocation of relevant feelings. In another context, Hume dismissively says of the possibility of an innate sense of rules of property, 'We may as well expect to discover, in the body, new senses, which had before escaped the observation of all mankind' (EPM3.40 SBN 201). In actual fact, he may well have discovered, along with some others, including Horace and recent psychologists, what we might come to call a sense: the sense of sympathy. It is a sense that is much more acute in Hume than in most people but that is clearly evident in large numbers of people, including newborn babies, and apparently other species as well.[43] It may be as hard-wired as the sense of taste or smell.

Hume says our sympathy for those on a ship sinking off shore will be greatly heightened if they are close enough for us to see their faces and their frightened responses. He does not explain this fully but only says that contiguity makes their suffering clearer to us (T3.3.2.5, SBN 594–5; also see T2.1.11.6 and 8,

---

[40] See various contributions to Meltzhoff and Prinz, eds., *The Imitative Mind*. Also see Miller, 'Reflecting on Another's Mind.'

[41] Miller, 'Reflecting on Another's Mind,' 947.

[42] Owen, 'Reason, Reflection, and *Reductios*,' 195. On Temple Grandin, see Sacks, 'An Anthropologist on Mars.'

[43] Chimpanzees and Macaque monkeys, even in infancy at three days, apparently mirror emotions of others (Bower, 'Copycat Monkeys: Macaque Babies Ape Adults' Facial Feats').

SBN 318 and 320). The fMRI studies suggest that the issue is not that we have to see their expressions in order to understand their emotions; our reason is adequate for such understanding. The issue is that *we have to see their expressions in order to trigger the mirroring of our own similar emotions.* This is a phenomenon that is not mediated by thought or reason, and perhaps it cannot be replaced by thought or reason when the actual visions are not available.

Suppose we accept this entire account of our moral sentiments and of their apparent mirroring. If they are merely a fact of our psychology, should they determine our morality? Yes, in Hume's functional way. That is, our sentiments about others evoke responses from us that are responses to the utility, pleasure, or pain of those others. What typically brings pleasure to others is their own benefit, which is *good for them.* We cannot go further to say it is good per se unless we go so far as to say that something like utilitarianism is the right moral theory. Hume does not make this claim, but in his analysis of the motivating force of mirrored reactions he does imply that he and we are psychologically utilitarian. One of the things we can tell about another through mirroring is how something affects their welfare, pleasure, or pain. This fact is important if we are psychologically utilitarian—and mirroring virtually makes us be, as though evolution has produced utilitarianism as our moral response. Psychological utilitarianism connects observation to judgment. These facts do not make utilitarianism the true moral theory; they merely characterize our psychology as moralized through mirroring. This psychology gives us a science of moral beliefs and approbations; it cannot additionally justify those approbations or make them right.

Mirroring is a major discovery for Hume despite the fact that seemingly all people experience it, so that it might well have been a matter of widespread common knowledge. It apparently remains unconscious and inarticulate to most people even while it often regulates their emotions and behavior. Hume is sufficiently perceptive that, once he has noticed the phenomenon, he finds mirroring to be a fundamental part of the psychology of sympathy and therefore a fundamental part of distinctively moral psychology. Mirroring makes Hume's theory psychologically richer than any of the then contemporary moral sense and sentiments theories, which are inherently psychological in their foundations. Their proponents are generally content to stop their inquiries at the point of asserting that we just do know right from wrong, that reason can determine these, or that god has given us such knowledge. Hume has empirically observed—and supposes we can all observe—the phenomenon of mirroring and sympathy.

There is a further trick that might still be difficult: evoking an emotional response of a similar kind in response to the interests *of society*. Identification

with the interests of society must be very weak psychologically and it is grounded in reason more than in sympathy. The neurophysiological studies probably
cannot address such an abstract phenomenon as responding psychologically to
the interests of society. Seeing the interests of society forwarded or abused is
not comparable to the visual cue of a smile or frown.

Natural and Artificial Virtues

Hume distinguishes between natural and artificial virtues.[44] The latter are his
category to handle a fundamentally important problem in the psychology of
our approbation of institutional arrangements. Natural virtues tend to produce
good in every case in which they are properly applied, and often the good of
the action is, in a literal sense, evident. Artificial virtues produce good effects
only through their general effect on social order and public interest, and the
good of any particular action from an artificial virtue may not be evident.
The exercise of a natural virtue has an *immediate* effect directly on its own, it
is self-contained and complete. An action from an artificial virtue has effects
that are *mediated* through institutions, norms, or further consequences beyond
the moment. The good of natural virtues results from each and every case of
their action; the good of artificial virtues results from the existence of a general
practice of following them.[45] Metaphorically, we might say that we can see
the good effects of action from a natural virtue but we cannot typically see the
good effects of any particular action from an artificial virtue.

Hume states the difference best when he turns to discussing the natural
virtues and vices of ordinary virtue theory:

The only difference betwixt the natural virtues and justice lies in this, that the good,
which results from the former, arises from every single act, and is the object of some
natural passion: Whereas a single act of justice, consider'd in itself, may often be
contrary to the public good; and 'tis only the concurrence of mankind, in a general
scheme or system of action, which is advantageous. When I relieve persons in distress,
my natural humanity is my motive; and so far as my succour extends, so far have I
promoted the happiness of my fellow-creatures. But if we examine all the questions,
that come before any tribunal of justice, we shall find, that, considering each case apart,
it wou'd as often be an instance of humanity to decide contrary to the laws of justice
as conformable to them. Judges take from a poor man to give to a rich; they bestow

---

[44] The discussion begins at T3.1.2.9, SBN 474.

[45] Schneewind, 'The Misfortunes of Virtue,' 52. Schneewind says that artificial duties, like the
perfect duties of traditional natural law theorists, cover the domain of clear and definite claims that may
be enforced by law (51); natural duties are not so clear and sharp.

on the dissolute the labor of the industrious; and put into the hands of the vicious the means of harming both themselves and others. The whole scheme, however, of law and justice is advantageous to the society and to every individual (T 3.3.1.12, SBN 579).

The introduction of the artificial virtues resolves a problem in Hutcheson's ethics. Hutcheson supposes that his god has arranged our psychology to approve those things that give utility.[46] Bishop Butler points out that sometimes we approve things that are contrary to any dictates of utility. For example, if an impoverished man returns the dropped money of a wealthy person who would not even notice the loss, we approve the poor man's action even though by keeping the money he might be able to prevent his children from going hungry.[47] Hume does not wish to give up the view that the psychology of moral approval turns on the pleasure we get from seeing the virtuous action, from our sense of its utility. He sees that the issue here is one of the systematic structure of the law and of social norms. These must be carried out or lose their effect. But this means that they will be carried out in some instances in which they do not immediately produce pleasing outcomes. One might call this an anti-utilitarian conclusion,[48] but it is merely a conclusion about the economy or psychology of thought, especially in institutions. Indeed, we take many mental shortcuts, such as finding beautiful or pleasurable an action or character trait that is useful without supposing someone actually enjoys or receives direct benefits from the action or character.

Natural duties may be characterized as part of a one-stage theory of responsibility; artificial duties as part of a two-stage theory. In acting on a one-stage natural virtue, we see the good effect of our action directly without mediation from institutions or other actors other than those we are affecting with our actions. In acting on a two-stage artificial virtue, we see only indirectly through the fit with the mediating institution or norm we are following, but we may not see the good effect of our action, because it may not even have a good effect. Rather, its beneficial nature depends on the beneficial qualities of having the relevant institution or norm to guide our behavior generally for overall good effects.

Incidentally, Hume's invocation of the artificial duties and virtues may have cost him dearly. In his view he was denied appointment as Professor of Pneumaticks and Moral Philosophy at Edinburgh University for a list of sacrilegious offenses in his *Treatise*, including 'sapping the Foundations of Morality, by denying the natural and essential Difference betwixt Right and Wrong, Good and Evil, Justice and Injustice; making the Difference only

---

[46] Hutcheson, *Essay with Illustrations*, 145–6.   [47] Schneewind, 'Introduction,' 8–9.
[48] See e.g. Hiskes, 'Has Hume a Theory of Social Justice?'

artificial, and to arise from human Conventions and Compacts.'[49] In any case, university and broader Scottish politics went against him and favored far lesser men both at Edinburgh and a few years later at Glasgow.[50]

In one of his most important (but apparently one of his least read) papers, 'Two Concepts of Rules,' Rawls presents a two-stage account of what we can call institutional utilitarianism. He keeps the shell of Hume's arguments for a two-stage (or two-level) justification: first we have institutions and then we have actions taken under the aegis of the institutions. If we want to accomplish certain ends, we must have institutions to do the central work of coordinating and mobilizing us and then, at a second order perhaps, we need institutions to secure essentially equal or fair treatment of us as we are being coordinated and mobilized. Then if we wish to justify an action taken in an institution, we must do so by deducing the action from the requirements of the institution. Rawls broadens this claim to include practices, such as moral practices, rules of a game, and, we might suppose, norms. This is precisely Hume's move: first a two-stage argument to justify the institutional (artificial) principles and then to judge individual actions according to their fit with these principles.

Rawls develops this analysis as a defense of utilitarianism against various claims that attempt to show that utilitarianism is inherently unable to take justice into account. He continues the two-stage scheme in his later theory of justice, which is concerned with the basic structure of society, with the arrangement of major social institutions into one scheme of cooperation.[51] A theory of justice determines social institutions that will distribute advantages from social cooperation.[52] As in the earlier argument in defense of utilitarianism, he proposes a two-stage theory that includes both institutional design and action under the institutions. Given the causal constraints of his time, Hume rules out concern with redistribution by the state or even Rawls's holistic design of institutions.[53] At the point of designing institutions of justice, Rawls's problem is almost entirely one of social science, not of moral theory. Hence, his solutions must be as indeterminate as social science is, a problem that Hume openly recognizes and accommodates his theory to.[54]

Here we may add, not merely metaphorically, that the good that follows action from an artificial virtue may not be seen at all. Rather, we have to consider the good of having the institution or practice or norm in place in our society. Once we have an institution for the good effects it has, we

---

[49] Hume, *New Letters of David Hume*, 17–18. See further Gaskin, *Hume's Philosophy of Religion*, 1–2.
[50] The story is complex. See Emerson, 'The "Affair" at Edinburgh and the "Project" at Glasgow.'
[51] Rawls, *A Theory of Justice*, 4, 47, 84.   [52] Ibid. 6.
[53] See Hardin 'From Order to Justice.'   [54] See further, Hardin, *Indeterminacy and Society*, chap. 6.

are then bound to a substantial degree to let it make decisions on certain matters. As in Rawls's two-concepts argument, there cannot be a person in the role of saying we should override what the system of justice requires in this case and therefore implicitly in each case.[55] Although Hume still makes such claims in the later *Enquiry*, he largely drops the terminological distinction between natural and artificial virtues there and relegates some of the discussion of the artificial virtue of justice to an appendix (EPM App. 3, SBN 303–11); and he qualifies the sense of 'natural' (EPM App. 3.9, SBN 307).

Unintended Consequences

Among Hume's most important arguments is that social institutions are largely unplanned, they are products of social evolution. In the phrase of Adam Ferguson, many of our institutions are 'the result of human action, but not the execution of any design.'[56] In the twentieth century, the strongest advocate of the thesis implicit in this phrase is F. A. Hayek with many discussions.[57] The principle is fundamentally important for Hume because he insists on naturalistic mechanisms against rationalist or teleological arguments for the creation of institutions of justice, the convention of promise-keeping, and the maintenance of social order—every artificial virtue—which commonly arise, to use a favorite word of Hayek, spontaneously and without plan or guidance. Hume repeatedly says such things as that the system of justice, 'comprehending the interests of each individual, is of course advantageous to the public; tho' it be not intended for that purpose by the inventors' (T3.2.6.6, SBN 529). It is a social institution to be judged for its overall social benefits, but it is the product of individual contributions to its structure and content. It is also true that even the maintenance of the system depends on individual actions taken for reasons other than concern for the public or collective benefit.

---

[55] Rawls, 'Two Concepts of Rules.'

[56] Ferguson, *An Essay on the History of Civil Society*, 122. Ferguson, writing nearly three decades after Hume's discussion, attributes this insight to Cardinal de Retz's *Memoirs*, which are available online from Project Gutenberg, where they can be searched for each of the main words in Ferguson's formula. I cannot find any near equivalent of his phrase there. The nearest is a strictly individual-level, not societal-level, claim: 'With a design to do good, he did evil.' Hayek, checking the *Memoirs* of de Retz, finds only Cromwell's supposed claim that one never climbs higher than when one does not know where one is going (Hayek, 'The Results of Human Action but not of Human Design,' 96 n). One would not have wanted to quote that line to Sir Edmund Hillary.

[57] See especially 'The Results of Human Action but not of Human Design' and *The Counter-Revolution of Science*.

This device, or something like it, is necessary if we are to avoid supposing that individuals in their own private interactions seek the overall justice of society. Knud Haakonssen says that, 'to see justice in this way, as an unintended consequence of individual human actions, must be one of the boldest moves in the history of the philosophy of law.'[58] The irony is that this bold move sounds like mere common sense. Law is not planned, it evolves from the inputs of thousands of people over centuries. Other social norms grow and develop in like manner. Oddly, however, Hume had almost no impact on the development of legal theory in Britain, perhaps merely from his timing. Jeremy Bentham and John Austin, whose views and approach dominated legal philosophy for nearly two centuries, were under the sway of continental rationalist legal theory. Hayek thinks Hume the greatest legal philosopher in Britain before Bentham, but his contributions are sorely neglected.[59]

Haakonssen argues that the insight into unintended consequences allows Hume to escape the rationalism of Hobbes.[60] It also lets him maintain his naturalist program of explanation of our sense of justice. He replaces natural law, in both its religious and its teleological variants, with a fully secular and empirical conception. And he replaces ideal theory of law with empirical explanation of it. The prior visions make law static, as though what is right today has always been right. Hume's evolutionary understanding allows us to fit today's law to today's conditions. Whereas killing in vengeance was once not merely legal but honorable, today it is murder. Property law under simpler conditions was less complex than it is today, when, among other things, it must take into consideration the external effects of the ways I might use my property. In essence, Hume sets the agenda for a modern explanatory understanding of law.[61]

Incidentally, it is in this developmental sense that we have to understand his so-called laws of nature. As with Hobbes, these are sociological laws, not moral or 'natural' laws (T3.2.1.19, SBN 484; T3.2.4.1, SBN 514). They therefore change as the sociological context changes. No one today would want to be governed by the laws of medieval Europe or feudal Japan—indeed, the very idea is revolting. But the laws of those eras probably made considerable sense in the conditions of their times and for the people they governed.

---

[58] Haakonssen, *The Science of a Legislator*, 20.

[59] Hayek, 'The Legal and Political Philosophy of David Hume,' 109. The situation is better today, especially after the publication of Haakonssen's treatment of the jurisprudence of Hume and Smith in *The Science of a Legislator*.

[60] Haakonssen, *The Science of a Legislator*, 18. As argued in chapter 9, this is one of three ways in which Hume's understanding of convention resolves a problem in Hobbes.

[61] There is still, of course, the positive law tradition, with its often deadly definitional approach to law.

The idea of unintended consequences seems very slow to affect our social theorizing. Probably the most important way in which it is brought to bear is through functional analysis.[62] Robert Merton is the major figure in the sociological analysis of 'manifest and latent functions'; the first referring 'to those objective consequences for a specified unit (person, subgroup, social or cultural system) which contribute to its adjustment or adaptation and were *so intended*; the second referring to *unintended or unrecognized* consequences of the same order.'[63] The argument for functional maintenance of some behavior or institution is that it has benefits that are commonly not recognized but that reinforce the behavior that produces those benefits.

Analogizing from biology in noting that the whole animal is easier to recognize and is more immediately accessible than its various parts, Auguste Comte supposes that societies and institutions must likewise be seen holistically from the highest level rather than piecemeal from the ground up.[64] Hayek argues against him and others for a 'compositive theory of social phenomena [of] how the independent action of many men can produce coherent wholes, persistent structures of relationship which serve important human purposes without having been designed for that end.'[65]

It should be obvious that an unintended consequence need not be good. We could, for example, contrive a functional account of racism or of other norms of exclusion.[66] The extremely perverse and self-destructive dueling norm among aristocrats of Europe over several centuries was functionally reinforced even during periods when large percentages of young aristocratic males died for frivolous 'offenses.'[67] There can also be unintended consequences of actions that are merely not well understood. Hume argues against individual alms giving in general (and presumably also against the Elizabethan poor laws) that its harmful effects might outweigh its benefits, but the latter are easily seen while the former require more difficult investigation (EPM2.18, SBN 180). Here Hume's empirical method is to check whether action from a particular virtue really does have beneficial effects. He also notes many unintentionally bad commercial laws made in ignorance of economic consequences. For example, under Henry VII, in 'order to promote archery no bows were to be sold at a higher price than six shillings and four-pence [in the currency values of Hume's time]. The only effect of this regulation must be either that

---

[62] See further the functional analysis of conventions in chapter 4.

[63] Merton, *Social Theory and Social Structure*, 117, emphases added. He treats manifest and latent functions in chap. 3. For the model of functional explanation, see this book chapter 4 and Hardin, *One for All*, 82–6.

[64] Quoted in Hayek, *The Counter-Revolution of Science*, 58.   [65] Ibid. 80.

[66] Hardin, *One for All*, chap. 4.   [67] Ibid. 91–100.

the people would be supplied with bad bows or none at all.'[68] Henry got the opposite of what he wanted.

Concluding Remarks

Rawls says that Hume does not address the 'fundamental moral question' of the correct normative content of morality.[69] On the contrary, Hume addresses that question by essentially dismissing it and saying there is no such thing as truth in morality, a point he makes repeatedly.[70] As noted, Rawls repeatedly says that Hume has no theory of practical reason and of its authority, that his account is purely psychological. This could mean that Hume is merely giving us a psychological account and has nothing to say about the actual content of a true morality—but in fact he gives us arguments for why there is no such morality to be shown, that moral views are subjective, not objective. Part of his psychological enterprise is to explain why we commonly think there is a true morality, or at least why we often think our moral views are correct in some sense. Rawls says Hume does not give an analysis of morality in the contemporary sense. He merely explains how we happen to make moral distinctions.[71] That is right and Hume is deliberate in this project and in the resolute rejection of the project of determining the content of 'morality in the contemporary sense' or in any other sense. That is an incoherent project because its central term—'correct normative content'—is meaningless.

Rawls also says Hume gives no answer to the standard twentieth-century query why we should be moral.[72] Here oddly he may be wrong for the opposite reason. Hume gives an answer in terms of my interests for why I should behave well in many contexts and he gives an account in terms of the interests of all of us for why we have certain of our political institutions and practices. He answers both the question why I should be moral in my behavior and the question why the larger society should be moral in some sense or should be structured to achieve public interests and mutual advantage.

Rawls supposes Hume wants to show that 'morality is a natural fact, explicable in view of our natural human interests and our need for society,' that 'morality and our practice of it are the expression of our nature, given our place in the world and our dependence on society.'[73] These statements should be qualified. Hume wants to show that *our views of morality* are a

---

[68] Hume, *History of England*, 3.78.   [69] Rawls, *Lectures*, 98.
[70] See for example, EPM App. 1, SBN 287–9, where his dismissal of rationalist ethics is harsh.
[71] Rawls, *Lectures*, 94–5.   [72] Ibid. 99.   [73] Ibid. 51.

natural fact, not that *morality in the contemporary or any other sense* is a natural fact—whether that 'contemporary' is Hume's time or ours. It is just the psychology of our views, not the truth of them, that Hume investigates. We might therefore wonder whether those who disagree with Hume have a different psychology.

Hume often speaks of obligations, especially 'natural' obligations. This is an entirely self-regarding principle. Once I have made a promise to you, I am not obligated to *you*. I am obligated in the mechanical sense that I will suffer losses from not keeping my promise. This is clearly the meaning of the claim that *interest is the first obligation to keeping promises* (T3.2.5.11, SBN 523) and to being obedient to government (T3.2.8.7, SBN 545). My obligation to keep my promise is my interest in maintaining good relations with you and others to avoid penalties such as loss of opportunity to exchange with you or others in the future. One can give a similar account of Hume's references to natural virtues. It is not clear why he has chosen to use the word obligation here and one might think this usage perverse. Substantive moral theorists must find Hume's formula jarring. Perhaps he uses the word obligation in order to make deliberately clear that he rejects any claim that I have a moral obligation that grows out of my voluntary act of will. He insists that there is no such thing. I might eventually moralize my own natural, self-interest-based obligation to keep promises, but that would be merely a trick of my psychology, and it would not make my obligation moral. The word we might prefer to use when Hume speaks of our being obligated in this way is to be obliged.

Hume and Hobbes blur the normative sense of obligation in the same way. Hobbes more often says we are obliged, for example, by our promise. He seems to mean, with Hume, that we will suffer costs if we fail to keep the promise (no one will ever trust us again—brutal thought). Hutcheson, writing a decade or so before Hume's *Treatise* gives at least three then-current meanings of obligation. One of these is that some action is 'necessary to obtain Happiness to the agent, or to avoid Misery.' Another is roughly equivalent to contemporary senses of moral obligation. A third is that it denotes 'an indispensable Necessity to act in a certain manner.'[74] He says many other confused definitions are at work and he wishes writers would simply use the phrase that connotes their intended meaning rather than the multifarious word 'obligation.' He further runs the terms 'obliged' and 'obligated' together, as Hobbes does.[75] The two non-moral senses fit Hume's claim that '*interest is the*

---

[74] Hutcheson, *Essay with Illustrations*, 146.

[75] Samuel Johnson's dictionary, dating from the same time, does not give Hutcheson's panoply of meanings of obligation, but gives only the moralized sense. Many dictionaries run obliged and obligated together.

first obligation to keeping promises.' We keep them because we are likely to lose if we do not.

Hume occasionally seems to commend substantive morality, such as being virtuous, especially in some of his later essays. But his explanatory theory does not entail or include any such commendation. After starting into one of his panegyrics, he ruefully says, 'But I forget, that it is not my present business to recommend generosity and benevolence, or to paint, in their true colours, all the genuine charms of the social virtues … our object here being more the speculative, than the practical part of morals.' If this were really a matter of mere forgetting, he might have deleted this passage before going to print. He implicitly attributes his panegyric to psychology, saying 'it is difficult to abstain from some sally of panegyric' (EPM2.5, SBN 177–8). He speaks here not from his theory, but from his own personal psychology.[76] He is the first to grant that he is as much subject to his psychological account of such feelings as are others, and he also asserts that his occasional sallies of panegyric are not founded in any moral truth of his own approbations and disapprobations. (Such sallies are more frequent in the *Enquiry* than in the more tough-minded *Treatise*, and more frequent still in those of his short essays that were seemingly intended to sway the public.)

Note that not all artificial virtues are political, as the account of promise-keeping shows. But all political virtues are artificial, as is implied by the fact that political society comes after society at all and is therefore itself an artificial construct. The political virtues involve institutions, conventions, and norms, all of which are artifices of human contrivance. They typically involve large numbers, even require large numbers of people in interaction for them to have any content or force. Indeed, even the norm of promise-keeping arises socially and not merely personally. It is implausible that we would have a promising norm in a family on its own without society. There we could harmonize our actions with the beneficence that families can generate. The norm of promise-keeping must have arisen as a convention, as a social construct. Moreover, promising requires for its meaning that there be a social definition of it, and the very idea of reputation that stands behind promises requires a social context.

Promising is the interesting, but not unique, case of a social convention that governs small-number interactions (although in a very large-number instance of promising, the elder President George Bush promised all Americans he would not raise taxes—at least some of those Americans may have been offended enough by his subsequent reversal to vote against his re-election).

---

[76] There is some justice in the claim that Hume is an emotivist in ethics. That his panegyrics are merely assertions of his own feelings is an instance of emotivism.

Other such norms are those of truth-telling, honesty, and politeness. Perhaps no such norm is more important to our social lives than that of fidelity in keeping to promises, although some might suppose fidelity in marriage is about as important in some societies.

Hume's associationist psychology, his category of artificial virtues, and his recourse to explanation of morals from the passions may have been the innovations that pleased Hume most, although many scholars today would put his analysis of convention in the list of his most impressive inventions and we might eventually rank mirroring high in this list. His political philosophy is principally compounded of the account of artificial virtues and the analysis of convention. With these two ideas, he explains much of politics and gives us an account of why, psychologically, we might approve of government, law, and other institutions of social order. The analysis of artificial virtues involves subtle complexities and Hume gives it far more space (most of T3.2, SBN 477–573) than he gives to the ordinary natural virtues (T3.3, SBN 574–621). Most of his natural virtues are well known from traditional virtue theory, and Hume's views of them are relatively standard, except that, of course, his purpose is to give them a psychological explanation—or to give our approbation of them a psychological explanation.

Note that if a single act of justice may violate the natural virtue of beneficence (T3.2.2.22, SBN 497), then the virtues can come into conflict with each other in their requirements on us. This fact is more or less obvious merely from the fact that there is more than one virtue. It is, however a problematic fact for traditional virtue theory, although not for Hume's theory, which is about the psychology of the virtues and about the complexity of fitting them into both one-stage and two-stage accounts.

3

Strategic Analysis

I learn to do a service to another, without bearing him any real kindness; because I foresee, that he will return my service, in expectations of another of the same kind, and in order to maintain the same correspondence of good offices with me or with others.[1]

Hume has two classes of structural arguments going at once: the division between natural and artificial virtues and the division into strategic categories of problems that we face and must want to resolve. There is a wonderful set of insights behind each of these divisions. The natural—artificial division is discussed in chapter 2, where it is characterized as a division between one-stage and two-stage (or individual-level and institutional-level) explanations of our moral approbations. Let us here address the strategic categories of the problems we typically face in moral and political choice. While Hume's discussion of artificial virtues is well understood by many writers, the full scope and significance of his strategic analysis is not generally recognized.

Game theory was invented almost whole by the mathematician John von Neumann (1903–57) and the economist Oskar Morgenstern (1902–77) during the Second World War. Their theory was less a theory that made predictions or gave explanations than a framework for viewing complex social interactions. It caught on with mathematicians and defense analysts almost immediately, with social psychologists much later, and with economists and philosophers later still.[2] But it has now become almost necessary to state some problems game theoretically in order to keep them clear and to relate them to other analyses. The game-theory framework represents ranges of payoffs that players can get from their simultaneous or sequential moves in games in which they interact. Moves are essentially choices of strategies, and outcomes are the intersections

[1] T3.2.5.9, SBN 521.
[2] An early exception is Braithwaite, *Theory of Games as a Tool for the Moral Philosopher*, which appeared already in 1955.

of strategy choices. If you and I are in a game, both of us typically depend on our own and on the other's choices of strategies for our payoffs.[3]

Of course, the role of self-interest in explaining behavior was not a discovery of very modern times. From Socrates to the beneficent utilitarians, interest has been of central concern. Indeed, it has long been common to view morality as action against one's own interest in the interest of others or for otherwise good ends or good reasons. For example, Henry Sidgwick (1838–1900) saw benevolence and self-interest as often contrary dual motivations.[4] Machiavelli and Hobbes were merely more insistent than many earlier philosophers on seeing the world as dominated by self-interest, and they were less ready to salvage social order in theory by supposing individuals just would or do behave well or public-spiritedly.

Both Hobbes and Hume have a grasp of the nature of strategic interactions and their role in social life that is articulate and remarkably rich in its implications for their analyses. This part of their theories was poorly understood before the latter half of the twentieth century, and they were often pilloried for getting things wrong by critics who did not understand their strategic analyses. They had the great disadvantage of discovering strategic patterns and structures only in the context of trying to resolve problems of social interactions without having a background general theory of strategic structures. Only with the rise of game theory did such a background theory become generally available. Hume has, as I will show, a fuller grasp of the range of strategic interactions. In particular, he adds the strategic effect of repetition or iteration onto static, one-time interaction between the same people.

Hume's account assumes three modal categories: conflict, cooperation, and coordination, all of which he fits both to small- and large-scale interactions. Hobbes sees all of these, but primarily only at the large scale of the whole society. He fails to notice the import of iterated interactions and therefore is never led to the idea of a repeated coordination problem; he analyzes only the one-time coordination on an initial sovereign and the general benefit of such a coordination. Indeed, the nastiness of Hobbes's state of nature turns on the absence of iterated interactions—a state of affairs that Hume thinks essentially impossible. This is Hume's great insight and it is the assumption behind his

---

[3] Hume notes that actions per se are neither virtuous nor vicious. The result of an action 'depends on Chance.' Brutus, seeking to defend liberty in Rome instead 'riveted the Chains of Rome faster' (*Letters of David Hume*, ed. Grieg, 1. 34–5). This could be read as the pre-eminent problem of choice of strategy in a strategic interaction. You choose a strategy hoping for a good outcome, but others' choices taken together with yours push you into a bad outcome. Much of contemporary action theory misses the fundamental significance of this issue in social choice and action (see Hardin, *Morality within the Limits of Reason*, 68–70).

[4] Sidgwick, *The Methods of Ethics*.

argument for conventions in his and David Lewis's[5] technical sense (as spelled out in chapter 4). This lacuna leads Hobbes to recognize a major problem in his theory of the creation of a state that he cannot resolve—the empowerment of the new sovereign—whereas Hume resolves it readily.

To begin, note that Hume does three things in his strategic account. Briefly these are as follows. First, in essence Hume divides all interactions into three modal types: conflict, cooperation (in the form of exchange), and coordination. To motivate these distinctions, note that simple benevolence fits into the conflict structure (I make you better off by making myself worse off). Ordinary exchange, reciprocity, and promise-keeping fit into the cooperation structure (which is the game theorist's prisoner's dilemma[6]) in which we both become better off through our cooperative interaction. Finally, our meeting for lunch tomorrow and Hume's example of two rowers, each with a single oar, who both want to get across some body of water, fit into the coordination structure. This sounds like—and is—relatively simplistic game theory, but it is still two centuries before any other such careful analysis of strategic categories and their implications for behavior. Indeed, perhaps the most original of the strategic categories is coordination, which was not well analyzed or widely appreciated before the 1950s, when Thomas Schelling wrote extensively on it.[7]

Second, Hume recognizes the difference in scale between dyadic and small-number interactions on the one hand and large-scale, even society-wide interactions on the other. It is at the larger scale that his political theory works, and that is where our main focus will be. But the strategic categories are essentially the same for the small- and large-scale problems. For example, distributive justice, as it is commonly discussed in contemporary political philosophy, is an instance of simple conflict generalized to the societal level. One social group is made worse off in order to benefit another group. Collective action fits the exchange category at the large-group or societal level—it is an instance of the n-prisoner's dilemma.[8]

Third, Hume introduces the possibility that a particular interaction or form of interaction is repeated regularly. When this happens, the incentive structure changes and we no longer focus only on the immediate payoffs from the present interaction but begin to focus on how our choice in the present interaction might affect future opportunities, including opportunities for further interaction at all. For example, if I do not reciprocate your action now, you may never attempt to cooperate with me again but will look for

[5] Lewis, *Convention*.

[6] This claim will be spelled out below. Also see Hardin, 'Exchange Theory on Strategic Bases.'

[7] Schelling, *The Strategy of Conflict*, 53–80, 89–99.

[8] Hardin, 'Collective Action as an Agreeable n-Prisoners' Dilemma'; *Collective Action*, chap. 2.

other partners. This effect is fundamentally important for promise-keeping and social order. Social conventions, such as those governing principles of succession of monarchs and rules for handling property, are the result of repeated coordination on a particular outcome, also at the large-number or societal level. Ongoing, repeated relationships are, more generally, 'requisite to support trust and good correspondence in society' (EPM4.14, SBN 209).[9] It is through ongoing relations that we structure most of our existence without reference to or regulation by government.

Hume's two grand divisions of his problems—implicitly into strategic categories and explicitly into natural and artificial virtues—might seem to be partly related, because, for example, the virtue of benevolence is a small-number issue and is a natural virtue, while the virtue of obedience to government is a large-number issue and is artificial. But the keeping of a promise is essentially regulated by a larger social convention, and is therefore an artificial virtue even though the keeping of any particular promise is typically at issue for a dyad. In general, Hume's distinction between natural and artificial virtues is a response to certain standard ways of conceiving morality in the generation or so just before him. Small-number relationships are typically the subject of moral theory; large-number relationships are usually the subject of political theory.

The division of Hume's issues into strategic categories often seems not even especially conscious. It is as if Hume simply sees the particular strategic structure of any specific issue he is analyzing at the moment and recognizes its significance for his analysis, as in table 3.1. His focus is so sharply on the problems of social order and interaction that he does not stop to put the strategic categories into order. Keeping the categories clear even without an analytical framework suggests a daunting intellect. Perhaps it is this remarkable capacity that makes him not be bothered by any 'inclination to set up axioms or to construct deductive systems.'[10] We often are inclined to do just that.

Strategic Categories

The argument that Hume is a proto game theorist cannot be that he says he uses standard game theoretical arguments or that he claims to give a

[9] See further, Hardin, *Trust and Trustworthiness*, chap. 1.
[10] Passmore, *Hume's Intentions*, 152. Hume's clarity makes it possible for others to do the cataloging, as Capaldi (*David Hume*, 131) does for his account of the passions and Baier (*A Progress of Sentiments*, 198–219) does for his virtues.

strategic analysis of his categories. Rather, the argument is that his categories are very consistently ordered as though they were derived or described game theoretically. This is true of his general discussions and also of his examples or accounts of specific problems in the world. To be so consistent required a sophistication and clear-headedness that is beyond most of us and that has been beyond many commentators on Hume. Yet, once we put what he has done into a strategic perspective—with the relevant terminology—we should have little difficulty seeing the arguments; and many of us can readily accept his theory. The frequency with which Hume is accused of erroneous argument by his critics and even his advocates is astonishing. Some of these claims are arguably just. Many of them are demonstrably wrong as we can readily see once they are set against the strategic structures that underlie his arguments.

Hume discusses broad issues that define six strategic categories, in the form of three strategic structures, each at small and large scale. Let us put them in order with examples of all of them:

Conflict: In the category of conflict at the small-number scale of individual morality, there is benevolence. Large-number conflict interactions include the problem of distributive justice. Hume mentions this issue but then dismisses the idea of distributive justice as unworkable and pernicious.

Cooperation: In the category of exchange and cooperation at the small scale, there are reciprocity and promise-keeping as well as ordinary exchange. In this category at the large-number scale of politics and political order, there is the commonplace problem of collective action.

Coordination: In the category of small-number coordination, Hume mentions specific examples, such as that of two people rowing a boat (T3.2.2.10, SBN 490; EPM App. 3.8, SBN 306–7). He gives too few details, but let us suppose one has an oar on the right and the other has an oar on the left. They share the strong desire to get to some destination but if they do not coordinate, they will get nowhere. Often in such cases, there is little at stake. You and I may coordinate in meeting for lunch today, but our coordination is not itself likely to be a significant moral issue. In this category at the large scale there are various conventions or norms for ownership, inheritance, succession to office or the throne, and the stability of government, all of which involve various rules for resolving social choices. Hume offers very clear examples and analyses of all of these. They are all grounded in large-number coordinations on resolutions of problems that recur, so that iteration can produce a standard response that is then a convention or norm to govern future behavior.

The strategic categories for two-person interactions are represented in games 3.1–3.3. All of these can be generalized in relevant ways to large-number interactions. In each cell the payoffs are ordered R, C (for Row and

Column), with ordinal payoffs, so that 1 is the first choice or best outcome for the relevant player, 2 is next best, and so forth. In game 1, conflict, Column has no choice. If the players are at one outcome, one of the players can be made better off only if the other is made worse off. In game 3.3, coordination, either can be made better (or worse) off only if the other is as well. Game 3.2 is a mix of conflict and coordination.

Game 3.1 Conflict

	Column	
	I	1,2
Row		
	II	2,1

Game 3.2 Prisoner's Dilemma or Exchange

	Column	
	Cooperate	Defect
Cooperate	2,2	4,1
Row		
Defect	1,4	3,3

Game 3.3 Coordination

	Column	
	I	II
I	1,1	2,2
Row		
II	2,2	1,1

Coordination and conflict are relatively transparent, but there can be difficulties in coordinating when, as in game 3.3, there is more than one possible point of coordination. There might then be a *coordination problem*. Such a problem can readily be overcome if we are in communication and can simply agree on joint strategy choices that make sure we achieve one of the two better outcomes. If there are very many of us, however, such communication might be very difficult, so that we might fail to coordinate. Hume addresses this difficulty with his analysis of convention, which is partially spelled out below and applied to government in chapter 4.

Let us say more about the prisoner's dilemma of game 3.2, because it is strategically more complex than the other two categories. It involves some conflict of interest in the choice between the two outcomes that involve one of us defecting and the other cooperating. And it involves a strong element of coordination in the choice between the both-defect and the both-cooperate outcomes. It is essentially the model of exchange when there is no state or legal authority or no ongoing social relationships to compel either of us to fulfill our half of the deal. If we are in a barter economy without money, we might simply trade what you have for what I have. If I am Row, I would ideally like our outcome to be in the lower left cell. That can happen, however, only if you simply give me what you have or I take it from you. In a Hobbesian state of nature, I might attempt to take it, but we would not call my action stealing because property or ownership has no meaning in that world, so that everything of any value can be taken by anyone.[11] Hume recognizes the strategic structure of exchange in commenting on a failure of it when I can do something for you today in return for your doing something for me tomorrow (T3.2.5.8, SBN 520–1).

If we have norms or government to control our interactions, however, the only way I can arrange for us to be in the lower left cell is by stealing from you. Then, of course, there is the threat of legal action to punish me and to rectify the theft. Hence, in the presence of a working legal system or of compelling norms backed by sanctions, the attractiveness of the lower left cell changes. Either I cannot get to it at all or, if I attempt to get there, I must expect to suffer costs external to the game matrix that make it not beneficial to me. For Hume, *the role of government is to give us incentives external to our immediate interactions that will affect the way we behave in those interactions.* It enables us to exchange to our mutual advantage by blocking the theft that would make any interaction not beneficial to one of us, hence not mutually advantageous.

In sum, we have a strategic analysis of the differences between numerous categories of moral and political problems, or rather of the problems that morality and political theory should address and that norms and institutions should manage. Justice as order is a large-number coordination problem; establishing a government to manage justice as order is a coordination problem that can be resolved with a convention. Collective action is a large-number exchange or cooperation problem. Distributive justice is a large-number conflict problem, and it would take either popular acquiescence or even support to establish any strong principles of distributive justice for a polity. It would also likely require fairly strong government imposition to make it work, with taxation of some to benefit others. Hume thinks this to be

---

[11] This is the major difference between Hobbes and Locke (and other Lockean libertarians, such as Nozick). Locke supposes that there are property rights independently of the existence of a state or government. Hobbes essentially supposes that a right that is not defensible has no content so that there is no point in saying there 'is' such a right. In a Hobbesian state of nature, no rights would be defensible. For Hume, as we will see, my control or 'possession' over something might prevail even without government to back my claims because there can be social conventions—norms in contemporary language—that give others incentive to honor my claims.

Table 3.1 Classes of strategic interactions

Dyadic and small-number	Large-number
Pure Conflict	**Conflict**
Benevolence (T3.3.3, SBN 602–6; EPM2, SBN 176–81)	Distributive Justice (EPM3.26, SBN 194)
Gratuitous promise	
Cooperation (exchange)	**Collective Action**
Exchange promise (T3.2.5, SBN 516–25)	Dredging harbors, etc. (T3.2.7.8, SBN 539)
Draining meadow (T3.2.7.8, SBN 538)	Draining meadow (T3.2.7.8, SBN 538)
Mutual help in harvesting (T3.2.5.8, SBN 520–1)	
Coordination	**Coordination/Convention**
Coordination promise	Royal succession (T3.2.10.9–13, SBN 559–61)
Two men in a boat (EPM3.8, SBN 306)	Inheritance rules (T3.2.3.11, SBN 510–13)
	Traffic rules for wagons (EPM4.19, SBN 210)
	Pedestrians (EPM4.19 n, SBN 210 n)

nearly impossible in his time, when government power and even government information on citizens were very limited.

Benevolence

It is sometimes argued that there is a significant change in views from the *Treatise* to the later *Enquiry Concerning the Principles of Morals*. The change is perhaps most often said to be in the apparent elevation of benevolence to a more prominent role in the argument.

It is requisite, that there be an original propensity of some kind, in order to be a basis to self-love, by giving a relish to the objects of its pursuit; and none more fit for this purpose than benevolence or humanity. The goods of fortune are spent in one gratification or another: The miser, who accumulates his annual income, and lends it out at interest, has really spent it in the gratification of his avarice. And it would be difficult to show, why a man is more a loser by a generous action, than by any other method of expence; since the utmost which he can attain, by the most elaborate selfishness, is the indulgence of some affection. (EPM9.20, SBN 281)

Here benevolence is foundational because it can be part of my desire to be beneficent just as it can be part of my desire to enjoy a hike in the hills, attendance at an opera, or a grand meal at Paris's Taillevent. But the issue is still deeper than this. 'Were there no appetite of any kind antecedent to self-love, that propensity could scarcely ever exert itself; because we should, in that case, have felt few and slender pains or pleasures, and have little misery or happiness to avoid or to pursue'(EPM App. 2.12, SBN 301–2). There is no part of Hume's theory that says what passions we can and cannot have. We can have passions for the welfare of our children, of our friends, and even of the farthest reaches of humanity, although the strength of these passions must wane dramatically as we reach farther from ourselves.

Hume clinches his case by appealing to a negative passion that many must feel very strongly. We can readily engage our resources in seeking vengeance, just as much as we do in seeking benevolence. We can feel with Isabella who, upon leaving the boorish Heathcliff, thinks 'what misery laid on Heathcliff could content me, unless I have had a hand in it? I'd rather he suffered *less*, if I might cause his sufferings, and he might *know* that I was the cause.'[12] She would happily bear costs to make him miserable. Hume chides his doubters: 'what a malignant philosophy it must be, that will not allow to humanity and friendship the same privileges which are undisputably granted to the darker passions of enmity and resentment?' Such a philosophy would be 'a very bad one for any serious argument or reasoning' (EPM App. 2.13, SBN 302).

Perhaps this difference between the earlier and later texts is little more than one of emphasis and wording intended to counter the chance of misreading Hume's views. Hence, it is an elaboration of the earlier views. Hume already says in the earlier book that our concern with all others taken together typically rivals our concern with our narrow selves (T3.2.2.5, SBN 487). Moreover, his greater use of the term utility rather than interest seems to be deliberately an effort to focus his claims on the role of utility and interest in our motivations to action *both for our own and for others'* benefit. Or perhaps action is too strong a term, because all he needs is approbation or judgment. As he emphasizes, feeling approbation does not require or entail any commitment to doing anything (T3.3.1.23, SBN 586).

Hume asserts that benevolence has two forms: the general and the particular. The first plays far and away the stronger role in his arguments for the institutions of justice and law; the second is more important in our spontaneous moral relations with others. In the first form, I have no particular concern with the other person or even very nearly the whole society, but I care somewhat for them through a general sympathy for others. The second, particular form grows out of actual relationships with others, so that I have an ongoing motive

---

[12] Brontë, *Wuthering Heights*, 179.

for reciprocal interaction. As Hume says, 'we may feel a desire of another's happiness or good, which, by means of that affection, becomes our own good, and is afterwards pursued, from the combined motives of benevolence and self-enjoyment' (EPM App. 2.13, SBN 302). This twofold view of benevolence is essentially identical to the account in the *Treatise*. Hume's great claim for both forms is that they are a real part of common human nature. He does not ground that claim in argument but only in observation. His further arguments start from this foundational point. He is especially assertive about the general form of benevolence, perhaps because it might be readily doubted. He says 'I assume it as real, from general experience, without any other proof' (EPM App. 2.4 n 60, SBN 290 n).

One might suppose Hume is consistent in his treatments in his two main works on morality and that benevolence in the later book plays the role of sympathy in the earlier book. This cannot be entirely correct, because the role of sympathy is to give us knowledge of another's pains and pleasures, merely to communicate, not to make us desire to do something for another. Benevolence might encompass the combined effects of sympathy and sentiment. Even then, we would need to add motivation with these two to yield benevolence because sympathy and sentiments together produce only approbation, not any desire to do something on behalf of the other. Ordinarily, we can assume motivations are there for our own interests. Beneficence is more nearly a matter of consuming something, in this case the pleasure of another. Some of us enjoy this more than others do and all of us enjoy adding to the pleasure of some people more than we enjoy adding to that of others.

Benevolence, like justice, is a social virtue, and even a dollop of general benevolence will be enough to support a sense of justice and an approbation for those institutions that help to achieve it. This passion may be quite weak and in particular it might be far too weak to trump our concerns with ourselves and with those closest to us. But when there is not any conflict between the general and the particular or personal, the passion is enough to give approbation of others for their character or actions or for institutional arrangements.

Here then are the faint rudiments, at least, or out-lines, of a *general* distinction between actions; and in proportion as the humanity of the person is supposed to encrease, his connexion with those who are injured or benefited, and his lively conception of their misery or happiness; his consequent censure or approbation acquires proportionable vigour. There is no necessity, that a generous action, barely mentioned in an old history or remote gazette, should communicate any strong feelings of applause and admiration. Virtue, placed at such a distance, is like a fixed star, which, though to the eye of reason, it may appear as luminous as the sun in his meridian, is so infinitely removed, as to affect the senses, neither with light nor heat. Bring this virtue nearer, by our acquaintance or connexion with the persons, or even by an eloquent recital of the case; our hearts are immediately caught, our sympathy enlivened, and our cool approbation converted into the warmest sentiments of friendship and regard. These seem necessary and infallible consequences of the general principles of human nature, as discovered in common life and practice. (EPM 5.43, SBN 230)

Hume supposes that the motivations of general benevolence may be so weak as not to induce us to lift a finger on behalf of others but only to approve arrangements that secure justice. This claim is so mild, he says, that even those 'reasoners' who insist on the elemental selfishness of human nature will not be scandalized to grant so little benevolence to us. But that little is sufficient to open the gates to a far-reaching concern. For his purposes it is sufficient 'that there is some benevolence, however small, infused into our bosom; some spark of friendship for human kind; some particle of the dove, kneaded into our frame, along with the elements of the wolf and serpent' (EPM 9.4, SBN 271).

What are his purposes in arguing for at least a bit of benevolence? To get a '*moral distinction*,' which is a general sentiment of blame and approbation. What is the content of a moral distinction? Apparently, it is psychological. That might mean that it could vary from one person to the next; to say it is the same for all would require a vast social science research project, although Hume might be confident of his judgment from a survey of those he has met. For Hume, its content appears to be utility, usefulness, pleasure, and this family of beneficial things that he constantly invokes. He seems to suppose we are all relatively alike in this psychology, in which case we would all reach the same approbations and disapprobations. This moral distinction is fundamentally important if we are to have a notion of morals at all. This claim is, again, still merely psychological. It is about the sentiments that are evoked in us in response to our sympathy, our reading or mirroring of others.

The very notion of morals turns on the empirical fact of some sentiment common to all mankind so that we share in our approbations (EPM 9.5, SBN 272). That sentiment must be very general or we would not have it in common, we would not feel approbation for the same things. It is, of course, utility and the pleasure that people find in it that gives us a sense of pleasure or benevolence in contemplating their enjoyments. The other passions can be very strong but they are not felt so strongly in common. They therefore cannot provide a foundation for a general system or explanation of morals. Whether we know it or not, that seems to make all of us psychological utilitarians.

As in the *Treatise*, the social virtues of justice and fidelity differ from the virtues of humanity and benevolence; the latter produce their good effects directly and not as mediated through institutions, conventions, or norms. When I help my child, I do not need even to think about my actions or about whether they are generalizable to others. When I feel approbation for actions or institutions of justice, I necessarily think of the causal relations that generally produce good results without necessarily supposing that there is a direct good result of the institutional decisions or actions.[13] Hume evokes one of his occasional metaphors to spell out this difference:

The happiness and prosperity of mankind, arising from the social virtue of benevolence and its subdivisions, may be compared to a wall, built by many hands; which still rises by each stone, that is heaped upon it, and receives encrease proportional to the diligence and care of each workman. The same happiness, raised by the social virtue of justice and its subdivisions, may be compared to the building of a vault, where each individual stone would, of itself, fall to the ground; nor is the whole fabric supported but by the mutual assistance and combination of its corresponding parts. (EPM App. 3.5, SBN 305)

Therefore, in the system of justice I do care whether others do as I do.

Distributive Justice

In contemporary writings, what is generally at issue in any argument for distributive justice is greater equalization of income, welfare, wealth, resources, or all of these.[14] This would be simple if our task were merely to equalize shares of what exists, as in Bruce Ackerman's theory of justice in the distribution of manna from heaven.[15] But the real world problem we actually face is to distribute what we produce. Possibly the only extensive theory that is concerned with production and that requires virtually pure equality is that of the Levellers of Hobbes's time, as represented in the writings of Gerard Winstanley.[16] Winstanley supposed that all should have equal holdings of land and all should spend their lives working the land for their own sustenance. His concern was with a peculiar view of the requirements of Christianity: that all work diligently all their lives and that none consume other than what is necessary for health and survival. There should be no excess. With equal plots of land and equal industry, we should all have equal consumption. This is an extreme version of the life-denying monkish virtues that Hume reviles.[17]

---

[13] EPM App. 3.2–3, SBN 303–4.

[14] In some accounts of distributive justice, there is some notion of what a person ought to get from the larger society or how the person ought to fit into the society. For example, Aristotle proposed distribution according to merit.

[15] Ackerman, *Social Justice in a Liberal State*.   [16] Winstanley, *The Law of Freedom in a Platform*.

[17] See his discussion of the deplorable, self-denying virtues of Pascal (EPM Dial. 54–7, SBN 342–3). Such virtues are not functional or consequentialist in the senses in which Hume's virtues are both.

No standard contemporary theory or principle of distributive justice values poverty as a positive good, as Winstanley did. They all build on the possibility that we are productive and that we can distribute our produce in a way that makes everyone relatively prosperous. The core problem is how to motivate people to be productive. The market motivates people by giving them profits or paying them wages for their production. This essentially guarantees inequality. There are basically two ways to achieve substantially greater equality in principle. The first is to reorganize production by putting productive assets under collective control. The second is to leave production up to the market and to skim off as much as possible of the produce of those who are productive without substantially reducing their productivity in order to be able to distribute the excess to those who are less well rewarded by the market. Socialism is an attempt to do the former; Rawls's theory of justice is a proposal to do the latter.

In either case, what we do is turn the produce of the society into a vast collective good that is then distributed to citizens. If we cast the issue this way, then we can see the incentive problem as essentially the incentive to free-ride on the collective effort to produce what will be distributed. Rawls addresses this problem by supposing we give individuals specific rewards for their own contribution to the collective effort but that we tailor the rewards in such a way as to reduce inequalities according to the formula of his difference principle. That is, we allot greater rewards to the very productive if in doing so we can increase the welfare or resources of the least well off. We eliminate your incentive to free-ride on our general collective action by splitting your production into two parts: a contribution to the collective produce available for redistribution and an individual reward to you as an incentive to get you to be more productive.[18]

Hume argued against redistribution in general terms that would block both these resolutions: socialist equality and Rawlsian distributive justice. He saw distributive justice in the egalitarian sense as pernicious. He attributed concern with such an abstract principle as egalitarianism to writers who argued from pure reason with no attention to the possibilities of their actual world and to such religious fanatics as the Levellers.[19]

Hence, they are neither natural nor artificial. Strategically, they are one-person virtues. In essence, they are about one-person ethics, not about the ethics of choices in strategic interactions. They are virtues for the sake of virtue or, in some cases, such as Pascal's, for the sake of salvation in an afterlife.

[18] See Hardin, 'From Order to Justice.'

[19] Hume may not have read Winstanley. He is very tentative in his statement of the views and program of the Levellers, whose religious fanaticism he detested. Hume, 'Of Superstition and Enthusiasm,' 77.

Although Hume may have had a lingering commitment to arguments from productive merit, his actual statement of the problems with egalitarian distribution could hardly be more modern in its main arguments. He writes that:

ideas of perfect equality ... are really, at bottom, *impracticable*; and were they not so, would be extremely *pernicious* to human society. Render possessions ever so equal, men's different degrees of art, care, and industry will immediately break that equality. Or if you check these virtues, you reduce society to the most extreme indigence; and instead of preventing want and beggary in a few, render it unavoidable to the whole community. The most rigorous inquisition too is requisite to watch every inequality on its first appearance; and the most severe jurisdiction, to punish and redress it. But besides, that so much authority must soon degenerate into tyranny, and be exerted with great partialities; who can possibly be possessed of it, in such a situation as is here supposed? (EPM3.26, SBN 194)[20]

In this passage, Hume raises two of the standard arguments against equality, which can be stated in contemporary vocabulary as follows. First, equality entails reduced incentives to those who are especially productive and leads to a trade-off between equality of distribution and efficiency of production.[21] Second, giving a potentially capricious government the power to achieve equality gives it the power to do much else, including very undesirable, tyrannous things.[22] One might add that such a powerful government might make its major office holders essentially wealthy, as happened in many Communist and other autocracies, in one of which the office of autocrat has become an inherited right.

Hume canvasses these problems after first granting that, with typical inequality, we must 'rob the poor of more satisfaction than we add to the rich, and that the slight gratification of a frivolous vanity, in one individual, frequently costs more than bread to many families, and even provinces' (EPM3.25, SBN 194).[23] This view was later developed further by Edgeworth and other utilitarians.[24] Hume did not imagine the vastness of the fortune of Bill Gates, whose wealth

---

[20] Hume also argued that 'Perfect equality of possessions, destroying all subordination, weakens extremely the authority of the magistracy, and must reduce all power nearly to a level, as well as property.' This sounds like an aristocratic concern, implying that hierarchy, and hence material inequality, is virtually necessary for achieving many desirable social goals, including governance. If so, this view is not spelled out by Hume, although it is soon announced by Burke ('Speech to the Electors of Bristol').

[21] Scitovsky, *Welfare and Competition*; Okun, *Equality and Efficiency: The Big Tradeoff.*

[22] Hayek, *The Road to Serfdom.*

[23] Also see Hume, 'Of Commerce,' 265: 'Every person, if possible, ought to enjoy the fruits of his labor, in a full possession of all the necessaries, and many of the conveniencies of life. No one can doubt, but such an equality is most suitable to human nature, and diminishes much less from the *happiness* of the rich than it adds to that of the poor.'

[24] Edgeworth, *Mathematical Psychics.*

exceeds that of some of the poorest nations in the world taken together. Despite this clear, essentially utilitarian appeal of equality, however, Hume thought it a bad idea to try to impose 'perfect equality' because it would be impracticable to achieve it.

However we decide the merits of redistribution, we finally have to contend with contingent facts of human nature and the conditions of our world, including those in Hume's discussion of the circumstances of justice. The moment we suppose, as Hume insists we must, that justice is contingent, we are in the world of social science and not only of political philosophy. No simple theory of equality of welfare or resources can stand against human nature if all or most or even very many of us would substantially slacken our efforts if our rewards were not related to those efforts. Rawls's difference principle[25] pays deference to this apparent fact of our nature.

In addition, the conditions of Hume's world would have blocked any substantial program of redistribution. Before and still during Hume's time, Great Britain was very loosely organized. The Elizabethan poor laws were national laws to require towns to take care of their own poor. That was a sensible way to organize such a program because only one's own locality could have much knowledge about one's poverty. Moreover, at that time, the tax base of the national government was very small. A large fraction of the taxes raised was on malt and beer, because, as Hume remarks, malting and brewing cannot easily be concealed.[26] It is hard to imagine running any significant part of a contemporary national budget on the taxes on whiskey and beer. Added to these considerations, Hume supposed 'giving alms to common beggars,' as under the poor laws, leads to 'idleness and debauchery' (EPM2.18, SBN 180). One might disagree with Hume on this point, but articulate observers—including the nearest thing to social scientists in his time and soon thereafter—often support his view.[27]

Still, Hume's rejection of distributive justice is too strong, even for him. As Mackie says, if Hume's arguments against perfect equality are compelling, 'it is by no means the only alternative.' We could at least reduce poverty and its ills. Among the circumstances that Hume supposes would not allow us to insist on justice, he notes that in a besieged city the strict rules of justice may give way to concern with survival: 'if a city besieged were perishing with hunger;

[25] The difference principle says we allot greater rewards to the very productive if in doing so we can increase the welfare or resources of the least well off.

[26] Hume, 'Of Public Credit,' 356.

[27] See, among many commentaries, Samuel Johnson, as quoted in Boswell, *Life of Johnson*, 947–8; Mill, *Principles of Political Economy* 5.11.13, p. 960; Tocqueville, 'Memoir on Pauperism'; Townsend, *A Dissertation on the Poor Laws*. Also see Hardin, 'Altruism and Mutual Advantage.'

can we imagine, that men will see any means of preservation before them, and lose their lives, from a scrupulous regard to what, in other situations, would be the rules of equity and justice?' (EPM3.8, SBN 186) Mackie supposes that a city in these straits would suspend the normal laws and would require that everyone make known what food and other supplies they have for the benefit of everyone.[28] One could suppose similarly that the indigent in a society with institutions of justice would not think the institutions were beneficial to themselves and their hungry children, and many others might agree. Hence, we might expect to see citizens choosing to adopt principles of at least modest distributive justice.

From many remarks one can infer that Hume had kinder views of attempting to alleviate poverty. For example, in his historical account of Wat Tyler's rebellion, Hume comments,

There were two verses at that time in the mouths of all the common people, which, in spite of prejudice, one cannot but regard with some degree of approbation:

> When Adam delv'd and Eve span,
> Where was then the gentleman?[29]

Hume was too generous a person to feel completely happy with his own strictures on perfect equality. That does not mean he did not believe what he wrote but only that he seemingly would wish the case were otherwise. Of course, mere approbation does not impel one to work for a policy change.

Even the supposedly more thoroughly self-interested Hobbes assumed that the commonwealth must be responsible for charity towards the very needy: 'And whereas many men, by accident inevitable, become unable to maintain themselves by their labour, they ought not to be left to the charity of private persons, but to be provided for ... by the laws of the commonwealth.'[30] Under his fifth law of nature, complaisance, 'a man that (by asperity of nature) will strive to retain those things which to himself are superfluous and to others necessary, and (for the stubbornness of his passions) cannot be corrected, is to be left or cast out of society, as cumbersome thereunto.'[31] Scrooges should be dispossessed and exiled. Few modern egalitarians would be so tough. If Hobbes's rule were suddenly imposed in the US, many corporate boards and executive offices would be depopulated.[32]

---

[28] Mackie, *Hume's Moral Theory*, 93–4.   [29] Hume, *History of England*, 2. 290 n.
[30] Hobbes, *Leviathan* 30.18 [181].   [31] Ibid. 15.17 [76].
[32] Such generosity fits Hobbes's character more generally. For example, he is not inherently anti-democratic in the sense of wanting to block or override the interests of the masses. Indeed, he is among the most egalitarian of all political philosophers. In the great Anglo-Saxon tradition he is arguably more

Promise-Keeping

Consider an important artificial virtue: fidelity in promise-keeping. Strategically, there are three categories of promising,[33] one for each of the large categories of strategic interaction: pure conflict, cooperation or exchange, and coordination. Promises in the category of small-number conflict include the case of gratuitous promises. For example, I simply promise to do something for you with no quid pro quo. Although there is some bit of law (with significant legal differences across nations) on gratuitous promises, they are generally of almost no importance.[34] They have had, however, a large role in the slightly weird philosophical literature on, for example, deathbed promises, such as my promising you to tend your roses after your death, even though those roses are hidden away from everyone's sight and it will take substantial effort for me to tend them. That this issue has provoked so much discussion is evidence of how silly and irrelevant high intuitionist moral theory can be. For Hume that would be a happy fact. He says, 'Generally speaking, the errors in religion are dangerous; errors in philosophy only ridiculous' (T1.4.7.13, SBN 272).

Some promises fit in the category of small-number coordination, as when you and I promise to meet for lunch tomorrow. Keeping a coordination promise, such as this, is not very complex morally; we make such a promise because we suppose that, when the time comes, we will both want to keep the promise. We commonly do not even use the word promise or any near equivalent. There might be some problem of how I should deal with our promise if, at the last minute and without a cell phone, I have reason to break our promise.

The most important of the three strategic forms of promising is the exchange variety because it enables us to do certain things through cooperation that would otherwise not be possible. It regulates exchange over time. Typically a promise addresses a problem that has the structure of the Prisoner's Dilemma. When I keep a promise, I do something that is against my interest in that moment, and that fact might seem to be a problem for people who act primarily from self-interest. Against that worry, I can be brought to understand that *having in place the practice of promising*, with its norm of reciprocating, enables me to do things I could not otherwise do and that therefore the

---

egalitarian than Mill, and surely more egalitarian than Locke or Hume. He is anti-chaos. He thinks, perhaps wrongly as it turns out, that participation is likely to be chaotic. Hence, he is anti-participation and in that sense anti-democratic.

[33] Pretz, 'Promises and Threats'; Hardin, *Morality within the Limits of Reason*, 59–65.

[34] Dawson, *Gifts and Promises*.

practice is beneficial to me even if, from the short-sighted perspective of this moment only, keeping my promise to you is not in my interest. This general understanding of the value of the practice still may not lead me to keep a promise in the relevant moment when my long-run view of the practice is trumped by my short-run view of my interests right now.

Let us focus here, as Hume does (T3.2.5.8–15, SBN 520–5), on exchange promises, which are substantively and perhaps numerically the most important of these three categories. They are also the category that seems to be in discussion in most of the philosophical literature on promising, although one cannot always be sure what is the strategic structure that writers have in mind. Moreover, writers often make their case by running together different kinds of promise, for example, defending gratuitous deathbed promises by generalizing from the seeming morality of keeping an ordinary exchange promise.

Clearly Hume is right to put promise-keeping in the world of artificial virtues because promising must inherently be a convention rather than something immediately and obviously a matter of right and wrong.[35] Hume concludes that keeping promises is one of the mainstays of social order if that order is to be prosperous. The marvel is that we are driven to keep promises by our normal passions, which would seemingly provoke us to be so self-seeking as to dishonor a promise in the moment in which we have to reciprocate someone else's prior action. But, whoever makes a promise 'is immediately bound by his interest to execute his engagements, and must never expect to be trusted any more, if he refuse to perform what he promis'd' (T3.2.5.10, SBN 522). We keep promises out of interest, not out of moral duty. Indeed, part of Hume's purpose in analyzing the practice of promising is to refute the idea that promise-keeping is a natural virtue. It is inherently artificial.[36] Promise-keeping is a convention, a social construction, not an a priori notion of the right, despite the massive literature that treats it otherwise. Under that convention, interest in maintaining a relationship or a reputation is the first obligation to the performance of promises (T3.2.5.10–11, SBN 522–3).

A common criticism of Hume's view that interest is the first motive to keep our promises is given by Barry Stroud, who queries: 'Does Hume really explain how a man could come to see, on each particular occasion, that it is in his interest to keep his promise on that occasion? If the man is naturally as selfish or self-interested as Hume claims, surely he will be motivated primarily

---

[35] Again, scale per se is not the defining issue for artificial virtues.

[36] Hume speaks of a convention *entered into* (T3.2.2.9, SBN 489). This phrasing can be misleading. He supposes that conventions can simply happen, without deliberate design. The phrasing here suggests something more deliberate. We might enter into a convention in the sense of making use of it, as when we make a promise.

to get others to *believe* that he will perform, or has performed, his part of the bargain.'[37]

The answer to Stroud's question is Yes, Hume does explain this. His explanation is grounded in his fundamentally important insight about how repetition and hence reputation change the strategic structure of our interactions. Stroud here evidently thinks of a single promise as a one-off experience in one's life. But we do not generally make promises to just anyone. We could not rely on vast numbers of people enough to enter into promising arrangements with them at all, and we do not. We make promises to those who are an ongoing part of our lives, and for such people it is in our interest to maintain, in Hume's vocabulary, good offices. I keep my promises in large part because *I want to be able to have you accept promises from me in the future*.[38] Indeed, as Hume notes, I am concerned not only with my relationship with you when I consider whether to keep my promise to you, but also with my relationships with all those others for whom my reputation might be affected. Those others might suppose you stand proxy for them, and they will act toward me as though my relationship with you had been a relationship with them. Similarly, I am concerned with my reputation in other contexts of acting justly or unjustly (T3.2.2.27, SBN 501).

There is a further issue in Stroud's question implicit in his phrase 'on each particular occasion.' Hume's answer is direct and clear. It becomes an acquired habit to keep promises and if we do acquire the habit, we will soon see our promises rejected, and the exchanges that they enable will not be available to us. What 'we have very frequently performed from certain motives, we are likewise apt to continue mechanically, without recalling, on every occasion, the reflections which first determined us' (EPM3.47, SBN 203).[39]

It is apparently a common experience of people today to be accosted by someone who begs to borrow, say, $20 to buy a train ticket or to catch a taxi

---

[37] Stroud, *Hume*, 213.

[38] Hiskes ('Has Hume a Theory of Social Justice?' 89) reads Hume's argument from interest in iterated interactions as the gradual growth of a commitment to altruism, as though keeping a promise were always against one's overall interests. This is not Hume's point. He means it when he says the first obligation to keeping promises—including this particular promise—is interest (T3.2.5.11, SBN 523). Stroud may not have got Hume's strategic analysis from iterated interaction, but he rightly supposes Hume really does mean to claim that the motivation to keep promises is interest.

[39] One might recall Mill's response to critics who suppose that utilitarians must spend so much time calculating what to do as never to get any utility out of actually doing anything. Mill says there is no need to waste time calculating as critics insist. 'Nobody argues that the art of navigation is not founded on astronomy, because sailors cannot wait to calculate the Nautical Almanack. Being rational creatures, they go to sea with it already calculated; and all rational creatures go out on the sea of life with their minds made up on the common questions of right and wrong' (*Utilitarianism*, chap. 2, 225). The last few paragraphs of this chapter are among Mill's rudest and angriest. He says that we can make any moral theory unworkable if we assume 'universal idiocy' among those who are to apply it (224).

home after having a purse or wallet stolen. Invariably, the request is coupled
with a firm promise to return the money by mail the next day. And equally
invariably, the mail never comes. Few of us genuinely believe the promiser in
such a case, but sometimes we give the money anyway, even while counting
it as lost. We might even reject the charade of writing down our address for
mailing the repayment. If this one-off con-promise is Hume's concern, then
Stroud is right and Hume has no way to defend the view that promising
is backed by interests. But this is obviously not at all the kind of case that
motivates Hume's analysis, nor is it a credible case of genuine promising. We
and the promiser who begs for taxi fare both know that both know it is most
likely a scam. Moral theory is irrelevant to this kind of case unless we cast it as
a con. Historically, a con was grounded in the mistaken hopes of the person
conned. This con of modest cost in likely full appreciation of its being a con
is more like begging than like conning. Moral theory, of whatever variety,
should have its attention turned to more serious matters. Hume's account is
irrelevant to the one-off promise from someone we will never see again, and
he does not mean to address such a promise in his several pages on promising
as a law of nature. He is strategically far more subtle than to think this even an
interesting issue.

Hume fully grasps the iterated quality of our relationships of promising
and promise-keeping. He notes that contracts and promises 'ought carefully
to be fulfilled, in order to secure mutual trust and confidence' (EPM3.28,
SBN 195). Ironically, still today, a vast literature on trust misses this essential
insight, as does the ridiculously large literature that uses promise-keeping as
proof that utilitarianism is a false moral theory because it cannot justify keeping
a promise.[40] Hume justified it in powerful utilitarian arguments more than
260 years ago, but the lesson is evidently very hard to grasp. Promises to
random others are not to be taken seriously. They are like the con-artistry
above and we should treat them that way when we encounter them (fairly
rarely, and maybe never in some kinds of community). Similarly, we should
not take claims that we do or should trust unknown others seriously either.
They are vacuous or weirdly misjudged.[41]

Note here that reputational effects, which Hume often takes into account,
are a proxy for iterated interaction with any particular person. I can trust you
as much from your reputation and your interest in maintaining it as from your
wish to maintain good relations with me in particular. The import of your

---

[40] See many of the items cited by Yeghiayan, 'Promises: A Bibliography.'

[41] Those who make such claims commonly speak of social or generalized trust. See further, Hardin,
Trust, chap. 3.

good reputation is future oriented. You want to maintain it in order to be able to interact beneficially with others by making promises to them in return for their beneficial action toward you in this moment. You want to maintain your reputation for the sake of your actual and potential relations with many other people, and therefore you treat me reasonably in our interaction even though you might expect never again to have reason to deal with me in such a way.

Finally, note that the rise of the convention of promising turns on the significance of the problem that it addresses. It is almost a sociological law that we should have such a practice available to us if our conditions are stable enough to make it work. Therefore, promising and promise-keeping are one of Hume's laws of nature. It is still true that, if we follow 'the natural course of our passions and inclinations, we shou'd perform but few actions for the advantage of others, from disinterested views' (T3.2.5.8, SBN 519). That is why it is especially valuable to generate the convention of promising and promise-keeping and to have our promises governed by iterated interactions and their proxy in reputation to motivate our adherence to the practice. Having the custom of promising and promise-keeping is mutually beneficial.[42]

Hume grants that, 'Afterwards a sentiment of morals concurs with interest, and becomes a new obligation upon mankind' (12, SBN 523). This is just another instance of a general phenomenon, that we in a sense 'elevate' our motives, supposedly making them good because moral. Perhaps our prior move is to generalize into the future our experience with promising and promise-keeping, so that we keep our promises with no calculation or even thought about the possible costs or benefits of reneging. Speaking of the analogous problem of acting according to principles of justice, Hume says we are apt 'to continue mechanically, without recalling, on every occasion, the reflections which first determined us. The convenience, or rather necessity, which leads to justice is so universal, and everywhere points so much to the same rules, that the habit takes place in all societies; and it is not without some scrutiny, that we are able to ascertain its true origin' (EPM3.47, SBN 203). We just become habituated. It is still the case that the sanction for violating a promise is harm to one's reputation and some loss of opportunity to make further promises. To make a promise is to subject yourself 'to the penalty of never being trusted again in case of failure' (T3.2.5.10, SBN 522). One need not 'calculate' this

---

[42] Few claims have been subjected to more ridiculous criticism than has this mutual-benefit defense of promise-keeping. That defense is essentially utilitarian. Hodgson (*Consequences of Utilitarianism*, 45) says, 'Because the making of promises and the communication of information would be pointless in our act-utilitarian society, so that these practices would not be engaged in, there could be no human relationships as we know them.' Thus utilitarianism is immoral. Warnock (*The Object of Morality*, 33–4) agrees with this absurd argument.

cost at every promise, but will simply take it for granted that, barring force majeure or somewhat less oppressive changes of circumstance, each promise should be fulfilled.

Collective Action

In many contexts, all of the individual members of a group can benefit from the efforts of each member and all can benefit substantially from collective action. For example, if each of us pollutes less by paying a bit extra for our cars, we all benefit from the reduction of harmful gases in the air we breathe and even in the reduced harm to the ozone layer that protects some of us more than others against exposure to carcinogenic ultraviolet radiation. If all of us or most of us prefer the state of affairs in which we each pay this bit over the state of affairs in which we do not, then the provision of cleaner air is a collective good for us.

Unfortunately, my polluting less does not matter enough for anyone—especially me—to notice. Therefore, I may not contribute my share toward not fouling the atmosphere. I may be a *free rider* on the beneficial actions of others. This is a compelling instance of the *logic of collective action*, an instance of such grave import that we pass laws to regulate the behavior of individuals to force them to pollute less.[43] Hume's example is the neighbors of a marshy meadow who wish to drain the meadow (T3.2.7.8, SBN 538). He supposes that if there are only two neighbors, they should be able to manage the necessary cooperation to drain the meadow. But if there are a thousand neighbors around a comparably larger marshy meadow, they will fail to drain it because each will attempt to free-ride on the efforts of all the others.

The strategic structure of this logic is that of the n-prisoner's dilemma.[44] If n is 2 and the two members are able to coordinate on whether they act together, there can be no free rider unless one of the members is de facto altruistic. As represented in game 3.4, prisoner's dilemma for two players is essentially the model of exchange.[45] This is merely a variant of game 3.2, with new labels on the strategy choices that produce specific outcomes. Suppose that, in the status quo, I have a car and you have $5,000 but that both of us would prefer to have what the other has. Of course, each of us would rather have the holdings of both of us: the money and the car. The second best outcome for both of

[43] Olson, *The Logic of Collective Action*; Hardin, *Collective Action*, chaps. 1 and 2.
[44] Hardin, 'Collective Action as an Agreeable n-Prisoner's Dilemma,' and *Collective Action*, chap. 2.
[45] Hardin, 'Exchange Theory on Strategic Bases.'

us would be for you to have my car in exchange for my having your money. The status quo is a worse state of affairs for both of us than that in which we succeed in exchanging. In the matrix, again, the outcomes are ordinally ranked from best (1) to worst (4) for each player. For example, the outcome (upper right cell) in which you yield the money and I keep the car is worst (4) for you as the Row player and best (1) for me as the Column player.

Game 3.4 Prisoner's Dilemma or Exchange of Car for Money

		Column	
		Yield car	Keep car
Row	Yield $5,000	2,2	4,1
	Keep $5,000	1,4	3,3

As an n-prisoner's dilemma for n much larger than 2, collective action is therefore essentially large-number exchange. Each of us exchanges a bit of effort or resources in return for benefiting from some collective provision. The signal difference is that *I can often cheat with impunity in the large-number exchange by free-riding* on the contributions of others, whereas such cheating in the two-person case would commonly be illegal, because it would require my taking from you without giving you something you prefer in return. Although there are other possibilities, suppose that provision of our collective good, if not an exactly linear function of the number of individual contributions or of the amount of resources contributed, is at least a generally increasing function. In such cases, if n is very large and you do not contribute to our collective effort, the rest of us might still benefit from providing our collective good, so that you benefit without contributing. You are then a free rider on the efforts of the rest of us.

Unfortunately, each and every one of us might have a positive incentive to try to free-ride on the efforts of others. My contribution—say, an hour's work or a hundred dollars—might add significantly to the overall provision. But my personal share of the increased provision from my own contribution alone might be vanishingly small. In any case of interest, it is true that my benefit from having all of us, including myself, contribute is far greater than the status quo benefit of having no one contribute. Still, my benefit from my own contribution may be negligible. Therefore I and possibly every one of us have incentive not to contribute and to free-ride on the contributions of others. If we all attempt to free-ride, however, there is no provision and no 'ride.'

For public and many other goods, Hume supposes that political society easily handles the problems of provision. 'Thus bridges are built; harbours open'd;

ramparts rais'd; canals form'd; fleets equip'd; and armies disciplin'd; every where, by the care of government, which, tho' compos'd of men subject to all human infirmities, becomes, by one of the finest and most subtle inventions imaginable, a composition, that is, in some measure, excepted from all these infirmities' (T3.2.7.8, SBN 539). This passage and similar claims in Smith have led some writers to associate Hume and Smith with public-goods theories of the state (as discussed in chapter 5). In those theories, the provision of public goods is commonly seen as the reason for the creation and maintenance of the state. For Hume and Smith, it seems more nearly accurate to say that the state's collective provision of such goods is a happenstance benefit. The state supposedly arose first for the defense of the community, and in this function it was the solution of a coordination problem of getting everyone behind a focused leadership. But with growing power, it might be able to amass the resources to provide collective goods.

Coordination

Coordination is the simplest of the three classes of strategic structure. It is represented in game 3.3. In this particular coordination game, there is a potential problem, because one of us might try to coordinate on the upper-left outcome while the other tries for the bottom-right outcome. There is no conflict in this case, there is merely a failure to coordinate. With even a little bit of communication—you might merely say bottom-right—we will immediately be able to coordinate. Moreover, if we encounter this form of interaction repeatedly, we might finally settle on one or the other good outcome and stick with it thereafter. The mere fact that we did coordinate on the bottom-right during our last round of play is a good hint that we should do so again. Schelling discovered that people, asked to try their best to coordinate, could do it in even seemingly implausible contexts.[46]

A simple example, noted earlier, of two-person coordination is Hume's case of two men rowing a boat (T3.2.2.10, SBN 490; EPM App. 3.8, SBN 306–7). Both must basically pull their oars with the same energy or they will not maintain their course and they will not get where they each want to go. Here, physics forces them to coordinate in the relevant way and neither of them can sensibly expect to cheat by throwing a disproportionate burden onto the other because then the boat will veer in a circle and not progress to their destination. In this case, there is no coordination *problem*, because there is only

---

[46] Schelling, *The Strategy of Conflict*.

one way for the two men to coordinate that serves their interests.[47] Such an interaction is sometimes called a game of harmony, because there is only one jointly plausible choice, which is to say there is no choice.

If we expand the simple coordination game to many players, the problem of communicating with each other might be insurmountable. But we might still be able to coordinate if we face the same interaction repeatedly. Once a large number of people are coordinating on one of the good outcomes (even if there are very many of these), the rest of us may recognize that we should follow their lead, so that we all coordinate to our mutual advantage. When this happens, especially when it happens spontaneously and without extensive communication, we may call the resulting pattern of choices a convention. We will take up the force of convention in Hume's political theory in chapter 4. It is not the whole story of his political theory, but it is a centrally important part, because coordinating citizens in a convention of social order can resolve the first, seemingly most difficult part of making life reasonably cooperative in a society. It can do this without the need for divine intervention or draconian political force.

Concluding Remarks

Again, Hume is a very clear-headed strategic thinker who manages to keep all of these strategic structures straight even without the benefits of a game theoretic vocabulary or the kinds of matrixes that we use with such facility today. No major thinker before Hume managed this trick, although Hobbes and many others saw parts of the larger system and saw the import of the strategic interactions. We could recount Plato's recognition of the free-rider problem of the logic of collective action in Glaucon's invocation of the legend of the ring of Gyges that would enable a person invisibly to steal and rape without being seen,[48] and Hobbes's recognition of coordination problems in choosing and sticking with a sovereign. It is not true that one cannot understand much of Hume without a grasp of his strategic assumptions, but one cannot readily understand the systematic nature of his claims without such a grasp. And even for specific issues, such as promise-keeping, coming to Hume with a prior understanding of the nature of the strategic problem—in this case, the incentives in the iterated prisoner's dilemma—is very useful.

---

[47] Mackie (*Hume's Moral Theory*, 88–9) supposes that this problem is a prisoner's dilemma, as though somehow one rower could cheat and still expect the other rower to do all the work. If the boat has an oar on each side, this is physically impossible.

[48] Plato, *Republic* book 2, 360b–c.

In addition, among the most important strategic insights is the recognition of the incentive effects of repeated interactions—the game theorist's iteration. The epigraph for this chapter is Hume at his clearest and best at seeing that self-interest alone is sufficient to enable us to cooperate in many contexts. Many people master the benefits that can come from the incentives inherent in iteration while many fail far too often. Some of those who master them may even be able to lay out the strategic nature of the particular interaction of the moment. Hume masters the entire panoply of strategic structures and, if we follow him, he alters the way we see the world and its opportunities.

4

Convention

Nothing appears more surprizing ... than the easiness with which the many
are governed by the few; and the implicit submission, with which men
resign their own sentiments and passions to those of their rulers.[1]

In Hume's time there were three main theoretical views of how we maintain
social order. These were based on fear of God, contractarian agreement
or consent, and draconian coercion by the state. Hume forcefully, even
dismissively, rejects all three if they are taken to be the whole or central story.
The theological views were simply false or at least beyond demonstration.[2]
Theological justifications of the state had already been undercut earlier by
Hobbes, Locke, and others, some of whom proposed contractarian consent as
an alternative justification for the state and an alternative ground for obligation
to the state. By now theological arguments are essentially without a camp in
Europe and North America, although they hold sway over much of the Islamic
world. Although Hume's attack on the emptiness of the contractarian vision
is compelling, the tradition continues. Hobbes's argument for the necessity
of draconian force seems empirically wrong for many societies and Hume
rejects it almost entirely,[3] although he shares many social scientific views with
Hobbes.

Having demolished all of the then acceptable accounts of obedience to the
state, Hume therefore has to propose a dramatically different, fourth vision from
his psychological theory of human nature coupled with his strategic analysis of
social interactions. What he has to explain is the epigraph above. In essence
his theory is that government derives its power to rule by convention and the

---

[1] Hume, 'Of the First Principles of Government,' 32.
[2] Hume reduces to silliness the idea that government is good or right just because it was installed by
a deity by arguing, in parallel, that that deity must also have determined everything else in the world.
Hence, 'a sovereign cannot, properly speaking, be called [the deity's] vice-regent, in any other sense
than every power or force, being derived from him, may be said to act by his commission' (Hume, 'Of
the Original Contract,' 467).
[3] Hume, 'Of the First Principles of Government.'

populace acquiesces in that rule by its own convention.[4] The pervasiveness and power of coordination is Hume's richest strategic insight. Indeed, it underlies his extraordinary theory of convention, which was largely neglected until a few decades ago. The strategic structure of Hume's coordination problems was more or less independently discovered by Thomas Schelling,[5] whose discovery of it led to David Lewis's resurrection and analysis of Hume's account of the effects of iterated coordination that can establish a convention.[6] Lewis was looking for a solution to the problem of the initial rise of language when there was no language in which to reach agreements on meanings. Hume twice resolves that problem in a clause (T3.2.2.10, SBN 490; EPM App. 3.8, SBN 306). If one were drawing up a list of the greatest insights of social theory, Hume's convention would rank high in the list. It is the core of his theory of social order.

Hume's account of convention denies Hobbes's claims of the necessity of an all-powerful sovereign and of the absolute need of government if we are to have social order. It is the answer to the epigraph above. Hobbes recognized the nature of coordination, which is the strategic structure faced by those deciding on an agreement on who will be our sovereign. Hume takes a further step and argues that, if we coordinate on some social outcome enough times, our coordination begins to carry strategic force through the expectations that build up and that give us an incentive to follow that same pattern of coordination in the future. Doing so is to establish a convention. Rawls rightly says that the few pages (T3.2.2.9–14, SBN 489–93) in which Hume introduces this idea 'are among the more wonderful parts of the text.'[7] It is a remarkable fact that it took so long for readers of Hume to think this.

Note that the word convention, although taken from the vernacular, is a fairly technical term in Hume's account. Its easiest explication is via the most often cited example of a compelling convention: the rule of the road that says we all drive to the right in North America and most of Europe (or to the left in many other nations). Once we have settled on this pattern, each of us then has very strong incentive simply to abide by the convention. If from whimsy or ignorance I choose to drive left in North America, I set myself up for massive harm. If, as Hume and Hobbes assume, we are all motivated at least in large part by interests and by concern for survival, I have very strong incentive not to violate our rule of the road. Moreover, there need be no law or sanction from

---

    [4] Hume argues, by example, that ten million British citizens simply acquiesced in the succession of William and Mary to the English throne, all by act of 'the majority of seven hundred' in the English and Scottish parliaments (Hume, 'Of the Original Contract,' 472–3). Acquiescence is Hume's term (see also ibid. 469).

    [5] Schelling, *The Strategy of Conflict* (published in 1960).   [6] Lewis, *Convention*.

    [7] Rawls, *Lectures on the History of Moral Philosophy*, 61.

outside the world of driving that enforces my sensible behavior; I do not need any such extra sanction to see my interest in following our convention, which could be and probably once was wholly spontaneous. Hume mentions rules of the road that prevailed in his day (EPM4.19, SBN 210). He also mentions the related convention that, when walking, 'the right-hand intitles a man to the wall, and prevents jostling, which peaceable people find very disagreeable and inconvenient' (EPM4.19 n16, SBN 210 n).

Iterated Coordination

The term convention is first used by Hume in a discussion of how property relations become stabilized (T3.2.2.9, SBN 489).[8] He applies the term very consistently thereafter, but he never specifically defines it. It is clear that the meaning he has in mind is that of Lewis's analysis.[9] Lewis supposes that our numbers are large and that we are essentially scattered in such a way that we cannot come together to decide on which of various possible coordination outcomes we should focus. Therefore, if we ever just do happen to coordinate on doing things in a particular way, that fact is a signal to us that we could expect to succeed in coordinating on doing things that way the next time we face the same or even a similar coordination problem. Since none of us has much if anything to gain from challenging our prior choice, we simplify life for ourselves by supposing that our prior choice is a strong signal that every one of us recognizes clearly enough to act on it.

Lewis spends a hundred pages spelling out the analysis, but this is basically it. He worries, as some philosophers or logicians might, whether our prior action is a signal that I recognize, that I know you recognize it, and that I know you know that I recognize it, and that I know that you know that I know that you recognize it, and so on ad infinitum. Most of us would act long before we would give ourselves over to such abstract play. Indeed, one suspects that Hume would be slightly offended by and would ridicule the attempt to make his analysis so abstract. He would pragmatically just get on with life and assume it will work reasonably well. Most people in the real world, which just might not be one of Lewis's possible worlds, would follow Hume's manner and would take a lot for granted here. Peter Ustinov parodies the infinite regress of knowing that the other knows in the Cold War movie *The Mouse That Roared*. He runs back and forth from the American to the Soviet embassies, saying

---

[8] See further, Rawls, *Lectures on the History of Moral Philosophy*, 59–61.
[9] Lewis, *Convention*.

'Did you know that they know that you know that they know?' After several roundtrips, he gets the response, 'What!! We didn't know.' He is startled to have reached the end of the chain, but he has seemingly done them a great service.[10]

Note that, in the argument for convention, we go beyond merely the strategic structure of a one-time interaction to consider the effect on our choices in this moment's interaction of past and future choices in the same or merely the same form of interaction. Hence, as with promise-keeping (chapter 3), which is motivated by expectations of further exchanges in the future, a convention plays out over repeated interactions. It becomes virtually a social structure, but one that is created by our actions, so that in Hume's vocabulary it is artificial.

Once a coordination is achieved in some ongoing or repeated context, it can have great stability because it can be self-reinforcing. The resolution of a collective action does not lead to such stability. Hence, *coordination is the dominant feature of stable social organization*. Indeed, our successes in resolving collective actions often turn on the prior coordination on some organization or institutional structure that enables us to cooperate or even enforces our cooperation (T3.2.7.7, SBN 538). For example, actual laws may often regulate interactions that have a prisoner's dilemma structure, either at the dyadic or the large-number level, even though the overall plan or idea of government has the structure of a coordination (T3.2.7.3–6, SBN 535–7). Hume adds force to this view with his comment that it is easy to assent now to a future rule for ordering society even though we might reject such a rule for present circumstances (T3.2.7.5, SBN 536).[11]

A varied array of conventions is listed in table 4.1. At the end of the table are conventions that are important in our lives today but that were not among those Hume discusses, because, in some cases, they were not yet relevant in his time. Note that virtually all of these conventions arose spontaneously, although many of them have long since become subject to legal regulation (including language in France). For example, Standard Time was invented by the US railways for the convenience of their scheduling. At the time it was invented, all localities were on local sun-time. This made scheduling nearly impossible. The new standard time was called railway time, but it very soon came to dominate local time in popular usage and, eventually, it was legally mandated by act of Congress.[12] When communication and travel were very slow, local

---

[10] This is told from memory and might be slightly off.

[11] Hobbes's theory is similarly grounded in the resolution of a coordination problem rather than in the resolution of a prisoner's dilemma problem. Once we coordinate on a government, that government supposedly then has the power to regulate our cooperation in resolving collective action problems.

[12] Bartky and Harrison, 'Standard and Daylight Saving Time'; Hardin, *One for All*, 27.

Table 4.1 Coordination Problems in Hume

Social order (this chapter)

Property rules [the concern that apparently drives Hume's own analysis of convention] (T491; T3.2.10.3, SBN 555; T3.2.3.4 n, SBN 504–5 n; EPM3.40–1, SBN 201–2; chapter 6)

Rules of justice (EPM3.31, SBN 195–6)

Acquiescence to government [dual convention] ('Of the First Principles of Government,' 32; chapter 4)

Promise-keeping (T3.2.5.10; chapter 3)

Royal succession (T3.2.10.10–13, SBN 559–61; *History* 3.3–12)

Inheritance rules (EPM3.43, SBN 202; T3.2.3.11, SBN 510–13)

Municipal laws [which vary from place to place] (EPM3.46, SBN 202)

Rules for murder (EPM4.20, SBN 210–11)

Incest rules (EPM4.8–9, SBN 208)

Manners ['a kind of lesser morality'] (EPM4.10–13, SBN 208–9)

Chastity (EPM4.5–7, SBN 206–8)

Gallantry (EPM4.17, SBN 210)

Traffic rules for wagons (EPM4.19, SBN 210)

Traffic rules for pedestrians (EPM4.19 n, SBN 210 n)

Two men rowing a boat [not strictly a problem] (T3.2.2.10, SBN 490; EPM App.3.8, SBN 306–7)

Rules of games, which may be capricious (EPM4.18, SBN 210)

Rules for sports contests (EPM4.20, SBN 211)

Language (T490; EPM App. 3.8, SBN 306) [The origins of language when there was no language for agreeing on meanings is the issue that drives Lewis's analysis of convention]

Gold and silver as money (T3.2.2.10, SBN 490; EPM, App. 3.8, SBN 306)

International relations (EPM4.2–3, SBN 205–6)

Rules of war (EPM4.20, SBN 211)

Coordination Problems not clearly discussed by Hume

Driving convention (see Hardin, *Morality within the Limits*, 50–3)

Traffic signals (see Hardin, *One for All*, 27)

Standard time (see Bartky and Harrison, 'Standard and Daylight Saving Time')

QWERTY keyboard (see Hardin, *Morality within the Limits*, 51)

Norms (see Hardin, *One for All*, chapters 4 and 5)

Slang terminology (see Hardin, *One for All*, 80–8)

Customs

Culture

Group identification [e.g., ethnic] (see Hardin, *One for All*, chapter 3)

Power (see Hardin, *One for All*, chapter 2)

time was adequate; when they became faster, it was a recipe for chaos. The driving conventions in many nations appear to have arisen spontaneously and only later to have been mandated by law. In some nations, especially colonies of more developed nations, the driving conventions were legally mandated to mirror those of the colonial masters.

Furthermore, there is a fundamentally interesting difference between the exchange and coordination games when they are expanded to large numbers of players. The more others there are in a prisoner's dilemma or collective action problem, the less incentive I have to be cooperative. The more others there are in a coordination, the less incentive I have to attempt to change our convention because the costs of doing so rise; and the greater the incentive I have just to go along with the convention even if I think it is suboptimal for all or less good than some alternative for at least me. Therefore, again, *large numbers stabilize social conventions in coordination contexts but undercut standard kinds of cooperation in collective action contexts*. Hume takes this theoretical fact so completely for granted that he does not even view the social conventions he discusses as problematic. And he assumes that large-number prisoner's dilemmas (collective action problems) will require government for their regulation.

The self-reinforcing character of a convention for social order coupled with the fact that large numbers stabilize social conventions gives us a powerful explanation of social order. We do not need the shared values on which Talcott Parsons[13] and others insist and we generally do not need the draconian force that Hobbes proposes. Hume's account is both the first modern theory and still the definitive theory.

The Force of Convention

The rule of the road is an ideal type of a problem of coordination that gets resolved by a convention. We seldom have such elegant evidence for the importance and applicability of social scientific ideas. It is the rare case in sociology and social theory of an ideal type that is actually instantiated in the world. The example of the rule of the road is so ideal and pristine and so powerful in its force, that we are apt to expect too much of other instances of conventions. Other cases commonly allow for a lot of slack and for some degree of failure to follow the convention that governs the behavior of most of us. Such cases are generally the ones with which Hume deals in his explanations of social practices and social order.

There are several quite different questions we might ask about any convention:

    1. Why it gets the content it has;

---

[13] Parsons, *The Structure of Social Action*, 89–94. See further, Hardin, *Liberalism, Constitutionalism, and Democracy*, 9–12.

2. How it arises spontaneously; and
3. What maintains it.

In giving and explaining several examples of political and social conventions that govern our lives in many contexts, Hume sets himself two of these tasks: to answer why a particular convention arose *with its actual content* and to say what keeps it going once it is in place. He mostly addresses the first of these in long footnotes that focus on conventions of property and rules for its inheritance (T3.2.3.4 n–11 n, SBN 504–13 n). Seeking to answer the first question is a mistake in many ways. Just how the convention of driving on the left in the UK arose, why it was on the left and not on the right, might not even be an interesting question. Moreover, for this and Hume's examples the answers are likely to be speculative guesses at best. Hobbes makes a related mistake in concerning himself with the origins of a government rather than with what he needs to explain, which is the maintenance of it.[14]

Lewis largely addresses the third of the questions above: what maintains a convention once it arises. For him, it mostly does not matter why a particular convention arose in its particular form, although often there might be clear explanations. His concern is with the spontaneity of the rise of conventions and of their 'enforcement.' His answer to the question what maintains a convention is that it is an equilibrium, and is therefore self-enforcing. It is self-enforcing in the way that the driving convention or the power of government is. Because almost all of us do coordinate on a convention it is the interest of almost all of us to do so.

That many conventions are powerful once they are established is a fundamentally important fact about them. Explaining that fact is a matter of addressing the third question here. Hume does address that question, but not as assiduously or transparently as one might wish for the reception and understanding of his theory. Indeed, Jonathan Harrison, an especially attentive reader of Hume, largely misses the point, as do John Austin and H. L. A. Hart in their contrary accounts of the force of law, although both of them appear to have read Hume and to be addressing his views of the law.

Consider Harrison's discussion of such conventions of justice as those that regulate the inheritance of property and succession to the throne. Hume notes that these conventions vary from one place to another but that this variety

---

[14] Hobbes has essentially two different theories: creation of government and maintenance of government. Part of the first theory is of the creation of a sovereign by contract. It is a lousy theory because it runs against the strategic problem of transferring power from all individual citizens to the sovereign and it is historically irrelevant. The theory of maintenance requires only Hume's convention for order and Hobbes does not give us an account of how ongoing order works.

of rules or laws is fine and people should follow the particular convention that contingently governs in their society (e.g., EPM3.35–48, SBN 197–203). Harrison thinks Hume should 'hold the view that what caused men to feel that they ought to obey one rule, in preference to any other, was always their *belief* that this rule was more useful than any other, and that they were justified in thinking that this rule ought to be obeyed, if this rule was *in fact* more useful than any other.'[15] This misses Hume's central point of seeing the choice of a rule we should follow as a *coordination problem* as in game 3.3. It is a problem just because there need not be any rule that is '*in fact* more useful than any other.'[16] Drive left, drive right—why should one rule be better than the other? Often only contingently. Drive left is definitively better today in Australia and the United Kingdom; drive right is definitively better today in North America and most of Europe, but only because those are now the conventions in those places.

For the rules of justice, the case for ambivalence might never be so clear cut as it is for the rule of the road but, given our relatively poor understanding of exactly how various rules might work out in the long run, we might find ourselves just as ambivalent about which of variant rules to adopt in many other contexts. In historical fact, it is often not a matter of choice anyway; one or the other convention just happens more or less spontaneously. But coordination problems are rife in social organization. Hume notes that sometimes mutual advantage may require a rule of justice in a particular case but may not determine the particular rule, *among several that are all equally beneficial* (EPM3.31, SBN 195–6). Harrison and, historically, many others have simply missed the point of Hume's analysis.

Now turn to Hart's theory of law, especially his account of authority. He is concerned to reject the so-called gunman theory of John Austin, according to which we are kept in order primarily by the threat that government or the sovereign will punish us for going astray.[17] Hart supposes that there are many sources of the authority of government, including its power and also moral commitment to it. People's allegiance to their government might 'be based on many different considerations: calculations of long-term interest; disinterested interest in others; an unreflecting inherited or traditional attitude; or the mere wish to do as others do.'[18] And in any case he thinks it impossible to keep us in order merely with force. But it would be perverse to say that the Czechs who acquiesced in Nazi rule, many of the Argentines and Chileans who acquiesced in rule by brutal generals, and countless other subjugated people

---

[15] Harrison, *Hume's Theory of Justice*, 214. The specific issue to which this remark refers is the varied range of rules on the succession to the monarchy.

[16] For further discussion see Hardin, *Morality within the Limits of Reason*, 50–1.

[17] Austin, *The Province of Jurisprudence Determined*.   [18] Hart, *The Concept of Law*, 201.

shared any relevant values with their overlords. Even in much more benign contexts, moral commitments might be irrelevant to the explanation of popular acquiescence in rule by a particular regime.

Explanations from Hart's catalog of reasons for obedience might fit some behaviors, but they are not necessary; and in some contexts—such as rule by foreign conquerors—they may all be absent altogether. In the main, the power of a government is derived from the fact that we almost all acquiesce in its actions and policies most of the time. A sufficient reason for us to do so is that almost all others acquiesce, so that *their coordination gives the government extraordinary power* to go after the occasional miscreant.[19] For the most part, we the citizens know very little about what our government is doing and yet we acquiesce. The fact that almost all of us do so *makes it the interest* of almost all of us to do so. We are coordinating on not acting individually, which entails not acting collectively against the government.

If Austin had had the analysis of convention available, he might have framed his argument this way, and then the criticisms of Hart would not score against him, although his theory would still have been based in the power of government. Hart says that, without citizens' 'voluntary co-operation, thus creating *authority*, the coercive power of law and government cannot be established.'[20] This is true but not in the sense in which Hart means it. It is true by definition, because the government's power just is the coordination of most citizens in acquiescence to it. Indeed, to give a full explanation of the power of government, we would require a *dual-coordination theory*. First there is coordination among those who are the officials of the government and, second, there is coordination of the citizens in acquiescence to the government.[21] But the latter does not require 'voluntary co-operation'—only acquiescence.

One might suppose that Hume indulges in a derivation of an ought from an is in his account of property conventions if he supposes that our convention for property is per se right-making. But if he supposes the point of the convention is only to establish a mutually beneficial regime, there is no slip from fact to value. This is clearly what he means to do. Indeed, the conventions he discusses are not conventions that establish property but only that establish how we are likely to think about it in contexts of handling it. Hence, there are conventions on acquisition, inheritance, and transfer. The specific content of these conventions may vary from one place or time to another. It is a task of municipal law to fix what the principles of human nature have not determined precisely (T3.2.3.10 n11, SBN 513 n).

---

[19] See further Hardin, *Liberalism, Constitutionalism, and Democracy*, 141–83, 305–9.
[20] Hart, *The Concept of Law*, 201. [21] Hardin, *One for All*, 28–32.

As is true more generally of his strategic grasp of the range of problems he wishes to resolve, Hume is remarkably clear and consistent in his use of the argument from convention, although he does not give us a theoretical aside to explain the strategic structure and force of conventions in the abstract. That task was left for more than two centuries to Lewis, who elaborates the pattern of mutually reinforcing expectations that lead us to follow a convention. I drive right because I expect you and almost everyone else to drive right, and all of you drive right for the analogous reason. Contemporary readers must commonly find Hume's explication clear and compelling, but his central claim here has not been well understood even by many writers in our time, and hardly at all by anyone before recent decades.

Lewis is concerned to answer the question how the actual vocabulary and rules of a language could ever get established if there was no vocabulary in which to agree on meanings for various sounds.[22] He supposes, with Hume (T3.2.2.10, SBN 490), that the vocabulary and grammar are created by convention without any need for prior linguistic agreement, just as many other social conventions often get established. In fact, even if we deliberately establish a particular convention, it can have the force of a spontaneously generated convention, because it too will turn on expectations that are mutually reinforcing. It appears that the initial driving conventions in the United States, England, and many other nations arose spontaneously; many driving conventions have, however, been deliberately imposed. In any case all of them get their force now from the mere fact that virtually everyone follows them all the time, so that our expectations today are our reason for following the conventions now.

To break a convention typically means to put a new one in its place outright through coordination on a different outcome or pattern of behavior. There are at least three ways this might be done: through imposition by government or other powerful actor; through the dominance of a 'market leader'; or spontaneously through individual actions. An example of imposition by government was the 1967 change in the driving convention in Sweden. This was done at 5:00 o'clock in the morning on 3 September, a Sunday. Most traffic was banned for a few hours and the final changeover required stopping all traffic while newly placed signs and traffic signals could be uncovered and all vehicles could be moved to the other lane.[23] The British might wish today that they had the driving convention—shared by almost all other Europeans—to which the Swedish changed, but perhaps the costs of a change there would outweigh the benefits despite the dangerous habits of European tourists in the United Kingdom.

---

[22] Lewis, *Convention*, 2, 87–8.   [23] Hardin, *Morality within the Limits of Reason*, 51–2.

Changes that are in a sense sponsored by market leaders are common. For example, the US railways were a market leader in changing the time conventions of North America. And in the heyday of the IBM Selectric typewriter, IBM could unilaterally have changed its keyboards to represent a more efficient layout than the then—and still—dominant qwerty layout, and their change might have worked (or they might have lost market share to other manufacturers).

Changing a convention through spontaneous individual actions is commonly hard to do, because the individuals first have to coordinate with each other on switching the convention. For example, spontaneous individual action would have been a disaster in the case of the suboptimal Swedish driving convention. In the age of the easily reprogrammed word processor, spontaneous change might work for overcoming the convention of the qwerty keyboard, although it seems not to be happening. Nevertheless, there frequently are spontaneous changes of various conventions, such as conventions on dress and vocabulary.

Conventions and Functional Explanation

As noted, the claim that we almost all have incentive to coordinate just because we almost all do coordinate might sound circular. This claim and therefore Hume's account of government imply that the maintenance of a convention is an issue for functional explanation. Such explanation is commonly to be sought when there are multiple causes of a rule or multiple rules that could handle a particular problem and when there is apparently feedback from effect to cause, so that superficially the explanation seems circular (T3.2.6.6, SBN 528). In such cases there is also reason to suppose that the relationship between actions one must take and the result of all our actions is artificial in Hume's sense in that it works through an institutional structure or a norm that produces good results from our patterned individual actions. In such cases we can tell how the convention works now but not necessarily how it got to be this way. That is to say, *we can explain the maintenance of a convention even if we cannot explain its specific content or its specific origins.*

Here is the form of a functional explanation of some institution or behavioral pattern.[24] An institution or a behavioral pattern X is explained by its function F for group G if and only if:

---

[24] Elster, *Ulysses and the Sirens*, 28; Hardin, 'Rationality, Irrationality, and Functionalist Explanation,' and, *One for All*, 82–6.

1. F is an *effect* of X;
2. F is *beneficial* for G;
3. F maintains X by a causal *feedback* loop passing through G.

Apply this paradigm to the driving convention. The rule of the road (drive right) is the behavioral pattern X; the group of all drivers is G; the function, F, of the rule is to keep us safe and to make driving fairly efficient. Now if all or nearly all of us drive right, then all of us as well as any newcomer will want to drive right. The feedback in this case is powerful and no one would want to violate the convention. An Australian who comes to drive in Austria will want to get it right. Few of the conventions we may wish to explain are so powerfully supported as this one and the support is entirely endogenous—it requires no coercion by government.

Suppose that the function of government is to maintain social order, as Hume insists (EPM3.1, SBN 183). X is government, F is social order, and the group G is the citizens. If our government succeeds in organizing social order, we the citizens will have an interest in going along with and therefore supporting that order. Social order is, as Hobbes supposes, clearly good for us. In fact, most of us will have an interest in following our government even if it is moderately abusive, because we cannot plausibly coordinate on putting an alternative government in place and we would suffer from any significant disorder that would result from efforts at regime change. The fact that you acquiesce in our government's actions strengthens the coordination on it and enhances the chance that others will acquiesce. As with the driving convention, you need not actually care very much which form of government or which leaders we have; you are not committed to our 'choice'—you merely acquiesce.

This says nothing about how X came to be. Hume supposes that there are mental associations, contiguities, sentiments, fancy or imagination, and so forth at play. That we cannot readily explain the actual form of the origins of many conventions bothers, even irritates, many social theorists. But that there can be a large variety of ways that a convention can get underway is a major theoretical insight. It is a fact we should proclaim, not be bothered by. Hume states the case very clearly in a footnote:

No questions in philosophy are more difficult, than when a number of causes present themselves for the same phaenomenon, to determine which is the principal and predominant. There seldom is any very precise argument to fix our choice, and men must be contented to be guided by a kind of taste or fancy, arising from analogy, and a comparison of similar instances. Thus ... there are, no doubt, motives of public interest for most of the rules, which determine property; but still I suspect, that these rules are principally fix'd by the imagination, or the more frivolous properties of our thought and conception. (T3.2.3.4 n, SBN 504 n)

One might suppose that the fact Hume relegated this point to a footnote suggests how easy the issue is, at least for him.

Hume's argument for the variety of origins of conventions is now widely understood to be a reason for resorting to functional explanation. Arthur Stinchcombe argues from equifinality that, if different structures in various societies seem to serve a similar interest or purpose in all the societies, the structures are to be explained functionally.[25] Variety will be maintained because in a given society the establishment of a particular convention to handle some coordination problem effectively excludes alternative conventions known to prevail elsewhere.[26] One should therefore hesitate to claim that an established convention was fittest to survive, because its establishment prevents other possible conventions even from being tested or compared to alternatives within the society, as is obviously true to a large extent for a general form of government once it has become stable.[27]

Hume repeats this point in a different way when he surveys the peculiarities of property law. The rules of property are artificial in his sense. They are far too varied to be natural, they can be changed by human laws, and they all tend to contribute to the public good. The last point is especially remarkable. First, despite the fact that their establishment was for the public good, they are nevertheless artificial. Second, if regard for the public good were a strong enough motive of people, they would not have reason to constrain themselves by these property (and other) laws. They arise from self-love, but self-love constrained by conflicting desires of others, so that our individual and conflicting interests are adjusted to produce an arrangement that is mutually advantageous although our individual actions do not have the mutual interest as a motive (T3.2.6.6, SBN 529).

It is, of course, just because conventions arise as resolutions of coordination problems that they can be quite varied. A coordination game might often be easy to resolve if there is one outcome that is best for everyone and is seen to be best by everyone. Its resolution might not even constitute a convention because it might be resolved anew every time it occurs without reference to past experience and newcomers to the group need know nothing of the past experience to get the resolution right. If, however, there are multiple possible coordinations, we face a *coordination problem* and this needs a convention.

---

[25] Stinchcombe, *Constructing Social Theories*, 90.
[26] Merton, *Social Theory and Social Structure*, 111.
[27] Hardin, 'Rationality, Irrationality, and Functionalist Explanation,' 764–6.

Conventions are therefore generally responses to the multiplicity of possible resolutions, institutions, or norms.

We might find regularities in the origins of some conventions but only wide variation in the origins of others. For example, driving conventions evidently arose more or less spontaneously in many nations not long before or soon after the arrival of the automobile. In some cases the convention was to drive left and in other cases it was to drive right. At the time the conventions arose, there was no clear reason to prefer either one to the other. At some point, however, many Swedes began to think that their convention of driving on the left was dangerous, because German and other tourists often forgot the Swedish rule and slipped over into the right lane on two-lane open highways. It was easier to change the Swedish convention than to change German and other tourists' habits.

Recall the three ways that conventions might be changed, as discussed above: through imposition of government or other power, through the effort of a market leader, and through spontaneous individual actions. Hobbes's account of government by conquest (or by acquisition in his terminology) is an instance of the first, and it has been a moderately frequent event in historical societies. Democratic governments set up a device that allows for relatively smooth change of direction even while keeping the nominal form of the government in place. Market leaders acting within the system can move government and its policies in new directions. This is, of course, part of the reason for the creation of parties; another part is to keep the government on course without such changes in direction. Both these purposes require coordinating large numbers of citizens. Arguably there have been important instances of spontaneous change as well, although eventually these must require coordination on a party or movement that helps to aggregate the spontaneously changing views, as in the case of the abolitionist movement against slavery in the United States in the nineteenth century and in many other nations before and after. In the United States the abolitionist movement gave seemingly spontaneous rise to the Republican party.

Hume gives us an example of the change of a major political convention when the British parliament deposed King James II and replaced him with William and Mary in 1688 after tumultuous events. James's sudden flight to France prevented what might have been a grim civil war.[28] Hume carefully canvasses the advantages and disadvantages of that change (more than twenty years before his birth) and comes down in favor of the change. The main advantage is that William and Mary were Protestants while James and his

---

[28] Hume, 'Of the Protestant Succession,' 511.

Stuart family were Catholic or had Catholic leanings. The major convention that was violated in this change was, of course, that of lineal succession within the royal family (then the Stuarts). By excluding the normal heir, Hume says, 'we secured all our constitutional limitations, and rendered our government uniform and of a piece [i.e., Protestant]. The people cherish monarchy, because created by it; The monarch favors liberty, because created by it.'[29] For eighty years, the nation had been 'in a continual fever' from the house of Stuart. As Hume notes, although reason might eventually end religious conflict in Europe, 'the spirit of moderation has, as yet, made too slow advances to be entirely trusted.'[30] Putting Protestants on the British throne at least reduced religious conflict within Britain itself. The convention of lineal succession soured in the era of the house of Stuart, and it was briefly abandoned to bring in the house of Hanover, which by Hume's time had established its own convention of lineal succession.

Allegiance to Government

Although it might at first seem odd that Hume gives so much space to the analysis of political allegiance (T3.2.8–10, SBN 539–67),[31] in fact that was the central problem of political philosophy for more than a century before his time, even though the term is not always a central one in that literature. Hobbes, Locke, countless religious writers, monarchs, popes, and many others provided theories or at least limited reasons for why people should obey their governments. The reason for allegiance was the core issue in dispute. The issue was heightened by the evident failure of the supposed divine right of kings when one of the best established kings was beheaded by order of a mere parliament in 1649. Some of the theoretical responses to the new world were to give reasons to citizens why it was for their own benefit that citizens should obey their governments. Some were to pose grounds for citizens to recognize an obligation to obey government.

Hume takes a very different tack. He sets out to explain the way government works by fitting it to the way people will deal with it. His is entirely *an explanatory theory*. Others had given explanations of various aspects of government and its rule, but no major thinker before Hume gives an essentially scientific account, without any normative trappings.[32] In the end, he shows

---

[29] Ibid. 506.   [30] Ibid. 510.
[31] Only property gets longer treatment, although only slightly longer (T3.2.2–4, SBN 487–516).
[32] As Hobbes does in part.

that it is a citizen's interest to acquiesce in government and therefore generally to obey it.

Government arose in the dark recesses of time and we may know little about its origins in general or even in our particular context. In the twentieth century many nations were created de novo and their origins are therefore clear enough for the actual government in place, but even in most of these cases social order long pre-dates the new governments. Hume supposes that social order at the scale of a very small society is not problematic. But when we move to the large scale at which citizens do not all know each other, indeed at which citizens know very few of their fellow citizens, spontaneous social order regulated by iterated interactions and communal norms can no longer work.

It is common at this point to bring in claims of moral commitment or shared values through Rawls's magical 'addition of the sense of justice and moral sentiment'[33] to make justice work at a large scale. (Hobbes, of course, brings in draconian enforcement.) Explaining the origin of such values must be far harder than explaining order without such values in play. Commonplace claims that citizens must consent to government for it to work or that citizens do consent to government and therefore it is justified are irrelevant and wrong for the large majority of all governments that have ever been in power for any length of time, as Hume argues in his brief against contractarian accounts of government. He is particularly harsh on Locke's supposedly moral claim that there should be no taxation without consent.[34] Imagine the collapse of all major governments today if their powers of taxation were suddenly surrendered for lack of consent.

Briefly, Hume's conventional account suggests, again, that a successful political regime is grounded in a dual coordination, first of those in the government who coordinate on their governing roles and second of the citizenry who coordinate on obedience or acquiescence to the governors. If we wish to explain the failure of a regime, we commonly need to understand the failure of this dual coordination. For example, the East German regime collapsed in 1989 when the governors lacked the commitment to resort to massive force against a population that was at least temporarily refusing to coordinate behind that regime, indeed was spontaneously coordinating on opposition. The result of the regime's failure was not chaos because there was an alternative available to make the transition work. During all the years in which that regime held sway, the populace mostly acquiesced, in part because there was evidently draconian force in the background, as East Germans

---

[33] Rawls, *Lectures on the History of Moral Philosophy*, 63.
[34] Hume, 'Of the Original Contract,' 487.

experienced when Russian tanks came in to stabilize the nation after strikes against changes in the wage system in 1953. Hungarians suffered the same lesson in 1956. As late as 1968 Czechoslovaks also experienced draconian force to maintain a particular order.

But these were relatively unusual cases, so unusual that virtually anyone trying to establish the importance of draconian force would elicit these cases and several cases in which the draconian force came from within the nation—as in China in 1989, almost every Arab regime in the late twentieth century, and Chile and Argentina under their respective generals—rather than from outside. The striking thing about the East European cases is not that there was real opposition to the regimes but that there was widespread opposition. Although they need not be strongly supported, governments do not often provoke such extensive opposition. Mostly citizens merely go along to get along. It is not in their power to make substantial changes; it is in their power to make the best of what they have.

To call what we see 'allegiance' is already too strong a word for many citizens. We actually know almost nothing of what the masses of citizens in various past states wanted historically. We know that they often eluded efforts to impress them into military service and to tax them. But we also know that the world that they inhabited was a far more fragmented and decentralized world than our own, so that information about that world would have been especially hard to collect even at the time. Austrian social theory describes that decentralized, information-poor world very well. For many people, therefore, government may hardly have mattered to their lives. As late as the years just before the First World War, 'a sensible, law-abiding Englishman could pass through life and hardly notice the existence of the state, beyond the post office and the policeman.'[35] By then there had been a developed system of policemen for only about a century and a postal service for not much longer.

So why did government work at all in such conditions? If government did not bother me, I did not need to bother with government. De facto, I merely acquiesced in its rule. This picture fits almost anarchically organized societies such as England, whose loose political organization arguably gave it tremendous advantages in enabling spontaneous revolutionary changes in its economy and its social order. The dual coordination that made for the English state grew out of what was earlier a small-scale coordination within the government itself and out of what was earlier a loosely connected collection of small-scale communities with many languages and dialects. Both of these—the state and the communities—could sustain conventions that were communal

---

[35] Taylor, *English History 1914–1945*, 1.

norms of cooperation and order through internally organized spontaneous sanctions.[36] Early volumes of Hume's *History of England* very well portray the very small scale of the government of those times.

As the government grew and the society became increasingly connected, there had to be conventions on a much larger scale. Those conventions have their force from the extreme difficulty individuals or even groups would face in going against them. Small-group sanctions of miscreant members do not work when the group is so large as to make members anonymous.

Note that a single citizen's acquiescence to our regime's rule could follow for either or both of two reasons. First, the citizen might comply with it out of anticipated reaction to the likely use of power to keep her in order. This might especially be true for criminal actions or even for traffic violations. Second, the citizen might see it as directly in her interest to comply not because the state will react to non-compliance but because non-compliance would directly bring harm or loss to her. This is trivially the motivation for driving on the correct side of the road and it might be the motivation for many other activities that are not so clearly defined. For example, I might readily comply with electrical codes not because I expect an inspection that would bring me a fine but because I want the safety of that compliance.

In Hume's day, the range of things that mattered and on which compliance with government might be at issue must have been far smaller and far less pervasive in his life than what we face today. Indeed, in his day even the driving convention might not yet have been established, although the analogous convention for sailing might have been. Still today, in my world, I am far more directly constrained by conventions than by legal strictures. That may partially be because some of the legal strictures are so compelling that behavior is readily fitted to them so that they are honored through anticipated reaction.

For such lesser matters as the electrical code, government is enabled to intervene by a kind of spillover of its power from the realm in which we might readily have conceded power to it into realms in which at least libertarians would sooner keep government at bay. For example, American government in the era of the anti-libertarian Attorney General John Ashcroft spilled its power into many aspects of American lives that no one might have even contemplated at the time that government was created with substantial popular backing in 1787–89.[37] That early government came to 'power' before it had much power,

[36] Hardin, *One for All*, chap. 4.

[37] Ashcroft was a civil libertarian on internet issues while he was senator from Missouri but, after he became attorney-general under President George W. Bush and was in charge of enforcement of

while it had little more than the power that came from coordination of a large fraction of the more powerful citizens—and even that was only tentative while the population could watch to see where the government might lead. After a dozen years, it began to have the power to keep itself in office against considerable opposition—had there been such opposition. By 1860 it had such power as to be able to crush the rebellion of the southern states; and now it has such power as to be able to crush nations almost at its choosing. Longevity can give governments and other institutions remarkable further staying power.

Consider one last aspect of life under real governments. Hume says,

Did one generation of men go off the stage at once, and another succeed, as is the case with silk-worms and butterflies, the new race, if they had sense enough to choose their government, which surely is never the case with men, might voluntarily, and by general consent, establish their own form of civil polity, without any regard to the laws or precedents, which prevailed among their ancestors. But as human society is in perpetual flux, one man every hour going out of the world, another coming into it, it is necessary, in order to preserve stability in government, that the new brood should conform themselves to the established constitution, and nearly follow the path which their fathers, treading in the footsteps of theirs, had marked out to them. Some innovations must necessarily have place in every human institution, and it is happy where the enlightened genius of the age give these a direction to the side of reason, liberty, and justice: but violent innovations no individual is entitled to make: they are even dangerous to be attempted by the legislature: more ill than good is ever to be expected from them.[38]

The stricture against violent innovations, as in revolutions, is similar to that of Hobbes. This is a central claim of both Hume and Hobbes, and from a quick glance over modern revolutionary changes it appears that they were right up until 1989 and arguably except for 1688 in Britain. But the main message here is that almost *all of what we enjoy in this world is an inheritance from others who went before*. Certainly most of the government that rules in any decent nation is something handed down to us, and most of us must be well served—even best served—if we keep it working well.

---

restrictions, and of choosing against whom to enforce them, he became anti-civil libertarian on those issues. As senator, Ashcroft wrote: 'The government's police-state policy on encryption is creating hindrances and hurdles that will eventually injure our ability to compete internationally.' Ashcroft, 'Keep Big Brother's Hands off the Internet,' final paragraph. See Corn, 'The Fundamental John Ashcroft.'

[38] Hume, 'Of the Original Contract,' 476–7.

Unequal Coordination

Many conventions, such as the driving convention, are entirely neutral in their impact on different members of the society who are coordinated by them. It is possible, however, to have a coordination that is unequal in its benefits. In such an interaction, we might all prefer any of two or more forms of order to disorder, anarchy, or rebellion. But some of us might strongly prefer one form of order while others want a different form. If one group manages to force its preferred coordination or even if the society merely happens to fall into that preferred coordination, the other group now might acquiesce just because the costs to it of attempting to change the coordination might be too great to justify the perhaps risky effort. Acquiescence would then be the whole story for the losing group, even though that group might undertake no action to show its concern over its status.

Game 4.1 represents a two-person (or a two-group) unequal coordination. In this game, suppose that the third best outcome for each participant is far worse than the second best outcome, so that each player would strongly prefer either of the coordination outcomes—(2,1) or (1,2)—to either of the (3,3) outcomes. But if you are Column you want the top-left outcome, and if I am Row I want the bottom-right outcome. If we resolve this coordination problem with a stable convention, that convention could be at either the top-left or the bottom-right outcome, so that one of us would be a relative loser so long as that convention lasts.

In democracies, the populace is often divided into parties, one of which might rule for a while and then another of which might rule. I might be distressed that your Column-party is in control right now but nevertheless be willing to acquiesce in your rule while waiting for my Row-party's turn later. In this case there might be alternating unequal coordinations so that on average each of us fares moderately well. I would acquiesce in your rule for various periods because, despite policies that harm my interests, I am still better off living in our democracy than I would be if I tried to change it to a very different kind of system in which my party would gain control for the long term. Game 4.1 represents the state of affairs for any given period. If there were

Game 4.1 Unequal coordination

		Column	
		I	II
	I	2,1	3,3
Row			
	II	3,3	1,2

a one-time choice of a coordination, as at (2,1), each side might have incentive to put enormous effort into securing the unequal outcome that benefits it. In such nations as Rwanda, an alternating coordination is not likely to happen and therefore the two large ethnic groups are often violently opposed to each other as each strives to fix coordination in its favor.

Hume does not appear to have foreseen unequal coordination problems, which may be more common in many political contexts than the more benign equal coordination problems. Barry Weingast gives accounts of several unequal coordination problems that led to major political conflicts and even break-downs.[39] When Hume speaks of knaves, one might suppose he has individuals in mind. The greater problem in many contexts is unequal coordination with parties contesting for control of the government. These are generally not issues of individual knaves out for their interest, but of knavish parties out for the interests of their members above all else. Hume is a contributor to the theory of liberal distrust,[40] which has essentially two parts defined by two different causal structures. The first is the problem of knaves who use office to benefit themselves in abusive ways. The second is the problem of parties that can gain control of government. There is apparently, in general, no simple coordination device to block such party action.

James Madison expanded the focus of liberal distrust to include not only a monarch but also to include an entire government. He wanted a weak national government primarily because such a government would not be able to intrude in the lives of individuals and would not have the power to impose, for example, a mercantilist economic policy.[41] It could block local or state-level intrusions into the economy but could make none of its own. The constitution he helped design is well over two centuries old and, as weak as it might initially have been, the state that it founded has become extraordinarily powerful, and it regularly intrudes into the economy, especially to benefit particular groups—such as farmers, the paper industry, the steel industry, friends of the Bush family, and so on. There are active groups that would like to gain control of the US government to impose a religious ideology. Such groups have gained some control over the Republican party. Coordinating against such politics depends on democratic mobilization of the citizenry and of certain agencies of government. It is not yet clear whether there is a convention strong enough to force government to stay out of many personal activities and civil liberties.

---

[39] Weingast, 'Political Foundations of Democracy and the Rule of Law' and 'Political Foundations of Limited Government.'

[40] Hardin, 'Liberal Distrust.'   [41] Hardin, *Liberalism, Constitutionalism, and Democracy*, 241–8.

This is not an issue that Hume addresses, largely because his view of the motivations of officials is quite sanguine. He speaks of 'the persons, whom we call civil magistrates, kings and their ministers, our governors and rulers, who being indifferent persons to the greatest part of the state, have no interest, or but a remote one, in any act of injustice; and being satisfy'd with their present condition, and with their part in society, have an immediate interest in every execution of justice, which is so necessary to the upholding of society' (T3.2.7.6, SBN 537). It is stunningly naïve for the empiricist Hume to believe that this describes the worlds in which we live. Hume's dual convention for the successful operation of government needs yet a third convention to block any large interest from gaining control of government and using it in their own interest. Hume's omission here is the single biggest flaw in his political theory.

Concluding Remarks

From his broad strategic grasp, Hume has a solution to Hobbes's central explanatory problem of how to empower a sovereign—hence giving the sovereign power to enforce social order—by a transfer of every citizen's individual power. Hobbes realizes this transfer is not really possible because the power is largely the individual's own person and capacities, it is not something tangible that they can simply hand over, as they might hand over a sword. Hume's solution does not occur to Hobbes, who is therefore conspicuously bothered by the seeming flaw in his argument for the transfer of power from the citizenry to the sovereign.[42] For Hume, power comes from convention and can evolve slowly as the society evolves from a primitive to a modern, complex state. In his theory, government is itself based on coordination for order, not draconian enforcement (as in Hobbes's theory). Hume speaks of opinion among the rulers, by which he means that they have incentive to keep to their coordination for power. Indeed, even the use of force against a populace depends on 'opinion' in Hume's sense. The incentives that back conventions can control even political office holders, who can be constrained in ways that Hobbes did not grasp, so that Hobbes's demand that the sovereign have absolute power is unnecessary.

Hume and Hobbes account for social order as the result of self-interested actions. This happens through coordination in two distinct ways. For Hobbes,

---

[42] As discussed further below.

the future citizens coordinate in selecting a sovereign. For Hume, they coordinate in acquiescing in letting the government govern. In both of these the result serves mutual advantage, which is the collective equivalent of self-interest. When we successfully establish a convention for handling some problem, such as the rule of the road that makes driving radically safer and more efficient, we all benefit, so the result is mutually advantageous. When we successfully cooperate in a collective action to provide ourselves some collective benefit, we again all benefit. The core of social order is not mere regularity—we could get that with a dead-hand rule that suppresses all beneficial activity. The core is organizing institutions to produce mutually advantageous outcomes.

The central focus of Hume's political theory is to explain social order from the fact that it serves mutual advantage. One way to do this, wrongly, would be simply to assert that we would, of course, benefit from mutual-advantage institutions and that therefore such institutions will arise. Émile Durkheim says, 'To ask what the function of the division of labor is, is to seek for the need which it supplies.'[43] If we simply identify the need and then assert that serving that need is why the relevant institution—for Durkheim here, the division of labor—arises, we make an argument from functionalism. This is not a useful explanation of the origin or even maintenance of the division of labor but is only a clear sign that we need an explanation of these. We should want to explain both the successes and the failures of relevant institutions to arise.

A seemingly related form of explanation is to say that some institution or norm is self-reinforcing, as in functional explanation in the account above. Once a conventional practice begins it can give people incentive to carry it further in minor ways that, when aggregated across all of us over time, may turn into major changes with highly refined and articulated institutions and norms. This is Hume's account of the rise of states that are as complex as his own England. Hume also gives an account of the beginnings of the 'partition of employments' (T3.2.2.3, SBN 485; see also T3.2.4.1, SBN 514) that actually explains, that is not functionalist in the manner of Durkheim's account. His account entails feedback from the result to its causes, so that the result is further 'caused.'

Today we would call many of Hume's conventions norms. And we would expect them to become moralized, as Hume says his conventions sometimes do. This happens because we tend to generalize our rules beyond their origins, and we may not make exceptions even when these would be grounded in the original reason for the rule (T3.2.9.3, SBN 551). For example, we begin to

---

[43] Durkheim, *The Division of Labor in Society*, 49.

think that our government is good and not merely that it serves our interests. When we do this, the norm can even become a residue in the sense of Vilfredo Pareto.[44] That is, we continue to moralize our government as good even though it no longer serves our interests. But because interest is the ground of allegiance, allegiance ceases when the magistrate violates interests of citizens. This argument seems to license some commentators to call Hume a rule-utilitarian, as though he elevated the rule of obedience to government to moral status. Against any such move, note that his point is psychological, not moral. To say that my allegiance ceases means merely that I no longer approve my government's serving of interests, because it violates interests. When my allegiance ceases, I do not lose a moral duty, I merely recognize that I have lost an interest.

[44] Pareto, *The Mind and Society*.

5

Political Theory

> It is evident, that, if government were totally useless, it never could have place, and that the sole foundation of the duty of allegiance is the *advantage*, which it procures to society, by preserving peace and order among mankind.[1]

Now we turn to the heart of Hume's political philosophy. Prior chapters have set up the discussion of politics and government, which are the topics of this and the next chapter. This chapter focuses on getting to the state and then making it work; chapter 6 focuses on what the state does (for us). Hobbes and Hume are primarily theorists of social order: how to establish it and how to maintain it. This issue is often taken for granted, but it is surely the most important single issue in all of political philosophy. There have been three general classes of arguments for how we maintain order. These are (1) draconian force, as represented by Hobbes, (2) shared values, as represented by many moral sense theorists in Hume's time,[2] many religious philosophers, Talcott Parsons, and contemporary communitarians, and (3) coordination on order as mutually beneficial even for people whose values may be widely varied. The last of these is Hume's theory and his unique invention. The most important move Hume makes is to eliminate the need for Hobbes's all-powerful sovereign by showing how we establish order as a convention that is commonly benign. (Hobbes and Locke had already eliminated theological versions of shared-value theories.)

In essence, Hume and Hobbes share the view that universal egoism, which is merely welfarism at the individual level, can be channeled by government to produce universal welfare and that egoists, for their own benefit, would therefore want government. Hume says, 'The same self-love,

---

[1] EPM4.1, SBN 205.

[2] The moral sense theorist Home (Lord Kames) argues against Hume's (and Hobbes's) view that property requires law to define it. Or, rather, he merely asserts that Hume is wrong, because we just all do share a moral sense about such things (*Essays on the Principles of Morality and Natural Religion*, chap. 7).

therefore, which renders men so incommodious to each other, taking a new and more convenient direction, produces the rules of justice, and is the *first* motive of their observance' (T3.2.8.5, SBN 543). Both philosophers also claim that most people are egoists, so that their prescription should apply to real societies. It would not apply if insufficiently many people were motivated by egoism—for example, if too many were concerned to promote particular religious views or to promote their honor or glory as defined by success in warlike endeavors. Hobbes supposes that it is such people who wrecked life in Great Britain during much of his century. His sovereign would be free to protect the mere egoists by killing or driving into exile religious fanatics and honor-bound warriors (generally Catholic aristocrats) who cause grievous disorder.

There are no terms to apply to politics and government that are strictly analogous to 'morality' and 'moral theory.' If there were, we would put them to use in the discussion that follows here. Our focus is on Hume's political theory, but not in the full sense of a theory of how politics does or ought to work. We have in Hume primarily an account of how citizens might evaluate government and its institutions and policies. Hence, as with his discussion of morality, he is concerned with the psychology of our approbation of government and its actions, approbation that derives from the impact of government and its actions on us and others. Hume does, of course, have a remarkably innovative and sophisticated descriptive theory of the realm of politics, just as he has of morals. In politics we are generally concerned with strategic interactions that involve substantial numbers of people. We are concerned with such problems as justice as order, collective provisions, and conventions for regulating social interactions and choices in recurring contexts. We might also be interested in distributive justice, but Hume is not.

It is sometimes noted that major philosophers, such as Kant, have a moral theory that does not lead to a political theory or, like Hobbes, they have a political theory that does not build on a moral theory. Hume is distinctively different because his moral and political theories are cut from a single cloth. The differences between the two are essentially a matter of scale or numbers involved. The main task in moving from his moral to his political theory is a task of social science: to explain the effects of large numbers on interaction. Utilitarians also typically have a unified theory of personal morality and political theory and they also need a social science to connect the two. The unity of Hume's theory makes it consistent with utilitarianism on this score.

In his political theory, Hume follows in the line of intellectual succession from Thomas Hobbes to contemporary political economy. Hobbes says that, where there is no government and therefore no positive law, the 'notions of right and wrong, justice and injustice have there no place ... They are qualities that relate to men in society.'[3] Hume partially disagrees, saying that justice can be prior to government (T3.2.8.3, SBN 541). His disagreement comes from his richer strategic understanding, which leads to the most important difference between the political theories of the two philosophers. Both are driven by what they think people actually want or value, and they both think roughly the same things are of interest to people: prosperity, safety, pleasure, and the absence of pain. Hobbes, writing in one of the most dangerous centuries of England's long history, especially focuses on safety; and Hume, writing in a society of relative stability and prosperity, focuses on pleasure and pain. Hume repeatedly speaks of utility, which, he says, pleases (EPM5.1, SBN 212–13). In Hobbes's words, 'The passions that incline men to peace are fear of death, desire of such things as are necessary to commodious living, and a hope by their industry to obtain them.'[4] All too often commentators reduce this list to fear of death. In certain grim times and places perhaps fear of death does come first in our concern, but Hobbes's commodious living or Hume's sweets of society (T3.2.7.8, SBN 538) must be the main concern for most of us most of the time in moderately prosperous peaceful societies. When this is true, utility is the dominant concern, and Hobbes and Hume are in close agreement.

The chief differences between the two philosophers are these. First, although Hobbes recognizes all three of the modal strategic categories in chapter 2, he discusses them primarily only at the large scale of the whole society. His is therefore entirely a political and not also a moral theory. Second, at the collective level, however, Hobbes fails to notice the import of iterated interactions. This lacuna leads him to recognize a major problem in his theory of the creation of a state that he cannot resolve, whereas Hume resolves it readily.

Both theorists depend on an understanding of power in achieving political order, although power seems to be a more fraught issue in Hobbes, for whom it is necessarily pervasive. For Hume it is often entirely in the background. Both have a conception of power that is largely founded in the coordination of large numbers of people. But Hume adds the effects of iteration to such coordination to yield an account of conventions that can govern individuals more or less spontaneously without the constant need of a Hobbesian sovereign threatening to wield a sword to keep us in line. Hume therefore has a strategic grasp of how power and social order work that is far beyond Hobbes's understanding. Hume is therefore able to resolve deep problems in Hobbes's account of the rise and maintenance of order under a supposedly all-powerful sovereign.

---

[3] Hobbes, *Leviathan* 13.13 [63].   [4] Ibid. 13.14 [63].

Power

How does a collection of anarchically organized people become a hierarchically organized society in which the sovereign or government has the requisite power to manage conflicts and coordinations? To answer this central question, first note that power is often conceived as roughly a category of resources. A modern nation may own a vast collection of weapons in which it has invested, and therefore it has power. For example, the United States used its weaponry in two brutally efficient wars against Iraq's military and government. Such power is produced by skimming off some of what is produced in the nation's larger economy. We may call it resource or exchange power, because it derives from value that is created by exchange and that can be taxed by the state. Clearly, a sovereign newly appointed in an anarchic society may not acquire any such power. Indeed, in Hobbes's state of nature, for example, there was too little exchange to allow the amassment of wealth to be taxed, and the first power an initial sovereign would need in order to acquire exchange power is the power to tax.

Prior to the accumulation of exchange power there must typically first be something vaguely like the power to maintain order in a fairly productive society. Such power can come from mere coordination, and we may sensibly call it coordination power. Such power can often be used in varied ways as though it spills over from one realm to others, but it commonly cannot be applied to just any purpose without undercutting the coordination of many.

Napoleon could coordinate several hundred thousand men to conquer much of Europe even with the limited weaponry of his time. Indeed, his defeat in his attack on Russia is dramatically portrayed in an 1861 graphic by the French engineer Charles Joseph Minard that displays the declining numbers of his men, from about 422,000 upon crossing into Russia at the Nieman River, to about 100,000 at Moscow, to about 10,000 upon recrossing the Russian border months later.[5] Weapons were not the central issue, which was manpower coordinated behind a leader, which Hobbes says is the greatest of human powers.[6] Napoleon lost his power in his awful winter in Russia.

When marauding tribes swept down on cities before recent times, they often had no greater wealth than what the tribe members individually created by fashioning their personal weapons and by raising animals. A leader behind whom enough other people coordinate has power from the potential efforts of those other people, not from stores of substantive resources. Hume's

---

[5] Tufte, *The Visual Display of Quantitative Information*, 40–1.
[6] Hobbes, *Leviathan* 10.3 [41].

and Smith's philosophical history of the rise of states is a history of the gradual growth of coordination that made taxation and the amassment of physical resources in central hands possible and that therefore eventually made exchange power possible.[7]

Hume's quick philosophical history of the rise of states is as follows. In a primitive society without law, there can be no property, although there may be conventions that define cruder forms of possession and justice. When there is war with outside groups, leadership arises; military camps lead to cities; republics arise to contend with despots (T3.2.8.1–2, SBN 539–41).[8] Smith's account of the stages of development of states is more expansive, but still speculative. In a pastoral society, Smith supposes that an individual shepherd will find it in his interest to be part of a group of shepherds because the group or tribe can better protect each individual against various depredations.[9] In a competitive world of pastoralists, one benefits best from association with the most powerful tribe. Hence, if someone rises to capable leadership within a tribe, others will be attracted to join with it. The result eventually will be remarkable power in the control of the leader of the tribe. Combination for the sake of survival then makes it possible not merely to survive but to thrive and even to plunder.

This is essentially an argument from coordination. We coalesce because it is individually in our interest to do so so long as others do so as well. What we need to guide us in coalescing with others is merely the evidence of sufficient leadership and sufficient numbers to make our joining them clearly beneficial. If others were coalescing around a different leader or group, we would be as pleased to join with them. On this evolutionary account of the growth of power, fitness leads not merely to survival but also to increasing fitness. Power may not simply be a resource that can be expended until it is gone; rather, it may derive from coordination that re-creates itself and expands the power as it is put to use. Harold Lasswell's famous definition of politics is who gets what, when, how. He saw politics as a matter of conflict. This is at best only half the truth. If we see government as, rather, a matter of coordination, then politics is who does what, when, and how.

Hobbes supposes that a government could come into power in one of two ways: by contract or agreement or by conquest or internal imposition.[10] Although most of his discussion is about the latter, his brief discussion of a social compact has dominated views of Hobbes's theory. Note that, because

---

[7] For a fuller account of power, see Hardin, *One for All*, chap. 2.

[8] See also Hume, 'Of the Origin of Government,' 39.

[9] Smith, *The Wealth of Nations* 5.1.2, pp. 711–15.

[10] Hobbes speaks of government by institution (*Leviathan* 18 and 19) or by acquisition (20).

they mistakenly focus (as Hobbes does not) on his brief discussion of the social compact, many and maybe even most scholars attribute a moral conclusion to Hobbes. They suppose he argues that we are inherently morally obligated to obey our sovereign because we promised or agreed to when we entered the social compact.[11] Ironically, if the two forms—compact or imposition—are essentially okay and equally obliging for us, then it cannot follow that we are morally obligated by any promise or agreement to obey our sovereign because we made none in the case of government by imposition. What the two cases have in common is that we are finally obliged by the power of the sovereign. Moreover, virtually all real cases involve government by imposition with no social compact.

Hobbes seems to grasp the nature of coordination in his contract argument for the selection of a sovereign, or de facto the creation of the state. In essence, he proposes that we coordinate on a form of government and on the selection of a particular sovereign. He goes much further in supposing that 'Reputation of power is power, because it draweth with it the adherence of those that need protection.'[12] That is to say, it augments itself through further coordination. Indeed, once there is a competent sovereign in place, the game we are in is a game of harmony, as in Hume's earlier example of two men rowing a boat. In this game of harmony, the only good choice for citizens is to acquiesce in the sovereign's rule. But Hobbes does not combine these insights with a grasp of the effects of repeated interaction. He therefore misses anything like Hume's argument for conventions and how forceful they are. In particular, he misses the fact that conventions can control the sovereign.

It is worthwhile to emphasize again, however, that Hobbes's move from disorder to order under a sovereign is *not a contractual relation*. There is no collective action problem in the sense of an n-prisoner's dilemma that must be resolved by agreement and then enforcement of the agreement. If we once do establish a sovereign, there is no prospect of free-riding on that choice. I might prefer to be able to avoid the sovereign's glare when I wish to steal from you in the political society on which we have coordinated. But I cannot free-ride on the initial coordination itself. We either coordinate or we do not, but there is no individual special action that is outside the coordination and that reserves for me the denial of the coordination. I might oppose it because, say, I want a different sovereign, but I cannot avoid the coordination that we achieve. That

---

[11] In any case we only contract with each other, not with the chosen sovereign, who obliges us to acquiesce without any reference to a contractual or promissory obligation, because we have none to the sovereign.

[12] Hobbes, *Leviathan* 10.5 [41].

coordination leads to power that can be used to keep me in line under the new order. Creation of such power is what the coordination is about.

Social Order

Turn to Hume's argument for the rise of government by convention and his justification of the state as provider of social order. Social order can take two quite different forms. First, in a very small society such as that of a small Indian tribe of North America in Hume's time, order can follow from conventions that can govern behavior in conditions of the general transparency of everyone's actions to everyone else. Such a society can be organized by norms, although this is not Hume's term (the term with its modern force would have been unavailable in his time).[13] He speaks of conventions. In Hobbes's state of nature there is neither justice nor property (nor right nor wrong). Hume says also that in a Hobbesian state of nature, 'or that imaginary state,' there is no justice or injustice and there is no property (T3.2.2.15, SBN 501). But for him, there is an intermediate position between this state of nature (which did not ever exist) and a large society that requires government. That intermediate position is a small society that is regulated by conventions, which must include some perhaps minimal sense of justice as order. This difference in views turns on Hume's richer theoretical grasp of strategic possibilities in his theory of convention as applied to the iterated interactions of a small society.

Instead of Hobbes's war of all against all in a state of nature, in a small society we face a substantially contrary condition: *the monitoring of all by all.* And we are therefore all basically reliable in our dealings with each other and toward our collective interests. As we now know from many anthropological studies of small, relatively primitive societies, they can work without any heavy machinery of government and with relative spontaneity of action by everyone. They enjoy spontaneous order. But if our exchange relations are restricted to the small numbers with whom we can repeatedly interact, we face a serious loss of opportunities that we could enjoy if we could guarantee reciprocal fulfillment of even isolated exchanges. Moreover, even in ongoing relationships, we cannot trust one another to abide by exchanges that involve very large values, so that our relationships will still be restricted. For example, to whom would you sell your house on a legally unenforceable contract to pay you a large monthly sum for the next twenty years? Hence, even if we do

---

[13] The first use of 'norm' cited in the *Oxford English Dictionary* is in 1821 and the term is used in the sense of a standard, model, pattern, or type. The next use in 1828 is in the relevant normative sense.

not go all the way with Hobbes in thinking that unregulated social interactions would be constantly murderous, as in his state of nature, we must agree with him that they would be radically poorer than what we could have under a properly functioning government.

The second form of social order is that of a large and at least moderately complex society in which we are not all known to each other and in which monitoring and individual-level sanctioning of miscreants therefore cannot be expected to guarantee generally good behavior by all. We need government to restrain us from harmful actions and probably even to compel us to beneficial collective actions.

In both these states there must be some sense of justice that provides for social order. Under a regime of such justice, there could arise principles of possession, although in the conditions of the tribe the range of things that could come under the rubric of possession might be extremely small and restricted. In a nomadic pastoral society, our goats, sheep, or cattle might count as individual possessions. In a hunter-gatherer society, almost nothing might count as individual possessions. In neither case would land count as a possession, although your tent might describe an area onto which others should not encroach while we are in this particular area.

Note that the small primitive society could lack government and could be relatively anarchic but nevertheless well ordered, with each of us free to do as we please much of the time but with very clear expectations about behaviors in many contexts of importance to our group. As anarchists have long insisted, there can be order in anarchy. Hume says, 'An *Indian* is but little tempted to dispossess another of his hut, or to steal his bow, as being already provided of the same advantages; and as to any superior fortune, which may attend one above another in hunting and fishing, 'tis only casual and temporary, and will have but small tendency to disturb society' (T3.2.8.1, SBN 539). Hence, despite its lack of government, the society need not descend into the violence and virtual war of Hobbes's state of nature. I have nothing to gain from attacking or stealing from my neighbor. Indeed, if I do steal, my theft will commonly be known to all in the society and I might suffer powerful sanctions.

Hume therefore specifically says that he disagrees so much with the vision of the state of nature of 'some philosophers' that he supposes government arose not in order to handle disorder within society but to allow for better organization of defense against those outside the society who might attack it (T3.2.8.1, SBN 539–40). Hume says the 'state of society without government is one of the most natural states of men, and may subsist with the conjunction of many families, and long after the first generation' (T3.2.8.2, SBN 541). The difference between Hobbes and Hume here might primarily be in the greater body of empirical evidence on the North American Indians when Hume wrote, almost exactly a century after Hobbes first wrote.[14] Hobbes presumably had no evidence for his speculative claim that the Indians lived in the brutish manner of a war of all against all.[15]

Although it would be possible to maintain a very small society indefinitely without government, "'tis impossible they shou'd maintain a society of any kind without justice,' which entails three fundamental principles concerning (1) the stability of possession, (2) its transfer by consent from one owner to another, and (3) the performance of promises (or contracts loosely defined). Hume adopts Hobbes's language and calls these laws of nature; they are among the far longer list of laws of nature in Hobbes.[16] These laws are antecedent to government in the sense that they are sociological principles (T3.2.8.3, SBN 541). Hume's three laws of nature are elevated to their high status by the fact that they are enormously useful in enabling us to have stable expectations and to invest our efforts in individually beneficial endeavors that have beneficial implications for the whole society. The three laws are, seen ex ante, mutually beneficial.

We can fully understand these laws of nature of Hume and Hobbes—or Rawls's principles of justice—and still act as though they did not govern our behavior. Indeed, in all three cases, it is not even always clear what it would mean for a single individual to act according to the derived laws or principles. Hobbes goes so far as to say that it would be wrong for a single person to follow the laws of nature in the actual world if no one else were following them because to do so would make one a prey to others and procure one's own certain ruin, 'contrary to the ground of all laws of nature, which tend to nature's preservation.'[17] Hume similarly says, 'I should be the cully [dupe] of my integrity, if I alone shou'd impose on myself a severe restraint amidst the licentiousness of others' (T3.2.7.3, SBN 535). That would be too much to expect, especially of a rational, moderately self-interested person. One can be obliged to follow the dictates of the laws of nature only in the context of a political society under a government that will enforce them as legal laws.[18]

Hume supposes that government would get its first authority from these principles (T3.2.8.3, SBN 541). It is only with greater prosperity and larger scale that we might come into such serious conflict with each other as to need

---

[14] We now have extensive evidence on various forms of societal development. See, for example, Johnson and Earle, *The Evolution of Human Societies: From Foraging Group to Agrarian State.*

[15] Hobbes, *Leviathan* 13.11 [63]. [16] Ibid. 14–15. [17] Ibid. 15.36 [79].

[18] Similarly, Rawls's principles of distributive justice should lead to the design of institutions that will produce just distributions, in part by giving people incentives for relevant behavior.

government to regulate our behavior. Although abiding by the principles of justice would be sufficient to maintain any society, it would be impossible for us to observe those principles in a large society unless we have government to enforce compliance with the principles (T3.2.8.5, SBN 543).[19]

In sum, the laws of nature are part of the mutual-advantage vision and not a moral alternative to it. That vision, of course, is grounded in self-interest, whose causal generalization is mutual advantage. The best way to secure our personal interest in survival and economic prosperity is to secure the mutual interest in these things through establishing or maintaining general order. To those who tend to see self-interest as a bad, this is a seemingly magic move, but it works as well as any fundamentally important move in all of political philosophy can be said to work.

As an aside, we may note that Hume finds in this argument the implication that observance of the law of nature that we honor our promises is 'an effect of the institution of government,' and obedience to government is not an effect of the obligation of promising, indeed, it logically cannot be. Moreover, the first motive for keeping promises is self-interest, and this is also the reason for having government. 'To obey the civil magistrate is requisite to preserve order and concord in society. To perform promises is requisite to beget mutual trust and confidence in the common offices of life. The ends, as well as the means, are perfectly distinct; nor is the one subordinate to the other' (T3.2.8.5, SBN 544), although our private duties of promise-keeping are more dependent on our public duties than the other way around (T3.2.8.7, SBN 546). Theories of the grounding of government in a promise or contract are therefore wrong (3.2.8.9, SBN 549).[20] For allegiance to government, he insists that there is no other principle than interest (T3.2.9.4, SBN 553).

One might argue against him here that, if promising could have arisen as a matter of justice in small societies, it could have been used to create government. Neither convention would be subordinate, but one might have been historically prior. But 'exact performance of promises' (that is to say, as in even moderately specified contracts) depends on government (T3.2.8.5, SBN 543), and without government-backing promises would be weak. And if there were no promises we would still need government (T3.2.8.7, SBN 546).

---

[19] In addition to thinking the focus on our interests or mutual advantage is the only morality Hobbes actually has in his account of the state, note that this focus is also the prior explanation of his laws of nature, which are laws to govern successful association, laws which must be made positive laws if they are to work in regulating our behavior. As laws of nature, they are of course prior to positive law, but that is because, again, they are sociological laws about what would work. Their workability makes them an appealing basis for positive law.

[20] Also see Hume, 'Of the Original Contract.'

This is not strictly the logical rejection of contractarianism that Hume asserts, but it is compelling.

Also, despite Hume's apparent criticism of Hobbes's state of nature (T3.2.8.1, SBN 539–40),[21] he says that, 'by preserving society, we make much greater advances in the acquiring possession, than by running into the solitary and forlorn condition, which must follow upon violence and an universal license'[22] (T3.2.2.13, SBN 492).

Government

Hume discusses government, its structure, and its value to us, in a long section of the *Treatise* (T3.2.7–11, SBN 534–69) and in several essays. Our approbation of government derives, of course, from our sense that it tends to serve mutual advantage, and hence our own interests. It does so because it protects us and enables us to do many things we could not do in a large society without the backing of government. Principally, it enables us to prosper and to enter into exchanges backed by enforceable contracts. I might not recognize the fact, but the state's benefits to you in this respect tend to my advantage as well. It is enough for Hume's account, however, that I have at least a modicum of sympathy for your welfare, so that I judge the government positively for its service to you.

One might suppose Hume's general view that we have a general interest in maintaining justice should mean that we can expect government to act well. So why would anyone act unjustly? Under the influence of our passions, we are governed by imagination, and this works far more strongly for what is near and contiguous than for what only reason can tell us (T3.2.7.1, SBN 534–5). One might suppose that this is a kind of akrasia or weakness of will, but Hume thinks it is normal, even universal psychology. It fits the account of mirroring because the nearer we are to someone the more clearly we can see their emotional reactions and, hence, the more likely we are to mirror them.

If we are generally self-seeking in our individual lives, then we must surely take advantage of public office to benefit ourselves against the interests of other citizens. Indeed, Hume says that every man ought to be supposed a knave in government office, and institutions that might happen to be staffed by knaves must be designed to handle that problem. Lest we think this is an excessive assumption, Hume notes that men are more honest in their private than in

---

[21] Also see Hume, 'Of the Original Contract'; 'Of the Origin of Government,' 37.
[22] Also see Hume, 'Of the Original Contract,' 472.

their public capacity. Honor is a great check on personal actions, but in a large-number crowd this check fails.[23] In fine, it is not from human goodness or morality that government works for our interests, but from the constraints of institutions that make even knaves work for the public interest.

Hume's task therefore is largely to show that government officials can be constrained to act for the general good. Why? In part because they usually act on general principles that do not directly affect their own interests. The consequences of a breach of equity are remote and cannot counterbalance any immediate advantage of better behavior (T3.2.7.3, SBN 535). When we consider things at a distance, all their minute distinctions vanish, and we give preference to whatever is preferable. When thinking of actions twelve months hence, I prefer the greater good (T3.2.7.5, SBN 536). The trick is to change our circumstances to make us observe the laws of justice as our nearest interest. We appoint magistrates who have no interest in any act of injustice but an immediate interest in every execution of justice (T3.2.7.6, SBN 537).

This last claim is perhaps overstated. Insofar as our magistrates have no interest in the injustices committed by others, we can generally expect them not to have a bias in favor of injustice. Indeed, through sympathy we can expect them to have at least a slight bias in favor of justice in any matter that does not concern themselves. All we need to do to constrain them from acting unjustly therefore is to block any actions that they might take on their own behalf or on behalf of their relatives and friends. We can do this to some degree by having different offices overseeing each other. This is not merely the separation of powers, which is typically intended to block institutions from acting on some institutional agenda rather than to block individual office holders from acting in their own personal interest against the public interest. It is more nearly James Madison's device of having ambition counter ambition, person to person.[24] Montesquieu argues for separation of powers. Hume and Madison propose the monitoring of all by all, which is Hume's device for a small society regulated by norms (or conventions). Although our present interest may blind us with respect to our own actions, it does not with respect to the actions of others, so we can judge the latter from sympathy with the general effect of those actions (T3.2.8.7, SBN 545).

How does Madison's device work? It has more in common with competitors in a market than with Montesquieu's hiving off some duties to one agency and others to other agencies. I block your action because I think it is wrong, meaning that it is harmful to the general interest, but I do so because I

---

[23] Hume, 'Of the Independency of Parliament,' 42–3.
[24] Madison, *Federalist* number 51, p. 322.

have a slight leaning toward that general interest through the influence of my sympathy for the public utility. My action against you is likely to be costless to me and it might even be rewarded by other office holders or even by the citizens who, if they have no direct interest in the matter at issue, also have a slight sympathy for the general utility. I therefore have both a motive from sympathy and possibly a motive from interest to block your illegitimate self-interested action. Government itself has more of the character of a small society than does the whole society that it governs. (This would have been far more true in Hume's day than it is today, with our enormous government agencies whose total populations exceed the populations of many nations in Hume's day.) Even Madison does not think that his device will work if government is torn by factions, that is to say, if there is an unequal coordination on rule as there has been most of the time in most representative democracies of modern times.

Justificatory Theories of the State

There is a lot of effort to justify the state, especially in contractarian theories, public-goods theories, and theories that ground the state in shared values. There was also a long tradition of justifying the state as the order of God in the world. By Hume's time, this traditional justification no longer made sense and was generally irrelevant, although it continues to have its retrograde advocates. The rise of contractarian justifications of obedience to the state is arguably a response to the loss of religious justifications. Contractarians of Locke's school attempt to ground obedience in the consent of the citizens to the government and its rule.

The main justification of the state for Hobbes and Hume (and many others, especially later) is that it maintains order. Unfortunately, to do that, it must have power that allows it to do much else. The state in Hume's time was ham-handed in many arenas. Domestically, it could generally keep the peace by using the criminal law and harsh sanctions to deter certain disorderly behaviors, although it was often draconian in its punishments, such as hanging countless people for extremely petty crimes. It could maintain harbors, lighthouses, some roads, and a few other infrastructural facilities. Beyond that it could do very little other than cause havoc in the economy and, of course, play favorites by extending grants of monopoly. It could raise taxes primarily through customs at ports and on land. It was not capable of the kinds of welfare policy that modern states often have. As a percentage of domestic product, its budget was a tiny fraction of the budgets of contemporary states. Yet at that stage of development, or soon thereafter, it already worried such libertarians as Wilhelm von Humboldt and John Stuart Mill.[25]

Let us consider the force of the three main justifications of the state other than that it merely secures order. Consent is the main theory that Hume addresses because it was more or less the reigning philosophical theory in his time. He and Smith actually contribute arguments that have been taken up as a nascent version of the public-goods theory (T3.2.7.7–8, SBN 538–9), although that theory reaches its articulate height long after their time. Theories of shared values might have been attributed to earlier thinkers, such as Socrates, who did not present justificatory theories of the state. The main claimants for shared values in Hume's era were later religious thinkers, especially in the Catholic tradition, who assumed we all must share the relevant religious views. Shared-values theories have since come back into debate through claims by sociologists in the tradition of Talcott Parsons and by communitarians. Hume speaks directly to contractarian theories, which he ridicules, as does Durkheim for similar empirical reasons, in particular the pervasive division of labor, which has wrecked any chance of broad contractarian agreement.[26] Hume does not address the public-goods and shared-values theories, but we can try to address them as Hume might have done.

Here we focus on justificatory rather than explanatory theories. In rough outline, political economists have contributed to three categories of explanatory theories of the state based on arguments from, respectively, public goods, coordination, and evolutionary stability. Hume and Hobbes give coordination theories of the origin of the state (or of states in general) and Hume and Smith add to this an evolutionary account of the growth and transformation of the state as a series of more or less unintended consequences. The best known of these and the most extensively articulated are theories that build on public goods, in part perhaps because the theory of public goods has long been relatively well understood in at least a crude form, and in part perhaps because the public-goods theory seems to yield not only an explanation for but also a justification of the state.[27] In any case, the long tradition that grounds the state in the demand for public goods and in the state's capacity to deliver such goods has been both normative and explanatory. The other two economic traditions—coordination and evolutionary stability—are primarily explanatory and not normative, and they are discussed throughout this book

---

[25] Humboldt, *The Limits of State Action*; Mill, *On Liberty*.

[26] Durkheim, *The Division of Labor in Society*, 1.7.1, 201–3.

[27] Hardin, 'Economic Theories of the State.'

as essentially Hume's theory. Here I will briefly address the contractarian, public-goods, and shared-values justifications of the state, all of which Hume does or would reject.

Contractarianism

Hobbes is the principal forerunner of the contractarian vision, as articulated later by Locke and others, but partly in a negative or provocative sense, as Euclidian geometry is a forerunner of non-Euclidian geometries such as Riemannian geometry. It is partly in reaction to Hobbes that the contractarian enterprise flourished. That enterprise is not merely an elaboration of Hobbes but is an alternative to what are often seen as the worst parts of Hobbes, especially the pervasive egoism. Or at best it is a very partial elaboration of Hobbes, because, although he creates government by covenant (which is merely a contract that is not immediately fulfilled), he often defies the central elements of contractarian thinking. He is not concerned to substitute consent for religious bases of obligation. Indeed, he can generally do without a notion of political obligation. In any case, he frequently denies that we do in any meaningful sense consent to rule by our sovereign, or that we need otherwise do something to empower the sovereign. Moreover, most of us do not even understand the issue. All that we need do is submit to a powerful sovereign who has devices for coercing us. This gunman view of the sovereign, who is not idly called Leviathan in Hobbes's greatest work, makes a mockery of contemporary contractarian paeans to the beauty of consent.

Hume wrote a devastating essay, 'Of the Original Contract,' against the idea of the social contract.[28] He agrees with Hobbes that in all probability no such thing ever happened. It is instructive to note Hobbes's full remarks on the supposed state of nature in which a social contract might have been entered:

> It may peradventure be thought, there was never such a time nor condition of war as this; and I believe it was never generally so, over all the world. But there are many places where they live so now. For the savage people in many places of *America* (except the government of small families, the concord whereof dependeth on natural lust) have no government at all, and live at this day in that brutish manner as I have said before. Howsoever, it may be perceived what manner of life there would be where there were no common power to fear, by the manner of life which men that have formerly lived under a peacefull government use to degenerate into, in a civil war.[29]

He adds much later that there is likely no government that came into power other than by conquest or violence.[30] The contractarian story is a myth and

[28] See also, Hardin, 'Contractarianism: Wistful Thinking.' [29] Hobbes, *Leviathan* 13.11 [63].
[30] Ibid., 'A Review and Conclusion' 8 [392].

has no role to play in actually motivating obedience to any actual state or in Hobbes's own explanations.

For Locke and for many other contractarian thinkers, an important part of the social contract theory is that, because we have agreed to the elevation of a sovereign, we have in a sense promised our obedience and we are therefore morally obligated to obey the sovereign.[31] They ground obedience to government in our consent to the government. Hume says that this view is particularly silly ('nothing could be more absurd' (EPM App. 3.7, SBN 306)). In addition to its logical absurdity, the view is historically absurd because no ordinary citizen then living in Scotland, England, or any other well-organized state had ever actually agreed to be obedient in that way.[32] Surely, Hume supposes, all these people could not be wrong about whether they had ever made a promise of obedience.[33]

Moreover, Hume supposes that conceptually and causally we could not have created an obligation of keeping promises by promising to do so (EPM App. 3.7, SBN 306). Therefore the supposed social contract could have no bite for us. In one of his harshest criticisms, Hume, perhaps in chiding humor, says that only someone 'trained in a philosophical system' could have made such an argument as that we are bound to obey because we promised to do so.[34] Of course, far more philosophers have lived after his time than before it, and remarkably many philosophers are tainted by this philosophical sin. Although he seldom explicitly identifies those with whom he agrees or disagrees, in an unusual move Hume flays Locke on this issue. This astonishingly smart essay, which is short and acute, should have put an end to contractarian political thought.[35]

Elsewhere Hume says, 'Were the interests of society nowise concerned, it is as unintelligible, why another's articulating certain sounds, implying consent, should change the nature of my actions with regard to a particular object, as why the reciting of a liturgy by a priest, in a certain habit and posture, should dedicate a heap of brick and timber, and render it, thenceforth and for ever, sacred' (EPM3.38, SBN 199). Hobbes says contracts are bonds 'that have their strength, not from their own nature (for nothing is more easily broken than a man's word) but from fear of some evil consequence upon the rupture.'[36] It follows that a contract in the state of nature is void; 'but if there be a common power set over [the contractors], with right and force sufficient to compel

---

[31] Locke, *Two Treatises of Government.*   [32] Hume, 'Of the Original Contract,' 470.
[33] Ibid. 487.   [34] Ibid. 481.
[35] For more of the historical background of Hume's remarks, see Haakonssen, 'Introduction and Commentary,' 405–8.
[36] Hobbes, *Leviathan* 14.7 [65].

performance, it is not void.' Indeed, to perform one's side of a contract first in the state of nature is wrong because 'he which performeth first does but betray himself to his enemy, contrary to the right (he can never abandon) of defending his life and means of living.'[37]

In sum, there is little or no objective moral content to the political theories of Hobbes and Hume. There is especially no reliance on the morality of keeping promises or contractual agreements. There is only social scientific explanatory content to any such agreement on a form of government or on a sovereign. Again, because Hobbes thinks we are obliged to obey even a government that has come to power over us via conquest, there is no moral claim for our obedience to it. Through its power, however obtained, government merely obliges us. Whereas for Locke, contract makes government right, for Hobbes, at best, it merely makes government happen, and for Hume the whole apparatus of contracting is a silly idea.

Public-Goods Theories

In its most literal variants, scholars in the public-goods tradition suppose that people deliberately create the state in order to provide themselves with goods they could not individually provide themselves, as, for example, by literally contracting to establish government. This bootstrapping move is circular if it is supposed that the state is itself a public good. In frustration at failing to provide ourselves some public good, we merely provide ourselves another that then provides us the one we failed to provide. Although it has not fully withered away and may occasionally betray signs of spontaneous regeneration, this branch of the tradition was finally cut off by Mancur Olson's argument of the logic of collective action.[38] According to this logic, I rationally contribute to the provision of a collective good only if I get more value from the bit of the collective good that my contribution buys than that contribution costs me. Commonly, in large-scale collective action contexts, my contribution returns

---

[37] Ibid. 14.18 [68]. It should be clear that Hobbes sees the strategic structure of exchange by contracting as a prisoner's dilemma because his ordering of the payoffs of the possible outcomes is that of the prisoner's dilemma. We both prefer the outcome in which we have exchanged to the status quo. To either of these outcomes, we each prefer to be the recipient of the other's half of our contract without having to fulfill our half. And it is obvious that Hobbes thinks the worst outcome for each of us is to fulfill first and then to have the other not fulfill—so much so, indeed, that he thinks it wrong of one to fulfill first as doing oneself too great harm. In addition to recognizing the payoff structure of the prisoner's dilemma in his account of contracting, Hobbes also recognizes the individual incentive to defect on one's fellow contractor, an incentive that he supposes can only be overcome in general through enforcement by government, so that without government enforcement we cannot rely on contracting. This is, of course, the central problem of the single-play prisoner's dilemma.

[38] Olson, *The Logic of Collective Action*.

vanishingly small benefits to me, so that it costs me more than it is worth to me. Hence, although all of us might receive a large net benefit if we all contribute, none of us may have any interest in contributing individually.[39]

In its credible variants the tradition that associates the state with public goods is largely about what difference it makes that some goods are more successfully or efficiently provided collectively through the state than individually through the market. The public-goods theory of the state seems to involve one or both of two claims. The first claim is that certain characteristics of public goods require that they be provided by a central agency acting on behalf of the larger group of beneficiaries. The second is that collective provision merely has advantages over individual provision. This claim is surely true in some cases, but it should be weighed against the disadvantages of a state empowered to provide bads as well as goods. The claim is consistent with the possibility of totalitarian and exploitative states as well as liberal states; totalitarian and exploitative states seem contrary to or outside the first claim. The sanguine view of Hume and Smith that the state can perform miracles of dredging harbors and raising armies beyond the capacities of individuals spontaneously acting together—which is often taken as a statement of the public-goods theory—is consistent with both the first and second claims (T3.2.7.8, SBN 538–9). For Hume, state provision of such public goods as harbors and roads is in modern language *a by-product of the rise of government, not the reason for the rise*—which was to secure defense against foreign attackers. Just because we are coordinated in support of the state, the state can exercise great power.[40]

Smith thinks there are three things that individuals acting in spontaneous concert cannot be expected to provide: justice, defense, and certain infrastructural goods that, 'though they may be in the highest degree advantageous to a great society, are, however, of such a nature, that the profit could never repay the expence to any individual or small number of individuals, and which it, therefore, cannot be expected that any individual or small number of individuals should erect or maintain.'[41]

In the normative variant of the public-goods theory, it is state provision of public goods that justifies the existence of the state and the use of its coercive

---

[39] For further discussion see Hardin, 'Economic Theories of the State.'

[40] Much of what makes the state plausibly valuable is not its provision of genuine public goods, many of which can successfully be provided by market devices. For example, radio signals are among the best examples of public goods, but they are commonly provided by the market unless the state coercively blocks private enterprise in providing such signals. The state's chief role in providing them in some cases is merely to regulate bandwidths and interference between stations. That is to say, the state mainly helps in the coordination of the multiple provision. That is often the chief value of the state as part of its maintenance of order more generally.

[41] Smith, *The Wealth of Nations* 2.5.1.3, §1, 723.

devices. If the theory is strictly explanatory, it is subject to the bootstrapping complaint above—we resolve the problem of failure to supply public goods by supplying a super-public good, the state, so that it can supply lesser public goods. If the government is an ongoing resolution of a continuing society-wide prisoner's dilemma or collective action interaction, it cannot be stable, because it can be brought down by free-riding at any time. Coordination is the dominant feature of stable social organization because its continuing resolution faces no such problems and is therefore stable.

In his just-so story of the origin of government, Hume supposes that the first step toward government and the state is more or less spontaneous leadership in war (T3.2.8.1–2, SBN 541). For that, the collective good and the individual good are almost inseparable. There is hardly any scope for free-riding, as there would be for public good provisions. The whole community acts together and anyone who attempted to linger behind would be left behind.

Shared-Value Theories

There have been many states and political movements that have coordinated around a particular value, often a religious belief. The coherence and even the solidarity of these states was perhaps secured by the common belief and commitment to it or to its leaders. In wars of religious conquest the armies might be coordinated by a common set of beliefs. It is harder to believe that ordinary states are successfully coordinated in this way, although there may be cases. Perhaps it is such experiences that lead theorists such as communitarians, Parsons, and, to a less comprehensive extent, Hart to claim that societies cohere because they have core values that keep them in order.[42] Unfortunately, these theorists typically do not follow Hume's experimental method of arguing from actual historical cases. Their view, seemingly not grounded in facts, is very hard either to defend or to criticize in any articulate way.

Against such theories is their susceptibility to one of the oldest problems of social theory: the fallacy of composition. In the social variant of this fallacy, it is supposed that many individuals, all of whom have some property or characteristic, such as rationality, can be composed into a collective of some kind that has that same property or characteristic and that acts from it. Xenophon justified Cyrus's despotic rule with the claim that Cyrus's interests

---

[42] Durkheim, *The Division of Labor in Society* 1.2.1, 79–80; Parsons, *The Structure of Social Action*, 89–94; Hart, *The Concept of Law*, 88. See also Wrong, *The Problem of Order: What Unites and Divides Society*; Almond and Verba, *The Civic Culture: Political Attitudes and Democracy in Five Nations*; Mackie, *Hume's Moral Theory*, 87. As with most of these scholars, Mackie merely asserts that legal sanctions cannot 'be effective without the support of widespread moral sentiments.' It would pay to look before we take such a leap of faith. Generally, see Hardin, *Liberalism, Constitutionalism, and Democracy*, 9–12.

were identical with those of his subjects.[43] Xenophon's argument is somewhat trivialized by his claim that what makes their interests common is that they have common enemies, whom they wish to defeat. Evidently Cyrus's rule would immediately have ceased to be just had he lived to see victory over those enemies (he died in battle).

Despots have commonly held Xenophon's view of themselves, with a slight twist—that the people's interests are identical with the despot's. With the possible exceptions of Hume's case of the very small primitive society cohering behind a leader to defend itself, and perhaps other small anthropological societies cohering over many generations as Rawls argues (ostensibly on Hume's behalf),[44] such claims seem likely to be instances of the fallacy of composition. It seems very likely that the men in Cyrus's army did not all fully share his interests and that many of them may have fought under duress or may have lingered behind to avoid the harshest prospects.

Contemporary proponents of shared-value theory typically claim sociological authority for their views, which, however, are grounded more in assertion than in anything even vaguely approaching empirical demonstration. The assumption is that a society cannot cohere if its members do not share important values. An especially important statement of this concern is Durkheim's *The Division of Labor in Society*. For Durkheim, the rapid process of the division of labor in industrial societies has 'irremediably shattered' our common morality. Hence we need to make a new moral code.[45] The prospect of a common morality might make sense for a religious order, but it is hard to imagine what the content of any such morality could be in a modern society as pluralist as the UK or US or even Durkheim's early twentieth-century France. It appears that we can live without such a morality or a collective conscience.

Hume could respond to the shared-values school that the most prosperous societies we have known are large, diverse, liberal societies in which the claim that there are major organizing values that make the societies cohere seems prima facie implausible. At the very least, we would want research to show how values are shared and how that fact makes for social cohesion. We might grant that in many states there is a minimal value in the acquiescence of citizens in the rule of the government. That this is a common value, however, is likely to be an odd claim in many cases. To say that I do not acquiesce seems, if it is a serious claim, to entail that I do something about the state of affairs. But as Hume argues for the psychology of approbation and disapprobation, we

[43] Xenophon (4th century BC), *Education of Cyrus* 8.1.4.
[44] Rawls, *Lectures on the History of Moral Philosophy*, 66–7.
[45] Durkheim, *The Division of Labor in Society* 3, 'Conclusion,' 3, p. 409.

cannot expect any action to follow. The only action that follows for me in my nation under what I think is awful leadership is merely to grouse and complain and—what is even less effective—to vote. And I can sympathize with those whom my nation abuses, both internally and externally. That does not sound like the social solidarity that the shared-value theorists want.

Absent more specific content, it is hard to criticize the idea that social order depends on widely shared values.[46] One is inclined to object to this vision the way Hume objects to the idea that we promised allegiance to our state via a social contract. Hume says that if we promised such a thing, surely we would remember that fact.[47] Similarly, if we share important values with everyone else in society, we should be able to say something about what those values are. Or at the very least, our value theorists should be able to tell us. Parsons and the current generation of shared-value theorists tell us almost nothing about what these values are. That makes criticizing their views difficult even while it makes ignoring them easy. The novelist, William Gaddis, with his grasp of vernacular syntax, has Elizabeth in *Carpenter's Gothic* bemoan the impossibility of reaching accord on much of anything. She says, 'I mean when you think that those grasshoppers probably all just know the same thing but I mean with all these people, with all these millions and millions of people everyplace that no one knows what anyone else knows?'[48] Grasshoppers and ants might erect a social order on shared instincts; people in liberal societies in our time cannot.

Those who hold that it is shared values that keep us in order under a government should be able to give us at least a crude sense of just what those values are beyond self-interest, which they generally insist cannot be adequate. One can read dozens of very general claims for the necessity of such values and never encounter a single such value. Or, if one finds a value in the discussion, it is not one that is generally shared—for example, it might be the particular religious value of the author. The literature on the centrality of shared values for political order is among the strangest literatures in all of the social sciences because it is empirically almost entirely vacuous; it is more nearly an article of faith than a genuine thesis to be shown.

Against the shared-value theorists, Hume thinks interest is virtually the whole story, although he thinks that commonly it is indirectly motivating through institutional structures that give us specialized incentives to act in ways that then aggregate into social order, which is an artificial virtue and therefore

[46] Rawls argues that social order is based on 'The Idea of an Overlapping Consensus'; Hume's coordination on order plus limited beneficence beyond close associates is plausibly the most that we can agree to. Hence, the consensus that Rawls needs for applying his theory of distributive justice may not ever be available.

[47] Hume, 'Of the Original Contract,' 460.   [48] Gaddis, *Carpenter's Gothic*, 168.

necessarily a two-stage achievement. Indeed, given his rough grasp of the logic of collective action, Hume cannot suppose that we have a direct interest in contributing to the stability and might of our government.

There are people who wish to reduce the breadth of values extant in various societies by, if necessary, imposing their political or religious views on others. Many American politicians, for example, have insisted that the United States is a nation organized on Protestant Christian values. Criticizing such views is easy. They are false to the facts. Their proponents would not need or bother to assert such views if they were true. But one suspects that if the shared-values thesis were to come true, it would be through a coercively imposed religious dogma, as was happening increasingly under the Taliban's brutally rigorous rule of Afghanistan.

Rebellion

The issue of allegiance becomes enormously complicated when a government uses its power to impose its vision on a substantial minority, or when a de facto minority government even manages to impose its vision on the majority, as was typical for perhaps almost all governments before the democratic era. Then we may face essentially an unequal coordination, as discussed in chapter 4. My group might be substantially worse off than yours because your group might use its power from coordination on the present government to suppress my group and to block any prospect that my group could ever come to power or even merely affect your policies to be more benign toward my group. When such a divide occurs, or when there is a particularly bad government in power, we might finally have incentive to attempt revolution or rebellion.

Of the three great early Anglo-Saxon political philosophers, Hobbes, Locke, and Hume, Hume has the most open view of the justification of rebellion and the clearest discussion of it.[49] Hobbes's view is essentially that an individual can refuse obedience to the sovereign when the individual's own life is threatened by the sovereign. The view is not collective, and rebellion by an individual, as opposed to a large group or class, would be a pitiful act. Hobbes has only scattered remarks about rebellion per se, all of them hostile to the idea. Once we have a sovereign, we are stuck.

Locke imagines rebellion by the whole citizenry who could abrogate the old and enter into a new contract. The argument is simple enough: 'The end

---

[49] Hume, 'Of the Protestant Succession.'

of Government is the good of Mankind, and which is *best for Mankind*, that the People should be always expos'd to the boundless will of Tyranny, or that the Rulers should be sometimes liable to be oppos'd, when they grow exorbitant in the use of their Power, and imploy it for the destruction, and not the preservation of the Properties of their People?'[50] Locke recognizes that the people will generally have a hard time taking such action, and therefore there is little fear that government will be unstable.[51] Government is dissolved when the governors violate their trust (government may still be in power), and the people have sovereignty and 'a perpetual residual power to cashier their governors and remodel their government.'[52]

Hume, typically, sets the tone of his lengthy remarks by reference to an actual rebellion: 'But here an *English* reader will be apt to enquire concerning that famous *revolution* [of 1688], which has had such a happy influence on our constitution, and has been attended with such mighty consequences' (T3.2.10.16, SBN 563).[53] As revolutions go, that one was relatively mild and amicable, although it could not have pleased King James II, the Stuart family, or Catholics except insofar as they might have believed it prevented a civil war. Hume notes that earlier theorists tried to make rebellion a matter of having a right to rebel in response to violation of the social contract. When the government is tyrannous, the citizens 'are free'd from their promises, (as happens in all conditional contracts) and return to that state of liberty, which preceded the institution of government.' He says that this 'conclusion is just, tho' the principles be erroneous.' They are erroneous because there was no promise (T3.2.9.2, SBN 550). This is not a correct reading of Hobbes's contractarian arguments, which do not seem to be about a contract with the sovereign but a contract among the citizens 'only of one to another,' and therefore cannot be about a broken promise by the sovereign. Hobbes explicitly says (the view is pervasive in *Leviathan*) that there can be no breach of covenant by the sovereign.[54] But Hume's reading of Locke and others is correct.

Hume's own account does not depend on claims of having rights but only on our moral psychology of reacting to a government that is harmful to interests and that therefore provokes disapprobation rather than the approbation of allegiance. Therefore Hume's argument for the reasonableness of rebellion against an actual government turns on whether the government is perceived

[50] Locke, *Two Treatises of Government* 1.229, 417; see also 1.221–2, 412–14.

[51] Ibid. 1.223, 414.   [52] Laslett, 'Introduction,' 115.

[53] Hume, 'Of the Protestant Succession.' Locke also commends that revolution, which changed his life for the better (Laslett, 'Introduction,' 116).

[54] Hobbes, *Leviathan* 18.4 [89].

to harm our interests, because *the only reason for having government is to serve our interests*. That it serves our interest is the original motive for its institution and is also the reason for continuing allegiance to it. That interest is the security, protection, and prosperity that political society offers and that we could not have outside of such society. If that interest fails, allegiance to government fails, and we can try to find a government that will do a better job. That rulers may become tyrants is merely human nature, and no one thinks ill of those who have historically rebelled against tyrants. We do not need the contrivances of promises and rights to justify our actions in such cases. Hume's justification for any such action is strictly welfarist.

Although resisting authority might be justifiable on some occasions, *in the ordinary course of affairs it would be pernicious and criminal* (T3.2.10.1 and 16, SBN 553–4, 563–4). Hobbes opposes rebellion very strongly. Recall his discussion of how the state of nature, which probably never existed, is akin to that state we fall into during civil war, a state that Hobbes thinks must be brutal, as it was in his time in England.[55] Peter Laslett supposes Locke's society after the dissolution of government is about equally bad.[56] One might infer that Hume nearly agrees with this judgment in his remark that an established government has an infinite advantage over any alternative because of the turmoil through which we would have to go to change our government.[57] But, as noted, he also praised the mild revolution of 1688, so 'infinite' is apparently not so great as we might think.

In the accounts of Locke and Hume, we may suppose that the government that is now reprehensible once was in the collective interest and was backed by a strong convention of acquiescence in its power. Once the regime has violated its role, continued acquiescence might be motivated by the virtual impossibility that an individual or small numbers could successfully go against it. At that point it will likely have some supporters so that the society is divided by an unequal coordination. Changing the coordination onto a new regime will require the coordination of large numbers, which would often be tantamount to establishing an alternative coordination or to mobilizing a large-number collective action to gain control of the government. We may generally, therefore, expect with Locke that the likelihood of such turmoil is very low unless the government becomes radically intolerable.

---

[55] Ibid. 13.11 [63]; see also 19.20 [94].   [56] Laslett, 'Introduction,' 116.

[57] Hume, 'Idea of a Perfect Commonwealth,' 512; see also, 'Of the Original Contract,' 472. Hume says there that if there is a rebellion, then every wise man 'wishes to see, at the head of a powerful and obedient army, a general, who may speedily seize the prize.' Perhaps this would have been the likely outcome in his day. In our day, it is more likely to be the army with a deplorable colonel or general in the lead that wrecks a long-standing civilian government.

It is often noted that constitutions typically do not include exit clauses for citizens, groups of citizens, or even sub-national territories. Naturally, therefore they do not include specifications of when it is legal for subjects to rebel. Although Hume's argument for rebellion is generally accepted historically and is, as he says, 'the practice of all ages, 'tis certainly impossible for the laws, or even for philosophy, to establish any *particular* rules, by which we may know when resistance is lawful; and decide all controversies, which may arise on that subject' (T3.2.10.16, SBN 563). Actual constitutions and laws typically make it illegal to do anything bordering on actual rebellion.

International Relations

Hume's principles of political morality apply as well to international relations as to domestic politics. Indeed, his vision of liberty applies directly to other states. Just how bold his position was in his time is suggested by the reaction to his declaration on how British prosperity depends on that of other nations. 'I shall therefore venture to acknowledge, that, not only as a man, but as a BRITISH subject, I pray for the flourishing commerce of GERMANY, SPAIN, ITALY, and even FRANCE itself. I am at least certain, that GREAT BRITAIN, and all those nations, would flourish more, did their sovereigns and ministers adopt such enlarged and benevolent sentiments towards each other.'[58] Dugald Stewart remarks that this comment was considered to be 'among the most paradoxical and dangerous parts of Mr. Hume's political writings.' As Stewart says, anyone with any sense—evidently very few people—would recognize that 'a commercial nation has precisely the same interest in the wealth of its neighbours which a tradesman has in the wealth of his customers.'[59]

The supposedly paradoxical claim is a simple and transparent one for Hume. It is merely an instance of his standard principle of mutual advantage. *Within* any of these nations, a good and possibly even the best way to improve the lot of any individual citizen is to improve the lot of the whole nation.[60] Similarly, a way to improve the lot of the people of any of these nations is to improve the lots of all of them together. As a British subject, Hume's prosperity was tied to that of Great Britain, whose prosperity was tied to that of its neighboring states. Case settled. Remarkably, this demonstration is a cousin of Hobbes's view that domestic peace is the key to the prosperity of the people of a nation.

---

[58] Hume, 'Of the Jealousy of Trade,' 331.   [59] Stewart, *Lectures on Political Economy* 2.32.

[60] The same is true for protection of liberties—protection of my liberty is best secured by protecting the liberties of all (see chapter 8).

So too is international peace the key to the prosperity of nations. More than two centuries after Hume wrote, much of Europe seems finally to have got the message. Clearly, liberty is a principle that applies at any level of political organization, and Hume argues for it in free trade both domestically and internationally.

Hume refers to the ostensible maxim that there is '*a system of morals calculated for princes, much more free than that which ought to govern private persons*' (T3.2.11.3, SBN 568). Although the maxim is well known, he says, it is not avowed by many politicians. Under that maxim, promises between national leaders—treaties—are violated with impunity. Hume gives an explanation of this phenomenon from the original grounds of the social practices of promising and treaty-making. J. L. Mackie and others reject his claims, partially on empirical grounds—a move Hume would applaud.[61] Hume's attempted explanation, however, is the right kind. As is true for the original justification of promising and promise-keeping, we should look for a ground in interests for why there is a difference for states as actors in treaty-making (a form of mutual promise) and for persons as actors in promising. We can do so in Hume's manner even though Hume did not say what follows.

First note that mutual promises, that is to say, promises for *future action by both parties*, are commonly not legally binding until one of the parties actually suffers a cost and therefore comes to have a reliance interest in fulfillment of the promise by the other party, as in the earlier case of Missy and Nekhlyudov. Abrogating such a promise or contract is therefore legally not problematic before there is a reliance interest (for one of the parties) in the keeping of the promise (by the other party). Treaties often have the form of mutual promises with no reliance until the conditions of the treaty might happen to be met, perhaps many years and even many regimes later. This peculiar structure of many, maybe even most, treaties might tend to be generalized, so that no one seriously thinks it wrong to abrogate a treaty if one at least gives timely public notice.

As a start on understanding the interests that back treaties, we could note that in actuality, just because the practice of abrogation is very well known, it is implausible to claim that treaties are expected to be permanently binding. If promises were more like treaties, with frequent lack of reliance, they too would commonly be unilaterally abrogated. They are not. Contemporary treaties include a very easy abrogation condition. But this does not justify the fact that the practice of treaty-keeping (as opposed to treaty-making) does not get under way in the first place; it merely acknowledges that it has not

---

[61] Mackie, *Hume's Moral Theory*, 114–15.

done so. In any case, treaties are seldom about matters of simple specific performance of a well-defined task, as contracts commonly are, although not always. Additionally, they often entail a large element of moral hazard. For example, if Poland has a mutual defense pact with France, it has some incentive to be more aggressive toward Germany. For France the point of entering that treaty is not to invigorate Polish ambitions but only to help deter German ambitions. To characterize such agreements as strict analogs of promises merely executed between states is grossly misleading.

For Hume, however, the main argument must take the form of a claim that the international world is less in need of treaties and treaty-honoring than the domestic world is of promising and promise-keeping. And this claim seems surely correct. Treaties often govern very important aspects of international relations, but it is typically not true that states will be unable to survive in the world and interact with each other with great prosperity merely because they do not make or keep treaties. Most of us in domestic life make dozens, maybe even hundreds of promises and contracts as we make our way through life. We rely on each other very heavily. Few if any states have ever relied so extensively and heavily on each other. (Some have 'relied on' their colonial overlords.) The natures of the two relationships are dramatically different not only in the scale of interaction but finally even in the character of it.

Hume thinks a small community of persons can be orderly and can even develop a sense of justice that can be enforced by all against all within the community. He clearly does not suppose that a small collection of states or even of their princes has these qualities. Hobbes and Locke both suppose that national leaders—princes in their time—are in a state of nature.[62] Hence, promise-keeping as a law of nature cannot apply to such a group. It is therefore a false analogy even to criticize abrogations of treaties as kin to breaking promises of the ordinary kind.

Perhaps in the increasingly globalized world in which at least economic interactions are thick and manifold, states will begin to seem like persons in the extent to which they do and must rely on each other. As that happens, it may not be treaties (promises) that organize their interactions, but only institutional arrangements that transcend national governments, as in the European Union or the World Trade Organization. The British, who hesitate in going very far with the Union often insist on calling its proposed governing document a treaty, while those more strongly committed to the Union would sooner speak

---

[62] Hobbes states the point forcefully: 'the law of nations and the law of nature is the same thing' (*Leviathan* 30.30 [185]). This is not strictly true. One of the conditions of Hobbes's state of nature is the near-equality of each person to kill any other. The difference between, say, the US and Sri Lanka today does not fit this condition.

of a constitution. There is clear wisdom in this difference, because mere treaties will not bring these nations into the thick pattern of relationships that ordinary persons enjoy as a defining aspect of their lives and as, so far, perhaps few or no nations have enjoyed with other nations. If the European nations do come to enjoy such close relations, that will probably mean that they have dissolved much of the apparatus of their separate statehoods, so that their governing document has become a constitution and not merely a treaty.

Concluding Remarks

Hume's account here is richly grounded in coordination and convention. He thinks that utility or interest is a major part of what motivates us in general and especially with respect to government. We might elevate this concern to the moral theory of utilitarianism, but Hume need not do so and does not do so in his explanatory accounts that are grounded in our psychological motivations. The result is a wonderfully spare baseline political theory. If it can plausibly work, no rich morality is necessary for explaining the partial success of government.

Finally, note that Hume seems to suppose there is a psychological variant of the derivation of an ought from an is in debates in political theory. He argues that there seems to be a psychological need for many people to find a justification of government. They once had the justification that government (the monarch) was selected by the deity. After the failure of that justification, they sought a justification in the supposed original contract.[63] Hume thinks that government can arise without justification in any such sense. We do not need the palpably silly argument from a social compact to generate government or to justify it. There are reasons grounded in our interests for the rise of government, but any government that arises is not therefore right or good.

Perhaps what is psychologically at stake for us is that government seems to make demands on us and we therefore find it easier to accept these demands if we think the particular government itself is justified. Or maybe we even find it easier to accept *ourselves* if we can give a moral justification for our obedience to government, so that we do not seem like loyal puppies or even slaves. We may be uncomfortable to believe with Hobbes and Hume that our 'allegiance' is merely acquiescence under some potential for duress if we do not acquiesce. But if we think how we would behave under radically different governments,

---

[63] Hume, 'Of the Original Contract,' 465–6.

we must recognize that acquiescence under duress would often be the only plausible story. It is probably the main story for the overwhelming bulk of all mankind throughout the history of civilization. Hume supposes that even tribal allegiance to a chieftain in the early stages of the rise of government was merely acquiescence.[64] Political theory is not a morally uplifting enquiry.

---

[64] Ibid. 469.

6

Justice as Order

> The same self-love ... which renders men so incommodious to each other,
> taking a new and more convenient direction, produces the rules of justice,
> and is the *first* motive of their observance.[1]

Once empowered by the dual convention of acquiescence by the citizenry and
cooperation among government officials, a government has the capacity to do
many things, including ancillary things unrelated to the purpose of maintaining
social order. In Hume's view, the first element of social order in the kind of
world in which we live is the establishment of stable principles for dealing with
property (meaning moveable or transferable property, not fixed property) and
social cooperation. If we first achieve order, then we can go on to achieve
liberty, justice, and prosperity.

Two of the three large-n categories of strategic interaction in chapter 3
include structures of justice in its two usual forms: distributive justice and
justice as order. These two categories are large-number coordination for
justice as order and large-number conflict for distributive justice. The third
of the large-n categories, collective action, includes many problems that can
be resolved by a competent state but that would be very hard to resolve
through spontaneous collective action. What cannot be regulated either by
self-enforcing convention or by government will typically not happen and is,
for a pragmatic theory such as that of Hume, of little interest other than to
explain *why* it cannot be well regulated.

Moreover, what will be regulated are those matters that are of greatest
concern in making society work. Theorists and political leaders are apt to
disagree about just what are the matters of greatest concern politically, but
Hume's focus is entirely on order that enables all parties to ground their actions
in more or less stable expectations of what will follow from their actions,
especially from their investments of their labor and resources. Thus enabled,
we will engage in mutually beneficial production and commerce.

[1] T3.2.8.5, SBN 543.

Let us begin with the barest story: the force that government has in mobilizing a populace or at least staying in power over it. Then we can expand the elements to include justice as order, the somewhat derisive term that Henry Sidgwick uses to characterize Hume's chief concern, which is a working legal system for maintaining order, especially in property relations and in the organization of commerce.[2] Then we will turn to general issues of making government work well enough to handle these and other problems we might want it to oversee.

Justice an Artificial Virtue

In Hume's vocabulary justice is an artificial virtue because achieving it requires institutional devices or norms for behavior. It cannot be achieved merely through uncoordinated spontaneous actions from individuals, no matter how well meaning—although it will also require such spontaneous actions. As noted earlier, there are two strategically different cases. The first case is a society so small that we all know each other and can monitor each other's behavior. Such a society can be regulated by norms and the monitoring of all by all.[3] Similarly, a small community within a larger society is likely to be regulated by norms for much of what happens. Even in dyadic interactions, interest can keep us in line, as it does for promise-keeping.

Hobbes misses this small-society case. He insists that an agreement is binding only if the parties to it face 'some evil consequence upon the rupture.'[4] He therefore concludes that a contract or promise in the absence of government to enforce it cannot be binding. Again, he does not grasp the force of convention and group norms in the context of a small society. If I agree to do something for you, you can inflict 'some evil consequence' on me through the sanctioning power of our community. Indeed, without this consideration Hobbes's remark would preclude ordinary promises over issues that could not rise to the level of government oversight and sanctioning even in a well-governed large society. We can see them as binding in Hobbes's sense just because our small community can sanction me if I fail to keep my promise, even though government could not be expected to sanction me. Even you alone can sanction me by withdrawing from future exchanges with me. The force of this sanction can be almost nil if we are in a large society in which I can

---

[2] Sidgwick, *The Methods of Ethics*, 440.
[3] Cook and Hardin, 'Norms of Cooperativeness and Networks of Trust.'
[4] Hobbes, *Leviathan* 14.7 [65].

readily find others with whom to cooperate through promising relationships, but it will take me time to develop any such relationship, so that wrecking ours will not typically benefit me in the longer run even if it seems beneficial in the short run to break my promise to you.

The second case is, of course, a large society which must have formal institutions to maintain order and to achieve certain good effects. Hume focuses primarily on the conventions and laws of property. Implicit in all his discussions, and sometimes explicit, is the problem of criminal law, which is necessary for protecting property. Without a system of law, an artificial construct, '[a large] society must immediately dissolve, and every one must fall into that savage and solitary condition, which is infinitely worse than the worst situation that can possibly be suppos'd in society' (T3.2.2.22, SBN 497). Many of the defects of the condition of humans can be remedied by a large society—especially including the advantages of the division of labor (Hume's partition of employments (T3.2.2.3, SBN 485, T3.2.4.1, SBN 514)) and commerce. The point of justice is to procure happiness and security by preserving order in society (EPM3.8, SBN 186). Indeed, justice and property per se are not laudable. Their indispensability to order, through which they serve our interests, is the sole foundation of their virtue (EPM3.47, SBN 203).

Hume generally supposes that the reason for the scheme of justice in either case—small or large scale—is to serve our interests. Society, through division of labor and cooperative endeavors, offers the best means of procuring and improving 'transferable goods.' Hume shares Hobbes's view that all are relatively equal in the ability to harm each other or to take transferable property from each other.[5] Therefore we need justice to protect ownership of transferable property such as the food and other goods we can produce (T3.2.2.9, SBN 489).

In essence, justice tends to be utilitarian and mutually advantageous. One might therefore suppose, in the style of much of twentieth-century utilitarianism, perhaps especially as presented by its critics, that we could instruct people what to do merely by weighing the utilities that would follow from various actions. This might sometimes work in a small-scale society governed by norms but it would not work in a society that requires institutions of justice. Public benevolence cannot merely be the sum of actions of private benevolence, because these do not reach that far or trump concern with self or family. The very idea of justice as an artificial virtue is that we must design institutions or norms to bring about just resolutions. We do this deliberately or by unintended consequence of various actions taken for other purposes.

---

[5] Ibid. 13.1 [60]; Hume, 'Of the Original Contract,' 467–8.

Hence, justice is inherently a two-stage concern. It will bring about welfare but each of the actions we take within the justice system will not itself necessarily bring about welfare.

Note, however, that it is the whole scheme of justice that is utilitarian, not its adjudications in specific cases. To hammer this point home, Hume invokes the lovely story of how Cyrus is instructed in the rules of justice: 'CYRUS, young and unexperienced, considered only the individual case before him, and reflected on a limited fitness and convenience, when he assigned the long coat to the tall boy, and the short coat to the other of smaller size. His governor instructed him better; while he pointed out more enlarged views and consequences, and informed his pupil of the general, inflexible rules, necessary to support general peace and order in society' (EPM App. 3.4, SBN 304–5). The general rules here are those of property, rules that define ownership according to procedural criteria rather than according to welfare criteria. In a society of the scale of that of Cyrus, these rules are part of the law (there is no property without law). They are second-stage institutional rules, not one-stage direct moral claims.[6] Cyrus thought he could allot the coats in the way that would produce greatest overall benefit, without looking beyond the instant case to just how bad it would be to have someone such as himself decide on allocations of property more or less at will rather than following the stable laws of property.

We might object and say that the system ought to be corrected when it does not produce the putatively just outcome in a particular case. In essence, this is what the English equity courts did. They reconsidered cases that supposedly had been decided correctly according to the law and then ruled whether the standard courts somehow produced an unjust result in a particular case. Rawls demolishes such schemes in his argument that we create an institution, whose design determines the roles of individuals within it, and these roles determine behavior.[7] In the stage of institutional design, we should do our best to make the institution achieve results that will be utilitarian overall. We might include a role within the institution that forces reconsideration, but we cannot have a role for someone who simply decides in each case what is the utilitarian thing to do. That would de facto eliminate the institutional devices that we have designed to accomplish our utilitarian goals and would reduce our principle of justice to the idiosyncratic intuitions of an equity official. Our institution of justice depends on this two-stage argument: in one stage, we create an institution with its role holders, then these role holders follow the rules of their roles as defined by the institution. The final result should be that the institution achieves welfare.

---

[6] See further, Rawls, 'Two Concepts of Rules.'   [7] Ibid.

Hume insists that there is no natural affection for or love of mankind in general. What could that even be? He therefore tells his just so story of how concern for others arises from sympathy—this is a naturalistic, explanatory story. Our concern is first with ourselves, then our families, then those near us, and the urge to help any of them trumps the urge to be concerned about mankind more generally. Hence, not only does our self-interest run against the common interest, but even our altruistic love of our families does as well. Indeed, our partiality affects not only our actions but also our conceptions of virtue so that we think a transgression of *our* partiality is immoral—hence, our natural ideas of morality only confirm our partiality (T3.2.2.7–8, SBN 487–9). This is, of course, a psychological and not a moral theoretic claim.

Here again, Hume's concern is with motivation, not with some underlying moral truth. The remedy to the partiality of all of us comes not from natural inclinations but from artificial devices, through reason and convention. The remedy does not arise from a promise, that is, not from a contract, because contracts have standing only after the convention is established. Establishment of the convention is like that of language—it happens piecemeal by slow growth. This slow evolution is important to our coming to understand the nature of the convention. Once we have a convention on the stability of possessions, then the ideas of justice and injustice arise. Ideas of property, right, and obligation make no sense without a prior notion of justice: 'Our property is nothing but those goods, whose constant possession is establish'd by the laws of society; that is, by the laws of justice' (T3.2.2.11, SBN 491).

Nozick, Locke, and Lockean (as opposed to Millian) libertarians make rights to property prior to social order and government—indeed, make them natural moral rights prior to any political rights. Hume shares the contrary Hobbesian vision that property and property rights are the creation of government. He holds that our relation to property is not natural, it is artificial in the sense that it is a social construct. This is the central burden of government: to regulate our powerful passion for acquisition. All other passions apart from interest are either easily restrained or of little consequence (for example, vanity). Hence, 'we are to esteem the difficulties in the establishment of society, to be greater or less, according to those we encounter in regulating and restraining [interest]' (T3.2.2.12, SBN 492). Realization of the advantages of cooperation and division of labor would not happen except by experience—sexual union and family get it started (T3.2.2.4, SBN 486).[8] That is a good thing because there would be no humans if Hume were seriously wrong here.[9]

---

[8] Hume, 'Of the Origin of Government,' 37.
[9] Hobbes's crudest vision cannot even get humanity started.

So how does society motivate us? By 'preserving society, we make much greater advances in the acquiring possessions, than by running into the solitary and forlorn condition, which must follow upon violence and an universal licence' (T3.2.2.13, SBN 492). 'By the conjunction of forces, our power is augmented: By the partition of employments, our ability encreases: And by mutual succour we are less expos'd to fortune and accidents. 'Tis by this additional *force, ability*, and *security*, that society becomes advantageous' (T3.2.2.3, SBN 485). In general, it is to our mutual advantage to preserve society because it is the interest of each of us that society be preserved. There may, of course, be collective action problems in preserving it, so that its serving mutual advantage does not guarantee its survival. Indeed, mutual advantage can have more than one implication in cases of unequal coordination.

So far the story is entirely one of interests. So why do we annex the idea of virtue to justice (T3.2.2.23–4, SBN 498–500)? Although self-interest is the driving force for the establishment of institutions and rules of justice, 'a *sympathy* with *public* interest is the source of the *moral* approbation, which attends that Virtue. This latter principle of sympathy is too weak to controul our passions; but has sufficient force to influence our taste, and give us the sentiments of approbation or blame' (T3.2.2.24, SBN 499–500).[10] This sentiment can be augmented through teaching and through the exhortation of politicians. A major incentive for our own commitments to justice, or at least for our actions comporting with it, is our reputation for keeping to justice (T3.2.2.27, SBN 501). Why would that matter? Because if my unjust action affects another, that person and perhaps many others may take my actions as evidence that I will be unreliable in relations with them. They might therefore avoid interactions with me, interactions that would be beneficial to me. The force of reputation here is the same as in the convention of promise-keeping.

Circumstances of Justice

Let us back up to put justice in its place. Hume supposes that there are two factors in morality: human nature and the conditions of the world in which we find ourselves. Hume's empiricism and naturalism (and by his lights his Newtonian stance) on these factors are forcefully represented by his discussion of the empirical circumstances of justice (T3.2.2.1–22, SBN 484–95; and more felicitously in EPM3.1, SBN 183–8). One could give a more or less

---

[10] The second sentence of this quote (given in full in the Norton and Norton *Treatise*) was added in the margin and it is in the textual notes in *Treatise* SBN 670.

parallel account of moral principles, showing them to be either ill or well suited to our conditions. Let us canvass his arguments here. Although they are about justice, his strictures are of more general interest to all moral issues. In a telling discussion Hume demonstrates that any notion of justice we might be committed to cannot simply be abstract or inferred entirely from reason or idealized circumstances. He shows that we cannot sensibly have a theory of justice that is not contingent on human nature and the conditions that humans face in their world.

When moral and political theory are argued at a level of abstraction from such considerations they are therefore suspect. Rawls, for example, wants to 'examine the principles of justice that would regulate a well-ordered society. Everyone is presumed to act justly and to do his part in upholding just institutions.'[11] This is not our problem. The main element of human nature with which we must contend, and which is part of the reason we are concerned with justice, is our relative selfishness and limited generosity, and the main problem with the world in which we live is its scanty provision for our wants (T3.2.2.16, SBN 494–5).[12] Therefore there is extensive conflict between us and therefore there is need for regulation of our interactions with each other. It is only this combination of facts that leads us to a concern with justice—or with most of morality more generally.

In Hume's view, to ask what would be the principles of justice in a society so well ordered that all act justly and do their parts in upholding just institutions is to take flight into the clouds. The point of justice as order is to deal with people who are not like that but who are like us, and we can imagine that it is also the point of an account of distributive justice that would apply to any human world. Rawls's idealized citizens would presumably voluntarily pay their taxes, would make sure that they paid enough, and would readily vote to raise their own taxes if that would produce better outcomes for the worst off in their society. There presumably are people like this in our societies, but they have not been in control of public policy in, say, the US or the UK.

Although they might be too ignorant to do it well, real people hedge their tax payments and do their best to reduce them. Real Americans spend billions of dollars every year to find loopholes and dodges for their taxes. They vote for candidates who will do this even better for them; and several recent

---

[11] Rawls, *A Theory of Justice*, 8. Insofar as his arguments live up to this billing, his is therefore an ideal theory and would not have been of much interest to Hume.

[12] Strangely, despite his own commitment to a theory based on the assumption of idealized, justice-seeking people (Rawls, *Lectures*, 57–9), Rawls seems to recognize the cogency of Hume's claims that ''tis only from the selfishness and confin'd generosity of men, along with the scanty provision nature has made for his wants, that justice derives its origin' (T3.2.2.18, SBN 495).

presidents have given the wealthiest Americans enormous windfall breaks from their taxes while reducing welfare supports to the poorest Americans. The grateful recipients of the windfall boons give vast sums to the re-election campaigns of those who rewarded them in order to keep their tax breaks secure and to block programs for the poor. Without genetic manipulation, it is virtually inconceivable that large fractions of real people will ever meet the Rawlsian ideal. The Athenian Aristophanes ridiculed views of Socrates and a contemporary Aristophanes would ridicule Rawls's supposition no less acidulously—and we would all laugh uproariously at a performance of his play. We would laugh because we would recognize the characters and their foibles as ourselves and our own and because we would recognize the elegant, sweet academic at the center of the farce.

Here Hume's arguments are so easy and so varied that he seems almost to be playing with us. Suppose there were extravagant plenty in the world; then there would be no need for a notion of property or justice (EPM3.2–4, SBN 183–4).[13] Suppose humans were creatures of universal beneficence; again there would be no point in justice. To show that this is not a completely frivolous idea, Hume notes that within families we can see a limited version of this stance.

Are we not yet convinced? Then reverse the conditions to the opposite extreme. Grievous shortage would wreck laws of justice. For example, in the fiction of a Hobbesian state of nature, there would be no justice. Or if people are entirely vicious, there can be no point in justice. We suspend justice in dealing with a criminal or when in war, all for the benefit of the larger society. If there were a race of helpless creatures, in dealing with them we might be bound by the laws of humanity, but not of justice—as is evident for those animals that we raise and then kill for food without the least qualm of acting unjustly, although some are bothered by the cruelty. If each individual were self-sufficient, there would be no point to justice. In sum, by 'rendering justice totally *useless*, you thereby totally destroy its essence, and suspend its obligation upon mankind' (EPM3.12, SBN 188).

In this account, it is utility that determines the nature of justice. For Hobbes it is the positive imposition by a sovereign that defines what is just in that sovereign's society. For natural law theorists, there is an abstract principle of justice (although that principle might well be dependent on human nature and conditions, but if so, the dependence is not recognized). Immanuel Kant deals with only half of this issue by stipulating the nature of the rational being who is an end in the kingdom of ends. Hume would suppose that there might be no

---

[13] The fuller version of these 'circumstances of justice' is that of the *Enquiry*.

need for justice in a world of such creatures—*if* there were no conflicts over consumptions and pleasures, as there would be if that kingdom had as scant provision for human needs and desires as our world generally does. Hume insists that our idea of justice depends on such contingencies. Kant's derivation seems to rule out considering contingencies.

Note that Hume's discussion cannot strictly be applied to distributive justice but only to justice as order, and we should not slip between these two. Some of the circumstances that wreck justice as order actually mandate distributive justice. Moreover, what enables us to establish a system of justice as order, with its stringent property rights, makes distributive justice an issue. I own the only orchard and deny you any of its fruit. The very protections of justice as order reinforce the inequality by making it possible for me to block your access not merely through my own personal force but through the force of legal institutions of police and courts. Those who sense that justice in the traditional sense is an enemy to greater equality are logically right, although it is difficult to imagine that there could be much to distribute if there were no protections of property, so that the critique of property in the name of equality is causally largely wrong. This is the central difficulty that Rawls addresses with his difference principle for combining concern for equality with incentives for productivity, which might entail inequality because of differential capacities or motivations for production. Insofar as greater incentives are necessary to produce more for allocation of part of the extra production to the poorest class of people, inequality is allowed.

Law and a Legal System

Among the most important classes of political conventions is a system of law. Although he does not seem to avow that his position is Humean, Lon Fuller speaks of the coordination function of laws in certain branches, which serve 'to order and facilitate interaction.' To say that such branches of law as contract, agency, marriage and divorce, property, and rules of court procedure 'would be unnecessary if men were moral is like saying language could be dispensed with if only men were intelligent enough to communicate without it.'[14] Fuller implicitly carries the argument further: having certain laws helps us to coordinate, hence to produce further laws, hence to coordinate better.

Not surprisingly, because a legal system is established as a convention, this is a functional explanation of legal development. Define: X is the legal

---

[14] Fuller, 'Law and Human Interaction,' 72–3.

system (even a very primitive one); F is the growth of law to coordinate the populace better; P is the populace. Now F is an effect of X; F is beneficial (hence functional) for P; and F maintains X by a causal feedback loop passing through P:

1. Growth of law (F) is an *effect* of the legal system (X);
2. Growth of law (F) is *beneficial* for the populace (P);
3. Growth of law (F) maintains the legal system (X) by a causal *feedback* loop passing through the populace (P) who in their own interest bring cases that push legal development.

Indeed, we might suppose that if law did not develop in the face of experience and changing circumstances, it would begin to break down. We may neither intend nor recognize the secondary coordination benefit of the development of laws. Moreover, our system of law will grow in various ways in response to contingencies along the way, so that it will likely be quite different from the system that grows in similar ways in a neighboring jurisdiction. As Hume says, it is the proper business of municipal law to fix what the principles of human nature have left undetermined, which is virtually all of the detail of the law (T3.2.3 n17.13, SBN 513 n). Fixing the law happens by trial and error and further fixing.

What is important, again, is that we have a structure within which to build stable mutual expectations. It is less important whether we have a French or English legal system than that we have some well-developed legal system. Which of a vast array of possible structures we come to have is a matter of convention and of happenstance. Overall what we have after a generation or more will be an unintended consequence and not a 'rational' design. For example, as Hume notes, the words 'inheritance and contract, stand for ideas infinitely complicated; and to define them exactly, a hundred volumes of laws, and a thousand volumes of commentators, have not been found sufficient.' Such complexity argues against a rationalist account of the rightness of these detailed laws. 'Does nature, whose instincts in men are all simple, embrace such complicated and artificial objects, and create a rational creature, without trusting any thing to the operation of his reason?' (EPM3.42, SBN 202) No, and therefore these laws are artificial devices for regulating social order.

To argue that a particular system is 'necessary' or 'right' is very hard, because there is commonly evidence that other possibilities are attractive, plausibly even superior in principle. But it may also be clear that to change from a system which we already have in place to some in principle more attractive alternative would be very difficult and plausibly too costly to justify the change.

The more pervasive, articulated, and important the system is, the more likely this will be true. Swedes could change their convention of driving on the left to driving on the right at modest cost; they could not change their system of jurisprudence at low enough cost to justify serious thought to select superior systems. To this day, the people of the state of Louisiana, formerly part of colonial France, live under a legal system that is based on the Napoleonic Code, while the US Federal system and the systems of the other forty-nine US states are based on the British common law. The only thing that might make an extant system right in many such cases is that it is extant. We could not expect to design an ideal or even a much better system. This is merely an instance of Hume's general claims that rationalist theories of morality and government are inherently irrelevant to our lives (chapter 1). We might, however, be able to revise our system by drawing on the experience of others.

That conventions are self-reinforcing means that they can be both beneficial and harmful. If we could redesign government, law, norms, practices, and so forth, we might immediately choose to do so. The very strong Chinese convention of foot-binding was horrendously harmful, and it was deliberately changed.[15]   The still surviving convention of female genital mutilation is similarly horrendously brutal and it is being eradicated in some parts of Africa. In the light of such harmful norms, we must grant in general that it is possible to contest whether some pervasive convention costs us more than it benefits us. This fact fits Hume's general view that conventions do not have a normative valence per se (almost nothing does). Some are beneficial and some are harmful.

Hume places such value on legal stability that he supposes it is necessary for us to accept the finality of judges' decisions in court cases: 'Judges too, even though their sentence be erroneous and illegal, must be allowed, for the sake of peace and order, to have decisive authority, and ultimately to determine property' (EPM3.42, SBN 202).

Property

The central importance of property to Hume's political theory is suggested by the fact that it is in trying to make sense of it that he first introduces the idea of convention (T3.2.2.9, SBN 489). It is also through his discussion of property and justice, which are closely related, that he introduces the idea of an artificial virtue. Of this latter, Mackie notes how:

[15] Mackie, 'Ending Foot-Binding and Infibulation: A Convention Account.'

Hume's skeptical temper has led him to make a significant advance in thought. Whereas Locke and many others thought that there is a natural law of property to be found out by reason, and Clarke thought that honesty is evidently more fitting than dishonesty, and Wollaston thought that to invade property rights is implicitly to deny that things are as they are, and even Hutcheson thought that the rules of justice are easily covered by the general notion of benevolence, Hume had the sharpness of mind to see how odd and initially inexplicable the ordinarily established rules and practices about property are, and how much they are in need of some further, more elaborate, explanation, which essentially involves interrelations within a general scheme. This is the real insight summed up in the phrase 'artificial virtue.' Those who came closest to anticipating this insight were other skeptically inclined writers like Mandeville and Hobbes. But in some ways Hume's thought is subtler than that of either of these predecessors.[16]

Instead of assuming that property is an easily explained phenomenon and an easily justified principle,[17] Hume takes it to be the main focus of political philosophy, the major problem whose resolution in successful societies is to be explained. It is important to keep in mind, however, that Hume's concern is with the foundational importance of property to social order. The management of property is not the value that we seek in social order but is, rather, a sine qua non without which social order cannot work in a larger society. It is not the only sine qua non of social order—Hume's catalog of the circumstances of justice includes others, as detailed earlier. Once we meet the circumstances of justice, transferable property is at issue in the foundations of social order because such property can be stolen with ease. But if it is readily taken from us, we will have little incentive to create it and our society will be relatively impoverished. It is through its incentive to production that protection of property is so valuable. Hume's concern with easily moved and therefore easily stolen property, not with fixed property, which is not generally at risk of theft, is very different from Locke's central concern with property in land.

Hume is not an ideologue who supports the class of those who own property, especially fixed property. On the contrary, he even supposes that class relations are accidental and may well be inverted with the passage of time. From a marginalist perspective, one might wish to criticize property laws—especially for fixed property—as they exist today and to redistribute some property in order to make life more nearly equitable across classes. Hume may be blinkered on this issue because he seems to think it a difficult task

[16] Mackie, *Hume's Moral Theory*, 82.

[17] Home [Lord Kames] (*Essays on the Principles of Morality and Natural Religion*, 104) trivializes the debate through shallow assertion: 'In opposition to this singular doctrine, there is no difficulty to make out, that we have an idea of property, antecedent to any sort of agreement or convention; that property is founded on a natural principle ... '

to design interventions into the actual property regime that would not topple social order while merely attempting to revise property allocations.

Incidentally, as noted in chapter 1, Hume is unusual among political philosophers in that he writes in a time in which the status of his concerns—especially property and justice—was not in active political dispute. Nevertheless, he saw the theoretical difficulties in explaining them. This fact is nowhere more extraordinary than in his elevating moveable property to so central a role.

A core point in Hume's discussions of property is that laws of property are not inherently right or good in the abstract, they are good only insofar as they contribute to our utility (EPM3.34, SBN 196). To deduce laws of property, we must look to human nature. Property is unusually important because the order of society depends heavily on it and because a properly designed regime of property has enormous benefits for us. A good property regime is beneficial because stable ownership of your property gives you the incentive to invest in producing goods for the market, so that the society generally becomes more prosperous. *Hence, having a property regime tends to be mutually advantageous. Property is important for social order because the productivity it enables gives all of us reason to support a stable government, without which we would have far less productivity.* There is a serendipitous feedback: Government secures property and property helps secure government. Protection of property is functional for social order.

Hume's analysis begins from concern with possession in a small society that has no government. Here it would be wrong to speak of property. Property is possession as defined and backed by law; hence it depends on the prior existence of government (EPM3.34, SBN 196–7). Before there is law, the slow evolution of norms or conventions on possession can lead to a sense of justice. When society is too large for such devices to work, we need government to oversee possession and then we begin to have property law and only therefore, in a meaningful sense, property. 'Property is allowed to be dependent on civil laws; civil laws are allowed to have no other object, but the interest of society,' to which a stable property regime contributes (EPM3.34 n, SBN 197 n). One might find the whole law of property arbitrary or founded in superstition, so that there is seemingly no difference between superstition and justice—but the latter is absolutely requisite to the well-being of mankind (EPM3.38, SBN 199). The apparent arbitrariness is typical of resolutions of coordination problems, especially when there are many possible coordinations.

Many writers, such as theorists of republicanism, have held that fixed property in land is centrally important for the reason that it was widely seen as the only bulwark against the power of government. Substantial property is a powerbase that can protect liberty, as shown very early in the Magna Carta of 1215.[18] In Hume's time it was de facto the only countervailing power other than religion, which was not a good bulwark for Hume, Locke, and many others, because its role had too often been oppressive and even brutally destructive in numerous wars of religion and in the imposition of pointlessly restrictive norms. Republican political theory from Nicolo Machiavelli and many other writers therefore centrally focuses on property and its political benefits.

To summarize, there are three different species of goods: 'internal satisfaction of our mind, the external advantages of our body, and the enjoyment of such possessions as we have acquir'd by our industry and good fortune. We are perfectly secure in the enjoyment of the first. The second may be ravish'd from us, but can be of no advantage to him who deprives us of them. The last only are both expos'd to the violence of others, and may be transferr'd without suffering any loss or alteration' (T3.2.2.7, SBN 487–8). For Hume, therefore, the main issue in the focus on property is moveable property and its exchange. If all of us have our moveable property protected, we will all be more prosperous than we could have been without the incentives of ownership. From exchange of our extra production we can benefit from each other's productivity. Justice as order is mostly about this string of relationships and the benefits they bring to us.

As does Hobbes, Hume speaks of laws of nature. In both cases these are sociological laws—they are laws which, if followed, will make social organization work in our interest.[19] For example, 'all contracts and promises ought carefully to be fulfilled, in order to secure mutual trust and confidence, by which the general *interest* of mankind is so much promoted' (EPM3.28, SBN 195). 'For what stronger foundation can be desired or conceived for any duty, than to observe, that human society, or even human nature could not subsist without the establishment of it ... ?' (EPM3.39, SBN 201). Laws of nature are therefore often good candidates for being positive laws of the land.

This account makes sense, but Hume wishes to strengthen it with an explanation of the rise of the actual property convention. For this he resorts to a just-so story of a kind that Rudolf Carnap might call a rational reconstruction, because the story makes sense of what might have happened.[20] With luck someday there will be evidence to corroborate or refute at least part of this story:

---

[18] See further, Jennifer Nedelsky, *Private Property and the Limits of American Constitutionalism*.

[19] There are several discussions. See T3.2.1.19, SBN 484; and T3.2.6.1, SBN 526.

[20] Carnap, *Logical Foundations of Probability*, 576–7.

'Tis evident, then, that their first difficulty, in this situation, after the general convention for the establishment of society, and for the constancy of possession, is, how to separate their possessions, and assign to each his particular portion, which he must for the future inalterably enjoy. This difficulty will not detain them long; but it must immediately occur, as the most natural expedient, that every one continue to enjoy what he is at present master of, and that property or constant possession be conjoin'd to the immediate possession. Such is the effect of custom, that it not only reconciles us to any thing we have long enjoy'd, but even gives us an affection for it, and makes us prefer it to other objects, which may be more valuable, but are less known to us. What has long lain under our eye, and has often been employ'd to our advantage, *that* we are always the most unwilling to part with; but can easily live without possessions, which we never have enjoy'd, and are not accustom'd to. 'Tis evident, therefore, that men wou'd easily acquiesce in this expedient, *that every one continue to enjoy what he is at present possess'd of;* and this is the reason, why they wou'd so naturally agree in preferring it. (T3.2.3.4, SBN 503−4)[21]

Note that choosing laws of property or contract is a coordination problem. Hume, in a just-so story, supposes that the first assignment of legal rights to property would start from the fact of our special fondness for our own holdings. Hence, of all allocations of our present property, maintaining the present allocation is likely to be mutually advantageous and Pareto optimal. This is a clever argument, perhaps even too clever.

Beyond this initial assignment, Hume holds that 'society may require a rule of justice in a particular case; but may not determine any particular rule, among several, which are equally beneficial' (EPM3.31, SBN 195−6). The possible variety is very large. Can we think that nature, by an original instinct, instructs us in all these methods of acquisition (202)? There could be no such thing as property in the (Hobbesian) state of nature (T3.2.2.28, SBN 501), and in a large society all questions of property are subordinate to the authority of civil laws (EPM3.34, SBN 196−7). Still, it is typically true that highly varied systems of municipal laws have similar outlines, because their general purposes are the same (EPM3.46, SBN 202). That is to say, again, 'The necessity of justice to the support of society is the SOLE foundation' of the virtue of justice (EPM3.48, SBN 204), and hence we may say of a system of municipal law, much of which, both in criminal and in contract law, concerns property, that it is utilitarian in this sense of serving mutual advantage.

This discussion gives Hume opportunity to state again his general view of all of the virtues, natural and artificial: 'this circumstance of usefulness has, in general, the strongest energy, and most entire command over our sentiments.

---

[21] The phenomenon of preferring what one has to something new is largely a matter of hysteresis in value judgments.

It must, therefore, be the source of a considerable part of the merit ascribed to humanity, benevolence, friendship, public spirit, and other social virtues of that stamp; as it is the SOLE source of the moral approbation paid to fidelity, justice, veracity, integrity, and those other estimable and useful qualities and principles' (EPM3.48, SBN 204).

Commerce

Stroud says that 'the well-being of other individuals does not further my own interests at all.'[22] As a claim about psychology, this is obviously false for Hume.[23] Also as a causal statement, Hume clearly thinks it is wrong, as is suggested by the fact that his central political principle is mutual advantage, under which my benefit is correlated with that of the larger society. More specifically I benefit from the general level of prosperity of my community or society.[24] As Mill says, prosperity is greater as the amount and variety of personal energies are enlisted.[25] He does not merely mean that the aggregate is greater but that there is mutual advantage in the greater amount and variety. This is also Hume's and Smith's view that the scale or extent of the market leads to greater division of labor and therefore greater prosperity for all. Indeed, my opportunities are largely structured by my society.[26] Hence, the better off others in that society are, the better off I am likely to be. There could be no Warren Buffet or Bill Gates if North America, and therefore individual North Americans, were not extremely prosperous. There is no Buffet or Gates in Zimbabwe, although there can be a wealthy tyrant who extracts what resources he can from an impoverished populace.

If commerce enhances overall production by providing outlets for the sale of the excess production, virtually all producers benefit from the enhanced sales and income. (This need not be true for literally all producers at all times. For example Bill Gates might be so good at marketing that he can destroy other producers. Still, it is the overwhelming tendency.) This is one of Hume's most important claims and it would be a gross error to reject it. Dugald Stewart credits Hume with being among the very first authors to push for liberalization

---

[22] Stroud, *Hume*, 196.

[23] Hume says, 'we may feel a desire of another's happiness or good, which, by means of that affection, becomes our own good, and is afterwards pursued, from the combined motives of benevolence and self-enjoyment' (EPM App. 2.13, SBN 302).

[24] See Hume, 'Of the Jealousy of Trade,' 329.

[25] Mill, *Considerations on Representative Government*, chap. 3, 404.

[26] Smith, *The Wealth of Nations* 1.3, 31.

of trade, both domestically and internationally. He credits Hume with the rare success of attracting public attention and even influencing policy, perhaps especially through his influence on his younger friend Adam Smith. He says the French political maxim, *Pas trop gouverner* (Do not govern too much), might be of greatest value when applied to trade.[27] It is the Humean liberal's maxim.

Hume's general argument is simple. 'Different parts of the earth produce different commodities; and not only so, but different men both are by nature fitted for different employments, and attain to greater perfection in any one, when they confine themselves to it alone. All this requires a mutual exchange and commerce; for which reason the translation of property by consent is founded on a law of nature, as well as its stability without such a consent' (T3.2.4.1, SBN 514). It is clear in this argument that Hume's concern with property, especially transferable property, is important not for the sake of ownership but for the sake of productivity. It is the difference between a world of subsistence farming, such as that favored by the Levellers of Hobbes's time, and an urban and urbane world of great ease, creativity, and liveliness.

Moving to the second world requires not only producers but also merchants, who give each producer reason to produce more because the excess can be put on the market and can yield the funds for buying the very different excess of producers of other things. They are therefore 'one of the most useful races of men, who serve as agents between those parts of the state, that are wholly unacquainted, and are ignorant of each other's necessities.'[28] Those who formerly railed against the payment of interest on loans often rail against merchants as people who profit from the work of others. Aristotle says that wealth acquisition 'that has to do with exchange is justly disparaged, since it is not natural but is from one another.'[29] This is simply a mistake. Merchants

---

[27] Stewart, *Lectures on Political Economy* 1.2.3, 31–4.   [28] Hume, 'Of Interest,' 300.

[29] Aristotle, *Politics*, 1258^{a-b}, pp. 18–19. Aristotle goes on to disparage interest as immoral usury: 'For money was introduced to facilitate exchange, but interest makes money itself grow bigger…Hence of all the kinds of wealth acquisition this one is the most unnatural.' Hume clearly thinks this view is wrong in that he thinks the level of interest itself is explicable from beneficial economic activity (see Hume, 'Of Interest'). In an unusual burst of humor, Bentham teases Aristotle for his view despite 'the great number of pieces of money that had passed through his hands; more, perhaps, than were passed through the hands of philosopher before or since!' Aristotle's view seems to be founded partly in the Greek language, in which offspring and interest are the same word. Bentham, himself a master definitionalist, supposes that a man of such sagacity should have noted, 'that though a daric would not beget another daric, any more than it would a ram, or an ewe, yet for a daric which a man borrowed, he might get a ram and a couple of ewes, and that the ewes, were the ram left with them a certain time, would probably not be barren. That then, at the end of the year, he would find himself master of his three sheep, together with two, if not three lambs; and that, if he sold his sheep again to pay back his daric, and gave one of his lambs for the use of it in the meantime, he would be two lambs, or at least, one lamb richer than if he made no such bargain' ('Defence of Usury,' 158–9). Stewart wrongly attributes this quotation to Edward Gibbon (Stewart, *Lectures on Political Economy*, 1.2.3.3, 147–8).

perform a function which is itself highly productive. And they increase the industry of others by enabling them to trade more widely from their own surplus production, thus giving them incentive to produce surplus.[30]

More generally, Hume notes that the main source of an economically advanced nation's wealth is what we now call human capital, or at least trained labor, and not resources of other kinds. 'Trade and industry are really nothing but a stock of labour, which, in times of peace and tranquility, is employed for the ease and satisfaction of individuals.'[31] He even supposes that the more extensive poverty of the common people of France, Italy, and Spain is 'in some measure, owing to the superior riches of the soil and happiness of the climate.' This seeming paradox is easily explained by the fact that, unlike the farmers in England, farmers in these regions are not forced to be careful and inventive and they do not get long leases that could repay any investments they might make in the land. Although liberty does not guarantee prosperity, it is an important part of the story of prosperity in England.[32] Even more than Hume does, Smith later associates such prosperity with the division of labor that leads to specialization and much greater productivity.

Politics and Parties

What are the prospects of creating a government that provides the benefits Hume wants? The answer turns on how well we can get ordinary people, who are likely primarily to seek their own interests, to staff government and to do a good job of fulfilling its mandate. Hume thinks we have to design government agencies to be proof against knaves.[33] But it also clearly depends on how extensively various interests can gain control of government, and this depends on how extensively they can organize into parties, as they did in England in the seventeenth century. Hume's views of political factions organized around interests—or parties—are very similar to those of James Madison at the time of writing his contributions to the 1787–8 *Federalist Papers*. Madison seemingly deplored factions, or parties. Later, while he was an active politician engaged in securing the predominance of Thomas Jefferson, himself, and their associates in their contest with the interests represented by Alexander Hamilton and John Adams, Madison created a party that would run the new nation for more than a generation. In the constitutional period, however, he argued that the larger size and variety of the whole nation, composed of all thirteen former colonies,

---

[30] Hume, 'Of Interest,' 301.   [31] Hume, 'Of Commerce,' 262; see also 'Of Money,' 293.
[32] Hume, 'Of Commerce,' 265–7.   [33] Hume, 'Of the Independency of Parliament,' 42.

would be an entity that would reduce the tendency to faction, because local factions would all be weak in the face of the larger national interests. In *Federalist* 10, he claims, as Hume does, that republican government would be relatively more stable in a large than in a small society.[34] In a larger commonwealth, 'the parts are so distant and remote, that it is very difficult, either by intrigue, prejudice, or passion, to hurry them into any measures against the public interest.'[35] Both Hume and Madison are surely too optimistic, but they might be right that democracy works better in a larger nation than in a city-state.

Hume sees three kinds of parties: those organized around interests, around principles, or around a person or family. He supposes that conflicts of principle are especially destructive because they admit of no compromise; there is likely to be no principled position that serves mutual advantage. A politics of principle could be mutually agreeable, of course, only if the principles were entirely shared, but the point of an active politics of principle is generally to impose principles on the whole polity, especially on those who do not share the principle. In office, the program of a party of principle is typically to restrict the liberty and influence of those who do not share their principles.

If they are to avoid such divisive politics, people must be politically engaged in the pursuit of interest, which is a central part of human behavior much more generally; and they must be enlightened enough to recognize that the public interest is in fact a major part of their own interest, is indeed the most important private interest. As already noted, mutual advantage is the aggregate analog of self-interest. A politics of interest therefore can be a politics of mutual advantage. It requires compromise to make such a politics peaceful and mutually advantageous, but compromise over interests is readily possible in a way that is virtually impossible for principle.

Factions that are driven by 'abstract speculative principle' are 'known only to modern times, and are, perhaps, the most extraordinary and unaccountable phaenomenon, that has yet appeared in human affairs.'[36] When Hume lived, the world had not yet seen Jacobinism, let alone Nazism, Communism, racism, or rabid nationalism. These are political principles that brook no compromise. At best the movements driven by such principles expel or subjugate those on the wrong side of their principles. At worst, they kill them. As Hume says, there is nothing in their principles that can be divided and shared among the pro and con parties, as there is in a politics of interest. Here he agrees with Hobbes in disparaging the possibility of good government under the hegemony

---

[34] Madison, *Federalist* 10.
[35] Hume, 'Idea of a Perfect Commonwealth,' 528.
[36] Hume, 'Of Parties in General,' 60.

of religious or other principle. Hobbes's sovereign is intended to impose order so that interests in prosperity may prevail and murderous brawls over religion might be banished. Similarly, Locke supposes that government should focus on interest and that religious views should be kept out of politics.[37]

Madison's account of these issues is more richly grounded in experience but Hume's account is more acute in its discussion of interests and principles. Madison addresses the particular experiences of the thirteen US states, although he seems to be unwilling to provoke anyone in these states by citing specifics of his case for the destructiveness of faction in those states. He, however, offers the more compelling account of how interests might already be divisive enough for a nation. It is the larger multiplicity of interests in a larger nation that makes politics less destructive in such a nation than in a small city-state or even a single one of the American states. A small society with direct democracy is likely to be dominated by a majority interest; a large society with representative democracy is far less likely to have a single majority interest to dominate politics.[38]

In the era of the younger George Bush, one might have difficulty deciding whether it is partisan interests or partisan principles that are the more divisive. During the final decades of slavery in the US, interests were elevated rhetorically to principle, and they were deeply divisive. Apologists in the South went so far as to proclaim slavery a great benefit to the slaves and a generous service from the slave owners. Much of US history, however, seems to fit Hume's view that a politics of interest is less virulent than a politics of principle.

Concluding Remarks

Institutions are artifactual incentive systems, and they are often partly to be explained in functional terms because they work by feedback to enhance the incentives to each individual to perform according to the institution's requirements. They do this as the law does it. Government and its legal system, once they get established, keep us in line through acquiescence because, once the law keeps most others in line, it has ample resources to direct toward anyone who fails to acquiesce.[39]

Hume grants that, once we have established conventions for behavior in some realm, we are likely then to moralize the conventions, to elevate them to

---

[37] Locke, *A Letter Concerning Toleration.*
[38] Madison, *Federalist* 10: 46–8.
[39] Hume, 'Of the First Principles of Government.'

the status of moral rules (T3.2.9.3, SBN 551). This can happen in two ways, one that is constructive and one that may not be. In the second of these, the moralized rules will be relatively particular rules that grow out of our very particular history and circumstances. They may not be rules that generalize readily beyond our context. They will be more nearly like patriotism, which is extremely particular. Indeed, patriotism often leads people to think their country not merely best for them but best *tout court*. This will not do for the theorists of shared values.

The more constructive elevation grows out of shared interests, which are minimal, because they are essentially the interest we all share in having an order that enables each of us to prosper. Although I may fail to notice how my own actions violate the common interest in order, I will notice when others' actions violate it. Hume says, 'we never fail to observe the prejudice we receive, either mediately or immediately, from the injustices of others; as not being in that case either blinded by passion, or byass'd by any contrary temptation' (T3.2.2.24, SBN 499). Through sympathy for those who are harmed by unjust actions, we come to a moral approbation of justice and a disapprobation of injustice.

7

Utilitarianism

> Usefulness ... is a principle, which accounts, in great part, for the origin of morality: And what need we seek for abstruse and remote systems, when there occurs one so obvious and natural?[1]

Hume is held by various scholars to be a utilitarian, a rule-utilitarian, a half-hearted utilitarian, or not a utilitarian at all, and he is also held to be either a consequentialist or not a consequentialist. The remarkable fact of many of these views is that they are grounded in essentially the same passages in Hume. It is trivially evident that he is not simply an act-utilitarian, because he does not think individuals have sufficient commitments to beneficence to act for the general welfare rather than for their own; they have no general love of humanity as such (T3.2.1.12, SBN 481). He thinks we can be generous and altruistic, but the strength of our altruism declines sharply as we deal with those increasingly far from us. In response to claims for a genetic basis for altruism, J. B. S. Haldane is supposed to have quipped, 'I would lay down my life for two of my brothers or eight of my cousins.' Hume roughly agrees, although his claim is founded in social preferences rather than genetic survival. He says, 'A man naturally loves his children better than his nephews, his nephews better than his cousins, his cousins better than strangers, where every thing else is equal' (T3.2.1.18, SBN 483–4). The 'every thing else' might be the intensity of the relationships and the time spent in them, which would be a social rather than genetic artifact. Hume is the Haldane of beneficence.

There is an important sense in which Hume cannot be utilitarian (or any other kind of moralist), because he rejects any claim of the truth of substantive moral views. He is, again, a psychological utilitarian—meaning that he finds utility pleasing. But he also focuses more on social institutions, which are fundamentally important for our personal benefit, so that one can call him an institutional utilitarian for the clear enough reason that he thinks we must

---

[1] EPM5.17, SBN 219.

want our social institutions to bring us utility and that we value them only if they do. In this I think Hume is clearly right and I will sketch the view of institutional utilitarianism below.

Hume is the first major thinker to invoke utility regularly as a ground for action and for justifying actions, and utilitarianism rises soon after him to dominate Anglo-Saxon moral philosophy and the long tradition of positive law in the spirit of Bentham, Austin, Kelsen, and Hart. Utility pleases and it is adequate ground on which to build morality. We do not need elaborate arguments or metaphysical systems when we have such a compelling principle (EPM5.17, SBN 219). In this view, Hume is foundational for the new era, the era of utilitarianism, even though he did not live to be part of that era.

Utilitarianism is a moral and political theory that can be characterized as the combination of a concern with *individual welfare as the good* and a *theory of welfare*. Although there are many forerunners, articulate utilitarianism arose in the Scottish Enlightenment in the time of Hume, with Hume as a major theorist of it and Francis Hutcheson as a forerunner. In capsule summary, after Hume utilitarianism was further articulated by William Paley and Jeremy Bentham, who applied it to the design of legislatures and other institutions and to legislation and law; it was applied to law by John Austin; and it flourished in the writings of John Stuart Mill, Henry Sidgwick, and many nineteenth- and twentieth-century economists, such as Edgeworth.[2] The focus on welfare as the good and as the object of action and policy has been virtually constant from the beginning, although the scope of that concern sometimes expands to cover animals other than humans. The theory of value, or what the content of welfare is, however, has undergone frequent, substantial changes, largely because it is central to the discipline of economics but also because it is a complex and difficult matter. For Hume the details of the theory of value cannot matter very much because they cannot be at issue for the general run of mankind, who are the subject of his theorizing and who cannot be apprised of the finer points of utilitarian value theory.

The most common complaints against utilitarianism are divided into these two categories: the value theory and the welfarism (or consequentialism). The value theory of Bentham is taken by virtually all critics of utilitarianism to be the last possible word on the subject, although Bentham himself did not commonly invoke that value theory in his most important utilitarian writings and Hume certainly did not invoke it. Mill, who in the view of many is

---

[2] Paley, *The Principles of Moral and Political Philosophy*; Bentham, *An Introduction to the Principles of Morals and Legislation*; Austin, *The Province of Jurisprudence Determined*; Mill, *Utilitarianism*; Edgeworth, *Mathematical Psychics*; Sidgwick, *The Methods of Ethics*.

the arch-utilitarian, often ignored the Benthamite cardinal, interpersonally comparable value theory. It was taken seriously by Sidgwick and, in his time, also by the economist Edgeworth. Economists gave up that value theory soon thereafter. Pareto scorned it as metaphysical nonsense and the ordinal revolution of the 1930s consigned it to history's intellectual trash bin. It is a matter of interest primarily in intellectual history, not in morality today (or in Hume's day). Apart from John Harsanyi, few utilitarians have taken it seriously in the past half-century; it is primarily those who wish to criticize utilitarianism who latch onto it.[3]

Some scholars trivialize the issue by saying that utilitarianism is only the theory of Bentham—specifically the theory when he invokes aggregate utility, but not the theory when he does not. If one wishes to insist that utilitarianism means only this variant of Benthamism, one can refer to the utilitarianism that many advocates such as Mill have actually invoked as 'welfarism.' The only specifically moral criticism of utilitarianism would have to be against its consequentialism, not its value theory, which clearly is open to theoretical development in Bentham's view. Hume's utilitarian views are entirely about ordinal moves of making people better off without any measure of how much better off. This has the major benefit of being realistic because we generally cannot do more than this. It also has the major cost that it means our recommendations must commonly be indeterminate. Pareto supposes we should adopt a policy only if it makes at least one person better off and no one worse off. That standard means that most policies of actual societies cannot be adopted.

Hume's view is that utility pleases (EPM5.1–47, SBN 214–32), and this psychological claim is as far as he thinks we can go in morality. He may have thought it pleases virtually everyone. I am less convinced of that although I find it hard to grasp how anyone could disagree. Some of my friends and colleagues have energetically disagreed over dinner at some of the world's best, most pleasing restaurants. The only issue must be not whether it pleases everyone at least some of the time but whether it is generally or only occasionally trumped by other concerns. That utility pleases is, however, a statement of self-love, not utilitarianism. Utilitarianism as a moral theory is universalistic and a moral utilitarian must be pleased by the utility accruing to others, indeed, all others. Hume does not claim that we are utilitarian in this way in our outlook. On the contrary, he says that the public good is indifferent to us except insofar as sympathy interests us in it when, for example, there is a matter in which

[3] Harsanyi, 'Cardinal Utility in Welfare Economics and in the Theory of Risk-Taking.'

we have no stake, and then we can prefer that the resolution be one which benefits the public (T3.3.6.1, SBN 618).

Even some of the strongest of Hume's seemingly utilitarian statements can be read as about one's self-interest. For example, he asks, 'For what stronger foundation can be desired or conceived for any duty, than to observe, that human society, or even human nature could not subsist, without the establishment of it; and will still arrive at greater degrees of happiness and perfection, the more inviolable the regard is, which is paid to that duty?' (EPM3.39, SBN 201) The answer Hume assumes to his question is that we must all want to secure the mutual advantage. Of course, the prosperity of my society is necessary for my prosperity. The utility that mainly pleases us is our own, but—more than either Hobbes or Locke might allow—Hume supposes that we also are pleased by the utility of others, especially for those close to us and less so for those far from us.

More people today may know utilitarianism from its critics than from its advocates. I will therefore start with two criticisms. The first is a charge leveled against utilitarians in general, but also specifically against Hume. The claim as addressed to Hume is that, because they focus on actions, Hume's arguments are not really consequentialist and therefore not utilitarian. The second is a criticism of utilitarianism that one might or might not think applies to Hume. It is Rawls's claim that utilitarianism denies distinctions between persons (he speaks of Benthamite utilitarianism and dismisses Hume's views).

Rawls says that utilitarianism assumes some fairly accurate measure of utility.[4] Benthamite utilitarianism does this, Hume's does not. Hume most likely would have thought this Benthamite idea incoherent but it is an idea on which he does not comment directly, although he often says that we evaluate things only relatively by comparison to other things. This is the central vision of an ordinalist, who must therefore reject the additive, interpersonally comparable utility of Bentham. This means, of course, that Hume's psychological approbations are not likely to lead to a very detailed organization of society but are likely to leave very much of it indeterminate in the sense that we could not say what organization of society is commended by utilitarian considerations. Let us examine the nature of the utilitarianism that Hume commonly invokes to see how different it is from what Rawls discusses.[5]

[4] Rawls, *A Theory of Justice*, 78.

[5] Rawls says that 'all Hume seems to mean by utility is the general interests and necessities of society' (*A Theory of Justice*, 29). This is an unusually careless comment for Rawls. Utility is regularly invoked by Hume as the concern of individuals for themselves. It is such utility that leads to the psychological approbation of the actions and character of others. Insofar as we even notice the utility of the whole

Consequentialism

On the account of the history of utilitarian thinking, the strongest form of claiming that some position is not utilitarian is to say the position is not consequentialist. Some critics say that Hume is not consequentialist. To address this criticism without getting bogged down in several pages of textual commentary, let us chiefly consider a single sympathetic critic: Richard Hiskes. His main criticism is that, 'when Hume speaks of what makes persons or their actions virtuous, he insists that the major criterion for such an evaluation is the motive upon which the agent acts. In the *Treatise* he states that "a virtuous motive is requisite to render an action virtuous." '[6]

This criticism is common throughout the history of utilitarianism and it has evoked sometimes confused responses from utilitarians. All that is needed here, however, is recognition that when committed utilitarians are deciding what to do, they should then think of what would have a utilitarian consequence. This is merely a question of how we must choose to act, which is, of course, ex ante, before we act. This is purely a logical constraint. We cannot act ex post after judging the actual consequence of our actions. For all their concern first and foremost with consequences, utilitarians cannot defy logic and decide how to act after the consequences have played out. For Hume, to judge whether my action was virtuous is to judge whether, at the time I decided on it after canvassing alternatives, I expected good consequences. If bad consequences followed, that could be because I failed to assess the situation adequately or because some chance condition that could not have been predicted intervened. Often the chance condition is the fact that the entire proceeding is largely stochastic so that the same action by me could have a variety of possible consequences. In such cases any choice of action is risky.

A rigid deontologist in the same context might have a fixed rule to follow, but the result would be just as stochastically messy as for the utilitarian. The deontologist could haughtily respond, yes, but I did the only right thing, it's just too bad the sky therefore fell. The utilitarian would have to respond, I tried my best but, alas, the world did not cooperate. All our choices are ex ante, no matter what our moral theory is. *There cannot be a valid criticism of the attempt to deal with that fact.* Hume deals with it as presumably anyone who sees

society, that is through sympathy and generalization and a kind of indifference that seems identical to Rawls's (*A Theory of Justice*, 112) own principle of 'mutual disinterest' among the parties to the original position.

[6] Hiskes, 'Has Hume a Theory of Social Justice?' 74. The passage from Hume is at T3.2.1.4, SBN 478.

the issue clearly must likewise deal with it. For the most rigid deontologist, this fact does not matter because the result of following a deontological rule does not matter morally. In the extreme, only the actor's adherence to such rules matters morally, the world be damned. What distinguishes the utilitarian from the anti-consequentialist is their reasons for choosing particular actions, which is what they focus on ex ante. What defines the utilitarian is that her choice is based on the expected consequences of her action for the welfare of humans (and maybe other animals).

On this account, Hume rightly assigns virtue to characters or actions that have the tendency of producing utilitarian results. He does this, in a sense, on behalf of or as spokesman for those who find utility pleasing (as Hume supposes virtually everyone does) and who feel approbation for anyone who acts in a utilitarian way or has the character of generally doing so.

Respect for Persons

Perhaps the most influential critic of utilitarianism in our time is Rawls, who unfortunately chooses specifically to exclude Humean utilitarianism and instead criticizes Benthamite utilitarianism. He mentions Hume's views in various contexts and he addresses Hume at length in his *Lectures on the History of Moral Philosophy*. That title is strangely misfit but also indicative of a central problem. Rawls's own work is almost entirely in political philosophy. But his favorite forerunner is Kant, whose normative work is principally in moral philosophy.

Rawls is part empiricist, part idealist. He wants his conception of justice to have a realistic content, and that content then recommends the construction of institutions that will give real-world political form to the vision of the theory. Those institutions will suffer under the ordinary constraints of human psychology and sociology, and they can generally be expected to entail the impure procedural justice that afflicts courts and legislative bodies we know in the real world.[7]

Even in some of his ostensibly empirical claims, however, Rawls tends to idealize. For example, he notoriously says that no one would acquiesce in permanent disadvantage in order to make others much better off.[8] This is a perverse way to put his issue. Rawls's is a psychological claim, and it is surely false, especially if properly stated for Rawls's purpose. In fact, of course, we might gamble on higher average well-being for all at the risk of suffering

---

[7] Rawls, *A Theory of Justice*, 75.   [8] Ibid. 13.

potentially lower status for ourselves than we would have had under Rawls's maximin status.[9] We take big gambles often. Or rather, we take gambles on potentially awful outcomes in order to accomplish even minor purposes, as when we drive on Highway 101 just to go to dinner in San Francisco. The worst outcome in that outing would be an appallingly bad encounter with an SUV; the best outcome would be a very pleasant evening. Substantial risk acceptance, rather than extreme risk aversion, is consistent with the psychology of many of us and probably almost all of us. In any case, Rawls's statement is an unwonted distortion. We do not 'accept permanent disadvantage *in order to make others much better off.*' Rather, we accept the risk of being worse off in order to have a better chance at being much better off or making others much better off.

Rawls says that utilitarian social justice is the principle of rational prudence applied to an aggregative conception of the welfare of the group.[10] But this need not be an additive conclusion. Humean, Paretian, and contemporary economic views are generally not additive, but they all conceive of social improvements that serve mutual advantage, which is surely the core of the moral thrust of utilitarianism. Utilitarianism does not stand or fall with Bentham's crude cardinal, interpersonally comparable value theory, which not even Bentham attempted to articulate fully. Hume's utilitarianism, which is about the core utilitarian value of enhancing welfare for all, would not serve Rawls's purpose in setting utilitarianism aside as the source of a plausible theory of justice, and perhaps therefore he rejects it and takes on Bentham's crude theory instead.[11] Such major twentieth-century critics of utilitarianism as G. E. M. Anscombe have rightly focused on its core concern with consequences, its welfarism.[12] Rawls cannot do that because his own theory is largely about consequences: how to distribute the wealth of the society.

Rawls's supposedly harshest criticism of utilitarianism is that it conflates all persons into one for the assignment of utility from our social organization. He says, 'Utilitarianism does not take seriously the distinction between persons.'[13] Why? Because my welfare after we have worked out the utilitarian dispensation is a function of how I fit into the larger scheme of things. Rawls has stopped too soon in his criticism. His own ordering of society does an exactly analogous thing when it elevates one arrangement of society above another—even though I am better off in the former and worse off in the latter—for the sake of making the worst-off class of people better off. That is to say, my welfare is a function of how I fit into the larger scheme of things in Rawls's ordering of society. We

---

[9] Maximin is the best of the worst outcomes. To choose maximin in a game, one would find the worst payoff in each strategy choice and then adopt the strategy whose worst payoff is best.

[10] Rawls, *A Theory of Justice*, 21.   [11] Ibid. 28.

[12] Anscombe, 'Modern Moral Philosophy.'   [13] Rawls, *A Theory of Justice*, 24.

are all slotted into the general plan. If aggregative utilitarianism violates respect for persons by submerging the individual's interests into the societal outcome, then Rawls's theory of justice violates respect for persons in the same way.

In ethics such clever phrases as 'respect for persons' seem almost always to be persuasive definitions that hector and plead rather than justify. They sound good but there is often little or no content to them. All utilitarians insist that each person is to count as one and one only, a principle that sounds like equal respect for each person. Rawls says utilitarianism fails to take seriously the distinction between persons when it aggregates their welfare in a way that makes some worse off in order to make others better off.[14] Any accusation that either utilitarianism or Rawlsian justice violates respect for persons is virtually meaningless and does not deserve to be taken seriously. Mill, in response to a standard, vacuous, highly routinized criticism of utilitarianism, says 'Men really ought to leave off talking a kind of nonsense on this subject, which they would neither talk nor listen to on other matters of practical concernment.'[15] That criticism—that utilitarianism is self-defeating because one would miss any opportunity to do the utilitarian thing because one would be bogged down in deducing what that thing might be—is still alive and intellectually destitute today.

Rule-Utilitarianism

Let us turn to the question whether Hume is a rule-utilitarian, that is, someone who supposes we can determine the general rules that should be followed in various contexts to produce utilitarian outcomes. Thereafter we merely follow those rules. There are many things Hume says that might seem to license this conclusion, but it is an entirely mistaken conclusion. Consider at least three statements that strongly reject the view, one statement from each of the three parts of book 3 of the *Treatise*—which is to imply that in every context of morality, rule-utilitarianism or any other kind of rule-based ethics is prima facie wrong. First, Hume notes, rightly, that reason cannot have rules for all possible moral problems (T3.1.2.6, SBN 473). Rule-utilitarianism would be a hopelessly inadequate theory. (One can say the same of all rule-based theories of morality.)[16]

Second, one of the strongest claims that might license the view that he is a rule-utilitarian is Hume's claim that we tend to generalize our rules beyond their origins, and we may then not make exceptions even when these could

---

[14] Rawls, *A Theory of Justice*, 24, 153–60, 163.

[15] Mill, *Utilitarianism*, chap. 2, 225, penultimate paragraph.

[16] Hardin, *Indeterminacy and Society*, chap. 6.

be grounded in the reason for the rule (T3.2.9.3, SBN 551). But Hume's point here is—it should come as no surprise—psychological and not moral theoretic. He is just saying that we may tend to hold to a pattern of behavior and even go so far as to claim that following the pattern is morally required even when it is not in our interest. He clearly thinks that this is a mistake but that our psychology is subject to such errors. In characterizing such reasoning he says that it is the result of our being 'mightily addicted to *general rules*, and that we often carry our maxims beyond those reasons, which first induc'd us to establish them' (T3.2.9.3, SBN 551). Again, this is a psychological observation, not a moral theoretic claim. One wonders how anyone could read Hume's view that rule-tropism is a standard, natural psychological distortion to mean he favors rule-tropist rule-utilitarian principles.

Third, Hume doubles the psychological deficit of rule-tropism with the claim that general rules 'create a species of probability, which sometimes influences the judgment, and always the imagination,' even though some circumstances for making the effect of the rule-following beneficial are lacking (T3.3.1.20, SBN 585; cf. 27, SBN 589–90).

A final passage that is used to defend the thesis that Hume is a rule-utilitarian is this: 'We must, therefore, proceed by general rules, and regulate ourselves by general interests, in modifying the law of nature concerning the stability of possession' (T3.2.10.3, SBN 555–6). This sentence is part of a long passage in the *Treatise* that is filled out more fully in the *Enquiry Concerning the Principles of Morals*. There Hume makes the case for explicit laws that are to be applied systematically. Following the law can hardly count as the exclusive domain of rule-utilitarianism.[17] The conventions (as usually established in the law) of property ownership cannot be overridden by a direct account of utility. Property claims depend on what the rules of law are, not on the utility of any allocation as of this moment (T3.2.3.2, SBN 502). This is not a claim of rule-utilitarianism, although it has led some to assert wrongly that Hume is a rule-utilitarian. *Every* utilitarian—and probably everyone else as well—wants a system of law to give us utility enhancing social order. If advocacy of systematic application of laws is rule-utilitarian, then all utilitarians (and probably all legal and political theorists of any credible stripe) are rule-utilitarians, and the distinction is trivializing.

---

[17] It is not always true that one should rigorously follow the legal rules. Tolstoy writes of the mobilization of a collection of prisoners to be marched from the prison to the train for shipment from Petersburg to Siberia. The prisoners visibly suffer from the brutal heat, and one of them faints and dies. Tolstoy (*Resurrection*, 447) remarks, 'Every one of them—Maslennikov, the inspector, the officer of the escort—if he had not been a governor, an inspector, an officer, would have thought twenty times before sending people off in such heat and such a crowd [but] they were thinking not of human beings and their obligations towards them but of the duties and responsibilities of their office.' Such officiousness is not what Hume has in mind here.

The only one of the early major utilitarian thinkers who genuinely argues for what would now be called rule-utilitarianism is Moore, but his particular argument is not compelling. He essentially resorts to the claim that common-sense morality is inherently utilitarian.[18] In answer to the question whether one can ever be justified in breaking one of the commonsense moral rules (do not lie, keep promises, doff your cap in church (men), cover your head in church (women)), he says, 'this question can definitely be answered in the negative.' Why? Because the social evolution of these rules is such forceful evidence of their utility that the probability that my calculation in this moment can correctly suggest overriding the rule on utilitarian grounds is far too small for me to prefer my calculation to the rule.[19]

On this account, what it may be utilitarian to do in a class of interactions in China or Texas is different from what it is utilitarian to do in, say, Moore's England, rest its soul. It is different not because of the contingent conditions that might require different actions in one case than in another, but because the social evolution has produced different rules, quite possibly for virtually identical contexts. Ironically, Moore is overweeningly confident of this rule of social evolution although it is not itself a rule of social evolution and therefore has no apparent backing other than his individual effort to figure it out.[20] He seems to hold epistemologically that socially derived knowledge must always be superior to individually deduced knowledge with exceedingly high probability. On that remarkable principle, common sense should long ago have put an end to science with all its individual efforts, as essentially the church tried to do against Bruno and Galileo in defense of the commonsense science of Aristotle.

Institutional Utilitarianism

Hume is not a simple act-utilitarian because he does not think our psychology fits the demands of such a morality. Also, despite a lot of argument to the contrary, he is not a rule-utilitarian, that is to say, he does not hold the view that we somehow reach a conclusion on what rules we should follow in order to produce good results, and thereafter we follow those rules without fail. Again, our benevolence is too limited to get us to do that and, additionally, Hume does not believe we are motivated very strongly by a mere sense of duty, and he dislikes those moral theories that stipulate duties (as does monkish

---

[18] Hardin, *Morality within the Limits of Reason*, 14–18. [19] Moore, *Principia Ethica*, 162–3.
[20] Others have reached an analogous conclusion, which is an essential part of commonsense morality. But see, e.g., Berkeley, 'Passive Obedience,' 120–1.

virtue theory). Still, the air of the *Enquiry Concerning the Principles of Morals* and of book 3 of the *Treatise* is overwhelmingly utilitarian. There are many utilitarian claims, such as pervasive claims that 'usefulness has, in general, the strongest energy, and most entire command over our sentiments' (EPM3.48, SBN 204). Hume constantly cites utility, pleasure, absence of pain, well-being, happiness, and interests, and all of these have welfarist implications when he discusses or mentions them. So what sense can we make of his seemingly utilitarian position?

First, of course, we have to grant his two pervasively general claims. Whatever our morals are, they are to be explained psychologically. And the truth of their content cannot be at issue because their content cannot be a matter of truth. Therefore, if we are to attribute a view to Hume, it must be a psychological view of his own sympathies and sentiments or a psychological account of the sympathies and sentiments of people in general. And we cannot expect him to argue for these views per se but only to acknowledge them, most often by associating them with the typical other person, who is not unlike himself. Such views he does seem to have, and he seems to hold them strongly—to the point of making policy recommendations, as in the discussion of his views of commerce in chapter 6. On his psychological account, again, his views cannot be simply utilitarian at the level of individuals' acting—their psychology will not allow them to count distant others' utility equally with that of their closer associates.

All of Hume's policy recommendations are, naturally, at the level of government or broad social institutions, such as the market, political parties, or the organization of parliament. But his comments on how individuals are to behave very often refer to institutions as enablers or constrainers to get us to be more utilitarian in our actions. He says of promises, by which he presumably means contracts in this instance, that if they 'had only their own proper obligation, without the separate sanction of government, they wou'd have but little efficacy ... This separates the boundaries of our public and private duties, and shews that the latter are more dependant on the former, than the former on the latter' (T3.2.6.7, SBN 546). Most of his greatest contributions to moral and political theory are similarly directed at institutions and institutional arrangements and at broad social practices, including conventions and norms. On his psychological account, therefore, Hume seems to be an institutional utilitarian, as spelled out below.

The mid-twentieth-century effort to read earlier utilitarians, such as Mill and Hume, as really rule-utilitarians misses the central point of their concerns.[21] That

---

[21] See e.g. Urmson, 'The Interpretation of the Moral Philosophy of J. S. Mill.'

point was with institutional arrangements that would secure good consequences and not with individual-level rule following. Hume, Mill, and other utilitarians do not have the deontological leanings that the critics assert. It is true that we cannot imagine living without rules in our daily lives, but the main body of such rules are those that are institutionally promulgated and institutionally enforced.[22] In any modern nation the main body of such rules is the body of law, but there are hundreds of others that are specific to particular organizations or professions. Institutional utilitarianism is about the structure of law and of other institutions, such as systems of rights, and of practices, such as the rule of the road.

To make sense of this position, first consider a standard criticism of Hume. Stroud and many others argue that Hume's move from moral to political theory does not immediately seem to be coherent in that the devices that secure moral action do not work to secure compliance with institutions of justice. Stroud, for example, supposes that Hume relies on arguments from interests to explain and justify the rise and existence of political institutions.[23] If so, this would violate his presumption that we see these institutions as virtuous because they are pleasing to us, just as I see your action of saving a child from harm as virtuous because it evokes a sentiment of approbation in me. He supposes I could support the general institutions of justice but still try to cheat when it seems I can get away with it—for example, by stealing your transferable property.

This criticism is couched at the wrong level.[24] Hume's theory is about the justification of the institutions of justice, and a part of the institutions will be the devices of the criminal law to block people from stealing. Approving the institutions in the first instance is to approve the use of these devices, which are part of the larger set of institutions. Of course, they might not work perfectly and Stroud might successfully cheat the system. Nevertheless, if they work well enough, the institutions are pleasing to us *because* they serve our interests—even to the point of going after Stroud for his misbehavior—just as various personal virtues are pleasing to us because we benefit from the fact that people act from them. In both cases, we generalize from our own case to the class of similar cases. Stroud and others seem to want Hume to engineer the institutions *to make people be moral by their own commitments*. This is no part of Hume's theory. He thinks we have moral approbations and disapprobations. This is merely a psychological claim, not a claim about our becoming moral in our commitments.

---

[22] Hardin, *Morality within the Limits of Reason*, 77–83.
[23] Stroud, *Hume*, 203, 206, 214, and passim.
[24] See Mackie, *Hume's Moral Theory*, 86, for a similar confusion.

It is outside Hume's program to claim that every individual action under the institutions of justice must itself be compliant with the principles of those institutions, as Stroud assumes. Hume says very forcefully that the sympathy we might have for anyone or even for the public *need not motivate us at all*. This is a central claim of his psychological theory of the distinction between reason and knowledge on the one hand and the passions on the other. My (very likely weak) sympathy with the public interest as it is affected by actions under the institutions of justice is a matter of knowledge and it does not motivate. Stroud says, 'Hume's account of the origin of justice is supposed to explain why we approve of, and how we can be moved towards, justice ... '[25] On the contrary, it is not supposed to say anything about such motivations, which Hume commonly denies we even have.

Hume says, 'experience sufficiently proves, that men, in the ordinary conduct of life, look not so far as the public interest, when they pay their creditors, perform their promises, and abstain from theft, and robbery, and injustice of every kind. That is a motive too remote and too sublime to affect the generality of mankind, and operate with any force in actions so contrary to private interest as are frequently those of justice and common honesty' (T3.2.1.11, SBN 481). Hume's theory is about this generality of mankind, whose approbations he means to explain and whose motivations to moral behavior are, Hume thinks, very weak at best, especially with respect to the general public.

Let us carry this point further. Sympathy with public interest is the source of our moral approbation, but that sympathy is 'too weak' to control our passions, hence too weak to motivate us to action (T3.2.2.24, SBN 499–500). Hume makes this point very forcefully: 'My sympathy with another may give me the sentiment of pain and disapprobation ... tho' I may not be willing to sacrifice any thing of my own interest, or cross any of my passions, for his satisfaction' (T3.3.1.23, SBN 586). He continues this discussion with examples, so intent is he on justifying the strong claim. The account of justice is entirely about the psychology of approbation, *not about actions motivated by approbation*; such approbation is essentially a form of knowledge (judgment) and it is therefore not motivating unless it is attached to some motivating passion. This fact vitiates several pages of criticism of the failings of Hume's political theory, which does not do, because it is not intended to do, what some other theories typically strive to do, which is to explain moral motivations to act as driven somehow by moral concern *and* to determine what is moral. Hume rejects both these projects.

---

[25] Stroud, *Hume*, 207.

So, one might ask, why does our benevolence work through institutions when it fails in direct application or in patterned rule following? A very large part of Hume's argument for sympathy in general addresses this point and his answer is among his most subtle arguments, which is almost magical in resolving a seemingly massive obstacle to his theory. If I am not affected by some collective device or policy, I can react to it psychologically with sympathy for those who will be affected. And if I am considering a general institutional arrangement, such as government, I can consider it wholly in the light of its likely beneficial impact on everyone. In neither of these contexts am I moved by my own immediate passions; these issues so distant from me do not provoke my passions, because I cannot see any effect that they have on my interests per se. Hence, when I am considering the overall arrangements for social order or even for social policy to do things such as building public roads, I can respond entirely from their tendency to the utility of all (T3.2.2.24–5, SBN 498–500). That is the limit of my likely commitment to the happiness of the general mass, because 'the pleasure of a stranger, for whom we have no friendship, pleases us only by sympathy' (T3.3.1.8, SBN 576).

Our very general sympathy defines our very general institutional utilitarianism even though it rules out our act–utilitarianism in dealings beyond our close associates. This is an extraordinary claim for Hume's view here. Institutional utilitarianism is ex ante about creating institutional arrangements and only later about affecting individual actions—it is a two-stage program. At the first stage, we have very little personal interests at stake but we can sympathize with the general interests of everyone to have the relevant institutional results. We judge from our own very small share in the mutual advantage. At the second stage we act under the influence of the incentives that the institution creates for us, as when we comply with a legal contract that is enforced, if necessary, by the courts. Again, however, the fact that our psychology commends this result does not make institutional utilitarianism the true moral theory—there is no true moral theory, there is no truth of any moral content. There is only scientific truth about our moral psychology and views. And it is these that entail institutional utilitarianism as the moral 'theory' on which we actually act or which we approve.

Hume's account of artificial virtues, especially those that are managed by institutions, yields a very clear statement of institutional utilitarianism. Instances of honoring the law of property may violate our interests and might seem to entail no good whatever, but having the law of property is in our interest, is indeed mutually advantageous (T3.2.10.3, SBN 555). The principle of mutual advantage is constantly in the background of Hume's claims.

In fact, the chief context in which Hume implicitly makes utilitarian recommendations is in speaking of institutions and conventions. For these, I can feel sympathy for the larger public that its interests are cared for or that its justice is secured. Hume, the Haldane of beneficence, cannot make act-utilitarian recommendations because, again, he insists that we are too selfish for the motive of caring for others to have much impact beyond our very close associates. And he forcefully rejects rule-utilitarian claims and by implication he would make no rule-utilitarian recommendations. One might conclude therefore that he is personally committed to institutional utilitarianism. To an important extent, of course, he is. Institutional utilitarianism serves mutual advantage, and through that the advantage of each individual, including Hume, you, and me. Each of us therefore can forcefully advocate institutional utilitarian moves. And insofar as any of us can effect such moves at low enough cost to ourselves, we can perhaps be expected to do so.

It is not necessary here to lay out an institutional utilitarian account of political institutions. I have presented such an account elsewhere. That account goes substantially beyond Hume's own programmatic statements,[26] although Hume presents the beginnings of a fairly rich institutional utilitarian program (T3.2.10.3–15, SBN 555–63). Such an account must necessarily combine welfarism, sociology, psychology, economics, legal theory, and social science more generally. In particular, it must consider what law and government can do to enhance utility for citizens. In general, if we can make no interpersonal comparisons, we can have only mutual advantage as our criterion for choices. Indeed, if we can literally make no interpersonal comparisons, we cannot meaningfully define equality of welfare. Hume is more or less ordinalist in value theory.[27] He is not very explicit on his views on interpersonal comparisons, but he seems occasionally to make them, such as when he comments that a very wealthy person must get less benefit from an additional bit of money than many poor people would get from that same addition to their resources (EPM3.25, SBN 194). This statement does not require a precise measure of utility.

Even without interpersonal comparisons, we can suppose ex ante that many institutional devices do serve mutual advantage—or rather, they serve expected mutual advantage. Hence, at a minimum, an institutional utilitarian will want legal protections of individuals. On Hume's account of the value of liberty, we might also suppose that we should have liberal protections of individuals

---

[26] In Hardin, *Morality within the Limits of Reason*, chap. 3 and 4. That account is motivated by Hume's theory, but it goes beyond Hume in considering institutional arrangements for contexts in which we can make at least some interpersonal comparisons.

[27] See further, chapter 8.

from many kinds of intrusion by the state into their lives. We would expect to have broad agreement on certain legal rights—not so-called human or natural rights but specifically institutionalized legal rights. Such legal rights are positive devices for handling individual-level information problems, for enabling individuals to determine their own lives within the constraints of the society, and for protecting them against each other (as in Hobbes's central concern). Some of these rights would be such individual protections, as against crime. Some of the legal rights would be de facto dyadic protections, for example, of exchange and of property ownership. Some would be collective, as with generalized political rights of free speech and of political participation (as in voting). Insofar as such rights generally serve for better government they are therefore mutually advantageous. Such rights would be institutionalized in the way Rawls commends in his argument for having roles within institutions for carrying out the protections.[28]

We might justify particular rights piecemeal, and in fact we are almost sure to develop them only piecemeal—they evolve with further experience. But we might suppose that the system of rights and other institutional arrangements should be somehow calibrated together to produce better overall effects than if the protections are developed in happenstance ways to respond to particular crises or problems. Hume would likely not expect us to be able to do an especially good job of such overall design—that is too great a task for us.[29] Hence, we might expect to have constant criticism of whatever arrangements we have made and even constant tinkering with the system and its details. Moreover, we would expect, as Hume suggests for municipal government, to have variation from jurisdiction to jurisdiction, variation that could not be defended as inherently justified but that could be explained as part of the unintended consequences that follow when large numbers of people act politically over time—which is the only way our institutions can have happened—and as a valued experiment in alternative ways to organize government and law.

There is likely to be a tendency to adopt arrangements that are ex ante mutual advantage—because such arrangements will receive broad support. But the only genuinely mutual advantage claim we might be able to make

---

[28] Rawls, 'Two Concepts of Rules.'

[29] Hume, 'Of the Rise and Progress of the Arts and Sciences,' 124. Perversely, however, Hume attempts to design a government de novo in 'Idea of a Perfect Commonwealth.' From the title of this essay and some knowledge of Hume, one must expect this to be a critique, perhaps even a parody, of utopian ideas. On the contrary, it appears to be a serious proposal for a wholly new government for England or some similar nation. This is probably the grossest violation of his own well-argued views in all of his works.

will be that having the system of government available to enable us to achieve such beneficial order serves mutual advantage. This is unfortunately a limited program and one might want much more from a moral and political theory. This is, however, a larger institutional agenda than any other moral and political theory has ever offered. Most such theories stop with ideal models and some hope that institutions will be designed to fit them. Hume stays almost forever on the ground.

One should not overdo the criticism of the indeterminacy of mutual-advantage devices. It is right for the theory to be indeterminate because the world it represents is indeterminate.[30] The theory is, after all, consequentialist, and causal possibilities are commonly indeterminate. Often, of course, they are simply stochastic, at least so far as we can judge. Far more important even than this, however, is that social outcomes are generally the result of interactive choices by more than one person. If there were a perfectly determinate theory of interactive rational choice, this might pose no problem. But rational choice is inherently indeterminate when one is choosing against other choosers. In social contexts I do not choose an outcome; I choose a strategy. The outcome that results depends also on what strategies you and others choose. The model of choice in game theory represents this indeterminacy, because my best choice in a game usually depends on what you and others choose. But your best choices depend on what I choose. There is therefore no general theory of how to choose best in games and there are even disagreements about the specific strategies to follow in specific cases.

Concluding Remarks

If there are principles of justice that will have general application to others and to me, I will want to have a well-developed system of law that is advantageous to society. The way to do that is to have it be advantageous to every individual in the society—which means me as well as all the others. This is simply Hume's mutual-advantage view of the role of justice and government. He says that justice is a moral virtue merely because it has a tendency to the good of mankind (T3.3.1.9, SBN 577). This seems to be an indirect claim that the good of mankind is a standard of morality for Hume. He cannot say that this good, or utility, is the true morality, but this indirect claim is about as far as

---

[30] Hardin, *Indeterminacy and Society*.

he goes—other than when he exhorts us to seek virtue and extols 'practical morality' (T3.3.6.5, SBN 620–1).[31]

Hume is often ambiguous in his wish to entertain panegyric in favor of virtues that he approves while insisting that his program is only to explain the psychology of morals. So too he is ambiguous here. Is Hume a utilitarian? As a speculative philosopher, no. But in his own psychology, clearly yes. Why? Because utility pleases.

---

[31] Also see much of his discussion of benevolence, EPM2.6–23, SBN 178–82, which is full of panegyric.

8
Value Theory

> This circumstance of usefulness ... is the sole source of the moral approbation paid to fidelity, justice, veracity, integrity, and those other estimable and useful qualities and principles.[1]

Much of modern political theory has focused on the problem of collectively providing for individual welfare. This was de facto the whole point of Hobbes's political theory and it is the central point of Hume's. Both of these philosophers assume that social order will serve mutual advantage. Although it is not a firm rule, Hume refers to mutual advantage as commonly a matter of fact: 'that close union of interest, which is so observable between the public and each individual,' although this union often fails (EPM5.16, SBN 219). Rawls's theory of justice, which is supposedly rationally mandated for anyone with a modicum of risk aversion, is also mutually advantageous.[2] Rawls refers to the mutually disinterested nature of the citizens, so that each person judges each possible state of affairs solely according to his or her own outcome.[3] The central move of such theory is typically to create an institutional structure that will guarantee the welfare of individuals who act sensibly, which is commonly to say, who act according to the simple canons of rational choice. We create institutions that will secure collective results through individualistic actions by citizens. Such political theory therefore does not require a specific moral commitment from citizens.

Why should we go this way? Why not build political theory on normative commitments that are not individualistic? After all, we know that people often do behave morally against their own interest, for example, when acting on behalf of their families or larger groups, when following moral rules of some kind, or when being altruistic. In general, however, these motivations are sporadic and particular; they do not govern all behavior and we cannot expect to achieve high levels of, for example, altruistic action if we design our institutions to work well only if altruistic motivations are common or pervasive.

---

[1] EPM3.49, SBN 204.　　　[2] Rawls, *A Theory of Justice*, 66, 110.　　　[3] Ibid., 111–12.

One might aspire to create a society of people for whom such motivations are very strong, as in the desire to create a new, publicly oriented Soviet man, a few of whom probably were created, or in the desire to create devout Muslims in Iran and Afghanistan, where many of whom surely have been created. But, in a mild variant of Hume's dictum that we should design political institutions that would work well even if they were staffed with knaves,[4] we can say that we should design social institutions that would work well even for citizens who are not generally and pervasively altruistic.

We commonly can expect non-interested motivations to accomplish relatively specific and idiosyncratic—and usually local—purposes, but not to accomplish systematic public purposes. Moreover, we can generally expect individuals to see public interests or welfare as analogous to own-interests or welfare. That is, public welfare is merely the aggregation of individual welfares, especially when a particular action serves the welfare of virtually all. Much of what we must want of our political institutions is that they provide the collective equivalent of own-welfare. In an ordinal assessment, this is simply mutual advantage, which is the collective implication of own-welfare generalized to the collectivity. When altruistic and other ideal motivations enter, they can produce results that mutual-advantage considerations could not produce, and some of us may be grateful for such motivations in helping to eliminate racial inequality before the law and in attempting to reduce economic inequality through welfare programs. But we should also be grateful that general social order and much of the vast array of welfarist policies do not require such motivations. Indeed, we might even be grateful that interests have generally displaced passions in public debate and policy in many societies, as they did in England a few centuries ago.[5]

There presumably are and often have been societies that were governed relatively systematically by religious views, so that on many matters individuals might act for collective purposes or altruistically out of religious conviction. It is the initial legacy of liberalism that it cannot be grounded in the hope of any such resolution, because it was historically a response to religious division and deep disagreement. The first and still a central tenet of liberalism in politics is the toleration of varied religious beliefs, as enunciated especially forcefully in the US constitutional provision of the separation of church and state. Moreover, much of the religious conviction at the time of Hobbes and Locke, who were among the progenitors of liberal thinking, was specifically

---

[4] Hume, 'Of the Independency of Parliament.'
[5] See further, Hirschman, *The Passions and the Interests.*

other-worldly and idealistic about life in this world.[6] The seventeenth-century English Levellers, for example, preferred that people engage in collective production in a basically agricultural economy on collectively owned land without money or merchants to control distribution. This supposedly would lead to proper Christian humility and fundamental equality.[7]

Virtually all of political philosophy in the rational choice mode has been directed at achieving relatively high levels of welfare, and Hobbes was very forceful in refusing to allow the focus of his concern to depart from welfare onto religious qualifications. Indeed, Hobbes's starting point is to found an all-power-ful government to secure the safety of individual citizens and to secure their possibilities of furthering their own welfare. We seek preservation and material prosperity.[8] Few western political theorists since Hobbes have looked back from this stance, which is essentially foundational for modern western political thought. Indeed, the nearest competitors with welfare as a moral political concern have been fairness and egalitarianism, which are themselves generally about the distribution of welfare and the resources for providing welfare, and consent, which is an ex ante concern and is often about welfare, fairness, or egalitarianism.

The rise of welfarist political theory was accompanied by the rise of individualistic economic theory, as developed by Mandeville, Hume, Smith, and many others.[9] Many of these theorists simultaneously presented rational-choice political philosophies and individualistic market economic theories. Perhaps no one integrated the two better than Hume and Mill, for whom the two are clearly of a coherent piece. Most of them were utilitarians in political philosophy and more or less laissez-faire market economists in economics. The development of economic theory and of political philosophy largely separated over the course of the nineteenth century in Anglo-Saxon thought, and economic theory left political theory and utilitarian moral theory far behind in their technical developments in the twentieth-century. Terence Hutchison quips that Smith, who insists on the joint enterprise of moral, political, and economic philosophy, is led as if by an invisible hand to bring about an end that is no part of his intention: 'establishing political economy as a separate autonomous discipline.'[10] The greater damage was done by philosophers themselves, especially by Moore and his influence. It is a peculiarity of

[6] Locke, *A Letter Concerning Toleration.*

[7] Winstanley, *The Law of Freedom in a Platform or, True Magistracy Restored.*

[8] Hobbes, *Leviathan* 30.1 [175]; see also 13.14 [63].

[9] Mandeville, *The Fable of the Bees: Private Vices, Publick Benefits*; Smith, *An Inquiry into the Nature and Causes of the Wealth of Nations*; Mill, *Principles of Political Economy.*

[10] Hutchison, *Before Adam Smith*, 355.

twentieth-century moral philosophy that it became almost exclusively personal or individual in its focus. The shift in thinking began with a flood of intuitionist moral philosophy (e.g., Prichard's writings) early in the twentieth century and Moore's (1903) idealistic and practically irrelevant variant of utilitarianism.[11] These works rightly lie almost entirely unread today, although intuitionism is still a big, if intellectually destitute, enterprise.

The last major theorists who gave relatively equal consideration to moral and political theory on the one hand and to economic theory on the other were the philosopher Sidgwick and the economist Edgeworth. The value theory of this entire school of economic and political theory—from Mandeville to Sidgwick—has been welfarist or mutual advantage. Just as he does not lay out his strategic analysis as an abstract theory, so too Hume does not lay out his value theory as a whole apparel for the body of his moral psychology. He makes points about values almost always only in the context of whatever argument is at issue. It is therefore instructive to try to pull his views together, at least on the more important issues that seem to drive his major conclusions.

Political and Economic Exchange

It is often supposed—as in the public-goods model of the origin of the state—that the essence of politics is collective action, which is large-number exchange or prisoner's dilemma. The essence of economics is dyadic exchange or two-person prisoner's dilemma in a market. Therefore politics and government provide collective goods (or at least provide goods collectively) while the market provides private goods. On the contrary, one can argue that the essence of politics is coordination, especially large-number coordination. This is the essence of Hobbes's theory, that we all coordinate—whether by compact or by imposition—on a sovereign, thereby empowering that sovereign to maintain order through the use of draconian power if necessary. It is also the essence of Hume's far more sanguine theory of the rise of conventions, especially conventions of order and government. The difference between economic and political theory is that economics assumes a resolution of the prior problem of coordination on social order, while for political theory this is the central issue. Political coordination makes economic exchange possible—or at least makes it easy and common.

Hobbes understands that exchange is not of 'equal values' but benefits both parties to it. Morally speaking, 'the just value is that which they be contented

---

[11] Moore, *Principia Ethica*.

to give.'[12] Hence, exchange has the payoff structure of the prisoner's dilemma and not that of a zero-sum interaction. This view contradicts Aristotle's view that exchange is of equals, and it vitiates the medieval Catholic doctrine of the just price, as though the price of some object is inherent in its intrinsic value. The ordinal revolution in economics in the 1930s finally resolved this issue definitively,[13] but Hobbes, Hume, and (sometimes) Smith already glimpsed the central issue: that value is subjectively measured by the preferences of the individual and is not objectively inherent in the objects that we value. It is a function of supply and demand.

Game 8.1 Prisoner's Dilemma or Exchange (value of holdings ex post)

		Column	
		Yield car	Keep car
	Yield $5,000	$5,100, 5,000	0, $9,900
Row			
	Keep $5,000	$10,100, 0	$5,000, 4,900

Note how the representation of exchange alters if the payoffs are cardinal. We would have to put in values of, say, $4,900 and $5,100 for the seller's and buyer's valuations of the car in the matrix of game 3.4 in chapter 3, to yield game 8.1. Exchange merely of resources makes no sense if the payoffs are in homogeneous units, such as money. That immediately means that each cell has only values of resources in it. Unless value is being either created or destroyed exogenously, the sum of the two payoffs in every cell is the same, so that the game is constant sum and there is no point in playing it, because one player is made worse off if the other is made better off by some change, and the game is one of conflict rather than exchange. Game 8.1 as represented is a *game of exchange only because the two players place different values on the car, so that there is a gain to be made from trade.* A mutual-advantage principle commends the top-left outcome as the only outcome that serves a mutual-advantage change from the status quo bottom-right outcome.

The point of exchange is that it increases value to both parties to the exchange. If all we have are resources, we have nothing to exchange and the resources are worthless. If there is to be exchange, someone must produce something. (It is then production and our differential valuations of goods that will introduce inequalities.) If the payoffs are represented in money values, then we can assess the total money payoffs in each outcome, as we would have to do

---

[12] Hobbes, *Leviathan* 15.14 [75].
[13] Samuelson, 'Complementarity: An Essay on the 40th Anniversary of the Hicks-Allen Revolution in Demand Theory.'

in a Benthamite interpersonally comparable cardinal utilitarianism (assuming that money and utility are comparable). What we find is that a rule that says we should go for the maximum joint payoff will commend that Column yield the car independently of whether Row keeps or yields the payment for it. It is only Column's action of yielding or keeping the car that affects the total value of the outcome. To make Benthamite utilitarianism work we would all have to be normatively committed to achieving the greatest overall sum of utility. That is surely implausible for a real society. To make Hume's mutual-advantage utilitarianism work is far less demanding.

Relativity and Ordinalism of Value

In one of the earliest explicit statements of the ordinal view of value, Hume supposes we only judge value by comparison, not by some supposed intrinsic worth or value (T3.3.2.4, SBN 593).[14] His claim might be merely a psychological claim, but it seems likely to be grounded in the supposition that we could not make sense of intrinsic worth but only of comparative rankings. It might seem to follow that we must be marginalists, that we cannot judge whole states of affairs. But this does not follow because we can make the kind of judgment Hobbes makes—order under government is better than violent chaos for virtually all—as a strictly comparative judgment. Thus, Hobbes, Hume, and ordinalists more generally do not require that we establish a zero-point or a metric for how good any state of affairs is or would be. Indeed, for any marginal or holistic claim of mutual advantage, we could do a set-theoretic comparison of each individual in one state to the same individual in the other state.

It is difficult in the abstract to appreciate the depth of Hume's claim that we judge only by comparison. A couple of literary examples might help to give it some feeling, some bite. Of one of his characters in the story, 'The Comet,' Bruno Schultz asks: 'Was he happy? One would ask that question in vain. A question like this makes sense only when applied to creatures who are rich in alternative possibilities, so that the actual truth can be contrasted with partly real probabilities and reflect itself in them.'[15] On Schultz's view, it might have made no sense to ask of the vast majority of all people who have ever

---

[14] In his words: 'We judge more of objects by comparison, than by their intrinsic worth and value; and regard every thing as mean, when set in opposition to what is superior of the same kind.' See also, Hume, 'Of the Dignity or Meanness of Human Nature,' 81–2.

[15] Schultz, *The Street of Crocodiles*, 150–1.

lived whether they were happy. They were not rich in alternative possibilities. Hume remarks that 'we are no sooner acquainted with the impossibility of satisfying any desire, than the desire itself vanishes' (T Intro. 9, SBN xviii). Perhaps here he overlooks the lingering power of romantic love as a desire, but the claim still has force.

For a second example, in a letter to her husband, Dorothy Osborne tells of her evening walk 'where a great many young wenches keep Sheep and Cow's and sitt in the shade singing of Ballads; I goe to them and compare their voyces and Beauty's to some Ancient Shepherdesses that I have read of and finde a vaste difference there, but trust mee I think these are as innocent as those could bee. I talke to them, and finde they want nothing to make them the happiest People in the world, but the knoledge that they are soe.'[16] In quoting part of this letter, Virginia Woolf might have noted, but did not, that the price of having such knowledge may be to wreck it.

Hume's insistence on judging by comparison anticipates John Dewey's pragmatic view. Dewey argues that we cannot have as our goal the achievement of the best overall state of affairs. There is no such thing as 'the best' state of affairs overall in our lives. All we can do is to improve on the state we are in. We can know a direction but not an end point of our progress. Our judgment of whether one state is better than another does not turn on our determining the values of the two states and then comparing these but only on our assessment of the relative change from one to the other.[17]

In addition to supposing that we judge only by comparison, so that there is no zero-point for valuation, Hume and Hobbes also assume that value is subjective, that there is no objective value scale for the utility of the objects we might use. Consider Hobbes's view: 'For these words of good, evil, and contemptible are ever used with relation to the person that useth them, there being nothing simply and absolutely so, nor any common rule of good and evil to be taken from the nature of the objects themselves ... '[18] He supposes that there cannot be an objective value of anything but only the value that we place on it.

There are at least three considerations at issue here. First, we judge only relatively so that there is no fixed point, no zero-utility level. Second, value is subjective to the beneficiary of any state or user of any good; it does not inhere in the state or the good itself. Third, there is no metric for comparison of two pleasures or states. We can say x is better or more enjoyable than y, but we cannot say by how much it is better.

---

[16] Osborne, *Letters to Sir William Temple*, 89 (quoted in Woolf, *A Room of One's Own*, 66).
[17] Dewey, *The Quest for Certainty*.   [18] Hobbes, *Leviathan* 6.7 [24].

Perhaps it is a psychological point that we have no innate standard of goodness or value, but it is also an important point in value theory. Psychologically it is easily demonstrated by the hysteresis of our valuations of at least many of our possessions. Hume describes the phenomenon: 'Men generally fix their affections more on what they are possess'd of, than on what they never enjoy'd: For this reason, it wou'd be greater cruelty to dispossess a man of any thing, than not to give it him' (T3.2.1.14, SBN 482). To say that there is hysteresis in valuation is merely to say that the initial valuation of increases in one's holdings is likely to rise more slowly than the initial valuation of decreases in one's holdings is to fall. It may be better to have loved and lost, but it is not generally better to have gained and then lost in the cases of many other goods or experiences. This is a strictly intrapersonal phenomenon and perhaps it can be given a compelling psychological explanation, although for our and Hume's purposes it is sufficient just to recognize the phenomenon.

Mutual Advantage

The ultimate collective value for an ordinalist is mutual advantage, which is the collective implication of self-interest. It is also the ordinal utilitarian principle of value or welfare for a group or a whole society. To say that an outcome of our choices is mutually advantageous is to say that it serves the interest of each and every one of us relative to the status quo before the choices. One could say that, in this view, collective value is emergent, it is merely what individuals want. To speak of collective value in any other sense is to import some additional notion of value into the discussion beyond the interests of individuals. Hobbes may have been constitutionally oblivious of any such additional notions of value; Vilfredo Pareto evidently believed them perverse.[19] Hume does not assert a position on this issue, but the central concern of Hume's vision is the interests and the psychologies of individuals, because understanding their interests and psychologies yields explanations of their social and moral views.

Frank Knight says, 'The supreme and inestimable merit of the exchange mechanism is that it enables a vast number of people to co-operate in the use of means to achieve ends as far as their interests are mutual, without arguing or in any way agreeing about either the ends or the methods of achieving them.'[20] Mutual advantage does not entail agreement on ends. Exchange requires either

---

[19] Pareto, *Manual of Political Economy*, 47–51, 105–6.
[20] Knight, *History and Method of Economics*, 267.

differential efficiency in producing things or differential tastes in consuming things. It also does not entail interpersonal comparisons of our valuations of things we exchange. Without such comparisons, we can have only mutual advantage, not equality, as a measure of improvement of our collective state of affairs.

Incidentally, mutual advantage is the *only* plausible collective analog of self-interest. Consider a cardinally additive measure, for example. More utility to you can compensate for less utility to me in such an additive measure. Of course, it cannot be my interest for you to benefit at my expense. Hence, a cardinally additive measure is not a collective analog of individual-level self-interest. If the dollars in game 8.1 are a measure of utility, then cardinal utility would not differentiate the two outcomes in the first column.

When Hume generalizes beyond the individual it is from the individual's limited sympathy with the general run of the populace that he can say individuals would tend to approve general laws and institutions that would be in the interest of everyone. That is to say, his public vision is of the mutual advantage of all. Very few specific programs are likely to serve the interests of everyone, but the general creation of social order is a mutual-advantage program. In the first instance, of course, the creation of government is to the mutual advantage. This is a vision that Hume shares with Hobbes, for whom this is the whole purpose of government: to create order in which individuals might by their own efforts come to prosper and, of course, in which individuals might be protected against violent harm from their fellow citizens and foreign invaders. Similarly the general appeal of contract theories of government is that a contract to which all assent must inherently be expected to serve the mutual advantage.

Pareto combined the normative principle of mutual advantage with marginalist concern. Indeed, Pareto formulated what are now called the Pareto principles to avoid interpersonal comparisons and attendant moral judgments.[21] Hence, Pareto was Humean and Hobbesian in his motivations, at least in part. The criteria were introduced by Pareto not for recommending individual action but for making ordinal value judgments about states of affairs. They might therefore be used by a policy-maker.

Hume states the vision of mutual advantage often. In his summary comparison of justice and various personal virtues and vices, he says of justice that its distinguishing feature is that it serves the mutual advantage, and not merely the utility or interest of particular individuals. 'The whole scheme, however, of law and justice is advantageous to the society and to every

---

[21] Pareto, *Manual of Political Economy*, 47–51.

individual' (T3.3.1.12, SBN 579).[22] The final phrase, 'and to every individual,' merely defines 'mutual advantage,' which is Hume's central motivating social principle. We all want the mutual advantage to be served because we all gain thereby. Brian Barry rightly characterizes Rawls's theory of justice as being a blend of mutual-advantage and egalitarian elements. He attributes to 'Rawls as well as Hume the idea that justice represents the terms of rational cooperation for mutual advantage under the circumstances of justice.'[23]

Mutual-advantage theories, however, have a major flaw that they share with the Pareto criteria: as noted earlier, they are radically indeterminate. As in a claim for a Pareto improvement from some state of affairs to another in which everyone is better off or at least some are better off and no one is worse off, the principle of mutual advantage gives no criterion for selecting one of many possible mutual-advantage forms of government. For Hobbes, the order brought by any sovereign, almost no matter how draconian, is better than the disorder in Hobbes's awful state of nature. This is the only determinate claim one can make for any particular mutual-advantage resolution: that it is better than the world with no resolution. Indeterminacy in the theory and the state of affairs here, however, is desirable. We can achieve much greater determinacy in combining individuals' values only by crude devices that would be far more objectionable than indeterminacy.[24]

Both Hobbes and Hume suppose that any extant government is likely to be better than what would happen if we try to change the government, because the change is apt to involve a chaotic and destructive period of transition. For them, this is not a conservative reluctance to see change or a mere prejudice in favor of the status quo, but is a deeply theoretical concern about causal relations. For Hobbes the hostility to changing the form of government would apply to a democratic as well as a draconian monarchical government. The problem is the costs and difficulty of re-coordinating from a present regime to a new one. One might suppose that these costs would seem even greater to Hume because it is not merely re-coordinating that is required but the creation of a new convention to replace a present convention.

Hume has a resolution of the general problem of normative indeterminacy. He supposes an actual government is an unintended consequence of actions taken for many reasons. We did not sit down to design our political order, and we therefore missed the opportunity to quarrel over exactly which form we should adopt. This dodge is especially apt for Hume because he generally does not make any normative argument in favor of a form of government beyond its

---

[22] See also, Hume, 'Of Commerce,' especially p. 255.
[23] Barry, *Theories of Justice*, 148.   [24] Hardin, *Indeterminacy and Society*.

serving mutual advantage, which includes the protection of individual liberties and the consequent enabling of economic creativity and progress.[25] What he wants is explanation, not justification. And the evolution of government from earlier stages of social organization is explanation without justification.

There is a branch of game theory that partially assumes away the problem of Hobbes's state of nature. In cooperative game theory it is assumed that players can make binding agreements. Of course, if we can make binding agreements, we can resolve ordinary exchange in two-person prisoner's dilemmas. One of the problems that provokes Hume's and Hobbes's concern in a large society when there is no government is the inability to make binding mutually beneficial agreements or exchanges. The creation of government makes it possible for us to reach such agreements in many contexts, so that it enables us to reach far better outcomes for ourselves. Hume recognizes additionally that we can be bound by the incentive structure of ongoing relationships and of conventions and their norms. This works in small societies and in subgroups within large societies.

One could make mutual advantage a normative principle, as it arguably is in Rawls's theory of justice. But for Hume mutual advantage is entirely functional in that it satisfies our interests to some degree. He argues for mutual advantage not because it is utilitarian but because it is the aggregate implication or version of self-interest. It is a value only in the sense that it gives each of us what we want in comparison to some other state of affairs. It is just self-interest in the sense that I get the improvement in my own state of affairs only through the mutual-advantage move that also makes others better off (T3.3.1.12, SBN 579–80). I therefore can be motivated for the mutual advantage entirely from my own interests. *If I view the fates of all others with at least mild sympathy and I also see that the improvement in their fates is coupled with improvement in my own, then I have very strong reason to support a mutual-advantage move for all of us.* Moreover, because I know that others will not favor special treatment of me that is not coupled with mutual advantage, I am likely to see any mutual-advantage move as about as good a public choice as I can expect.

Incidentally, contractarianism in Hobbes's limited variant, in which the compact does nothing more than select a government, is a mutual-advantage theory. It becomes a normative theory only if it is further assumed, as by Locke, sometimes—but sometimes not—by Hobbes, and by many contemporary contractarians, that our agreement to the social compact gives us an obligation of the kind that promising is also thought by many philosophers to give us.

---

[25] A slightly weird exception is Hume, 'Idea of a Perfect Commonwealth.'

Hobbes supposes that the agreement has no binding force over us but that the regime, once in place, does have and can then give the agreement forceful backing. Hume thinks the whole exercise of asserting an argument from a social contract is absurd.

In discussions of these arguments, by far the most common query or challenge is to pose a particular case in which a person is a loser from the application of the law, the rules of property, or some other convention that is justified by an argument from mutual advantage. Such an objection is based on a fundamental misconception. The argument for a mutual-advantage convention is that having the overall system, for example, of law makes us better off than we would have been without the system of law. This is an ex ante argument. The formulation of the commonplace objection is wrong-headed in that it typically supposes a one-off example. To be a credible objection it must be formulated as a whole-cloth rejection of the idea that the chaos of an unordered society would be preferred by at least one person over a well-ordered society. Ex ante it is virtually inconceivable that this is true. Even a devoted thief must prefer a society that is well enough organized to produce enough to steal.

What is true, of course, and what might be objectionable, is that any change of current rules or institutions is likely to have losers who would have been better off keeping the old rules or institutions. But if the possibilities for change are themselves part of the old system, this objection does not work either. One can object that replacing the former Soviet system with a developing market economy and an open democracy has produced many losers. That is true. Indeed, a large fraction of those over age 50 at the time of the initial change must have been big losers and must have little hope of ever being winners. But one probably cannot design the institution that would have guaranteed the permanent stability of the prior system, which, as static as it may have been, was inherently subject to endogenous change, such as economic collapse that would have made far more losers.

Hume lived before the age of the democratic revolution, which we could date with the Declaration of Independence of the US colonies from Great Britain in the year of Hume's death. But his political philosophy is democratic in the sense that it commends aggregation of the individual interests or welfares of citizens into a mutually advantageous outcome under mutual-advantage political institutions. Of course, even in liberal nations actual political institutions often fail to represent mutual advantage, perhaps because they are captured by well-organized groups or corporations that can use the institutions to their own advantage. Seeking one's own welfare is not equivalent to seeking mutual-advantage outcomes. Institutional design can mitigate these problems by channeling the urge to enhance own-welfare in less destructive ways.

Contemporary Humean political philosophers would put such design issues at the core of their applied theory.

Liberty and Individualism

Hume uses the term liberty in two very different ways. First, there is liberty in the sense of freedom of will.[26] Second, there is liberty in the sense of political freedom to do as one pleases with one's life and to engage in whatever economic activities one wishes. It is the second that is relevant here because such liberty is of value in political theory. Hume writes in an age of liberty and although many think him deeply conservative, he is also strongly in support of liberty in ways and to a degree that are inconsistent with the views of standard conservatism in his time. He shares with conservatives a sense of history and its role in our beliefs and possibilities, but he does not share with them their sense of the relations between citizens and government.

Hume clearly supposes that it is individual and not collective values that motivate activities of many kinds.[27] He also seems to suppose that these are the only values there are, that there are no collective or societal values. The nearest thing he has to a collective value is the mutual advantage discussed above. But, again, that is simply the aggregation of individual interests. By implication, we might assume that he must be a strong advocate of individual liberty. He is, but his reasons are commonly causal rather than conceptual or moral. He supposes that liberty enhances creativity, motivation for production, commerce, and all economic activities that make the society and hence its members better off. Liberty is beneficial and not merely desirable in its own right. Indeed, in his discussions of liberty, the main benefit is to the mutual advantage of all of us. As Duncan Forbes says, the arts and sciences 'can only take their first rise in free governments which infallibly produce laws and the necessary security.'[28] For later libertarians, such as von Humboldt and Mill, one often has the sense that the main concern is the value of liberty to the individual per se, not the value of it to all of us together. They commonly focus on autonomy, and their claims sometimes seem to be deontological. For Hume the main concern is clearly the benefit of liberty to all of us together, and his claims are essentially utilitarian.

---

[26] Hume, EHU8.23, SBN 95.
[27] Venning, 'Hume on Property, Commerce, and Empire in the Good Society,' 92.
[28] Forbes, Hume's Philosophical Politics, 226.

Austrian Social Theory

Hume is often accused of excessive conservatism in defense of social order as it is. Because he has a theory of convention at the base of order and government, he is not given to the Hobbesian excess of preferring tyranny to an open government because he thinks order can be created out of more or less spontaneously coordinated individual actions. But given his understanding of convention and the unintended consequences of institutional arrangements, he thinks we should be slow to adopt new schemes. Rather, we should defer substantially to experience. 'To balance a large state or society, whether monarchical or republican, on general laws, is a work of so great difficulty, that no human genius, however comprehensive, is able, by the mere dint of reasons and reflection, to effect it. The judgments of many must unite in this work: Experience must guide their labour: Time must bring it to perfection: and the feeling of inconveniencies must correct the mistakes, which they inevitably fall into, in their first trials and experiments.'[29]

Against his reputation for conservatism, note that Hume uses this analysis to argue against the virtue of an absolute monarchy, which, he supposes, will be unable to harness the creativity latent in the larger society because the monarch will tend toward hierarchical organization of the society with deliberate designs and attempts at control. An open, liberal society is much better for progress than such a monarchy. In his arguments here, Hume precedes Smith, Humboldt, Mill, Hayek, and many others.

A regime of liberty has advantages for me directly, but also indirectly through the fact that your liberty is likely to lead to your greater inventiveness, productivity, and so forth, all to the greater advantage of the whole society, including me. Liberalism in economics is similarly mutually advantageous. Hume complains of the system of royal patents under which Queen Elizabeth invaded a surprising number and variety of activities. The queen 'granted her servants and courtiers patents for monopolies; and these patents they sold to others, who were thereby enabled to raise commodities to what price they pleased, and who put invincible restraints upon all commerce, industry, and emulation in the arts.'[30] Any patent holder or anyone who had a credible hope of gaining such a patent would be a loser in eliminating the system. James I declared such patents to be 'contrary to law, and to the known liberties of the people.'[31] Anyone who lost a patent then was a loser, so that the change was

---

[29] Hume, 'Of the Rise and Progress of the Arts and Sciences,' 124. But see his 'Idea of a Perfect Commonwealth,' published the same year.
[30] Hume, *History of England* 4.44, 344.   [31] Ibid., 5.49, 114.

not strictly mutually advantageous. But ex ante and very generally, the bulk of citizens are beneficiaries of the regime of economic liberty.[32] They must benefit from lower prices and the greater innovation that comes from competition. The earlier rule under Henry VI was that 'it is lawful for any man to trade and store himself with any wares and merchandise at his own pleasure, and that every inhabitant of England by law enjoyeth all the fruits of his land, with all the profits he gaineth by his own labour.'[33] James I essentially restored that rule.

One might defend individual liberties on some ideal ground. For Hume, mutual advantage is the compelling claim. As noted in chapter 5, he held the same view of international trade. Liberty to trade as one pleases is beneficial not just to the individual but, through the general pattern of free trade, can be beneficial to entire nations. Again, anyone with a protected industry is apt to be a loser in the short run from losing that protection, but the general regime of free trade is mutually advantageous.

In his mutual-advantage vision of liberty, Hume suggests the views of the later Austrian economic and social theorists. In the Austrian view of economic relations, the knowledge how to produce and market vast numbers of commodities cannot be centralized in any person or agency. Knowledge is inherently distributed and local, and most of it is inaccessible to any one person or agency. This is an unchallengeable descriptive claim from which various theoretical implications seem to follow. Hume essentially assumes an Austrian social theory of distributed knowledge and he supposes therefore that an autocratic government cannot know enough to run the society well.[34]

The chief policy implication of the Austrian vision of the nature and distribution of knowledge in a society is that the central design and very extensive management of a modern economy are unlikely to be as effective in creating great prosperity and innovation as is a relatively loosely run market economy. This claim could turn out to be false under certain circumstances such as, for example, conditions of extreme exigency when central management might, for all its inefficiencies and errors, get us through better than an unmanaged system could. For example, during wartime when the value of immediate production overrides various economically future-oriented values, central managerial control of production might be far more successful for the short term than operating by standard market principles would be. It might be wasteful and inefficient in many ways and might slow some kinds of innovation, but it would be highly efficient in the ways that matter most at

---

[32] See further, Stewart, *Lectures on Political Economy*, 2.17–18.   [33] Ibid., 2.19.
[34] See further, Mill, *Considerations on Representative Government*, chap. 3, 399.

the time, such as in producing vast numbers of jeeps or other military vehicles rather than in innovatively redesigning them.

In essence, Hume has an Austrian theory of social relations more generally and not only of economic relations. These cannot be managed or even overseen by any central agent or agency. Indeed, the argument for an Austrian social theory must be even more compelling than that for an Austrian economic theory. The earliest understanding of liberalism is that individuals should be allowed to go their own way on very many social issues. That vision is the equivalent of the social version of Austrian economics.

Much of the argument for Austrian economics is predictive and explanatory, although it is motivated by a central normative concern, which is productivity. That concern is imputed to or assumed for virtually everyone, so that the normative concern is itself factually determined and not theoretically imposed. It is a concern with mutual advantage. Arguably, normative concerns are more important in an Austrian social theory because it must often say simply that we should let people go their own way merely for their own sake and not for the sake of greater productivity in the larger society or anything else that would have such universal collective appeal. While virtually all might acknowledge the value of greater productivity, many might not grant the value of letting others lead their lives in certain ways. In many societies, however, it seems that the common view of politics is that it is to serve the welfare of citizens, so that its normative vision is the same as the normative vision of Austrian economics. The causal argument of Austrian economics is that, typically, individual welfare and aggregate productivity will be enhanced by decentralization of decisions that matches the actual decentralization of knowledge. The causal argument of an Austrian or a Humean social theory is the same. That social theory is welfarist and mutual-advantage.

Time Preference

Hume often resorts to a kind of time preference in explaining actions in the short run that do not benefit the individual in the long run. For example, his account of the failure of cooperation of two farmers who might help each other harvest their corn turns on a calculation that does not even take a very long term view. The problem is akrasia or weakness of will, which Hume calls the want of strength of mind, 'which might enable [us] to resist the temptation of present ease or pleasure, and carry [us] forward in the search of more distant profit and enjoyment.' So we settle for a small benefit now (or we avoid a small cost now) in lieu of a large benefit in the future. 'But when some of these objects approach nearer to us, or acquire the advantages of favourable lights and positions, which catch the heart or imagination; our general resolutions are frequently confounded, a small enjoyment preferred, and lasting shame and sorrow entailed upon us. And however poets may employ their wit and eloquence, in celebrating present pleasure, and rejecting all distant views to fame, health, or fortune; it is obvious, that this practice is the source of all dissoluteness and disorder, repentance and misery' (EPM6.15, SBN 239–40).

Yet we are also able to recognize, when we are far enough away from either benefit, that the more distant one of them is greater and we even prefer to arrange to get it. George Ainslie presents these two different choices graphically. Metaphorically we may think of them as visual effects as follows. Before us is a short building and farther off there is a much taller building. In each case, the height of the building is proportionate to the benefit we would get from choosing it. If we are far away, the farther tall building looms high over the shorter building. But as we approach the two buildings, we eventually reach a point at which the shorter building completely blocks the view of the taller building, as though in fact the shorter building were taller than the other. Our changed perspective misleads us, and 'poorer goals that are close can loom larger than better, distant goals.'[35]

If we are designing institutions for more distant futures, we can readily see what is the greater prospect and we can design to cause us to get the better result. Specifically, we can design to block short-sighted actions in distant future times. If we are acting without the benefit of planning and using institutional devices, we may fail. We may therefore want to have institutions that seem superficially to be paternalistic. But if we choose to constrain ourselves, the arrangement is ours and is not paternalistic. In some of Hume's accounts of collective actions we might similarly choose to constrain ourselves if we can set up the relevant institutions while we are far enough away (in time) from having them help us make better choices. It would therefore be wrong to say that this device infringes our liberty.

Rights

Perhaps the most important single category of constraints to deal with perverse time preferences is the collection of rights that protect individuals against larger

---

[35] Ainslie, *Picoeconomics: The Strategic Interaction of Successive Motivational States within the Person*, 82–3.

groups and against the state and that therefore help to guarantee liberty. Hume is reluctant even to use the term rights because of its perverse associations. As Haakonssen notes, there were two traditions of rights prevalent in his day, both of them objectionable to Hume. On one view, rights are 'qualities of the person as a moral agent'; on the other they are derivative from Christian natural law.[36] Still, Hume's libertarian views require a positive regime of individual protections that we could only refer to as legal rights. The larger groups—and even the state—against which we might want protection may be extremely short-sighted in acting against the liberty of some individual and, by implication, setting up the possibility of such actions against others, including themselves in future contexts.

When we have a regime of legal rights, there can be collective implications of individual liberty and these may actually entail benefits to others from our own private liberty. In brief, the argument is this.[37] If, for example, my rights of free speech are abridged, typically by some local authority, I can take that authority to court to seek to have my rights protected and honored. When I do that, I automatically help to secure the rights of others in my society. Hence, although I ostensibly seek an individual benefit, I effectively help to provide a collective good. One might speak of this, in Mancur Olson's terminology, as an instance of a group that is privileged in the provision of its collective good.[38] One person values the good highly enough to provide it essentially for all.

Collective action on behalf of a whole society is typically hard to motivate. Action that has benefits to an enormous collection of people but that is justified already for a single individual is a rare category. Yet, through a bit of legal magic, the defense of individual rights often has this extraordinary collective quality. One commonly hears of the logic of rights. Securing collective interests through individual actions is the grand logic of rights that protect liberties. This logic also connects individual interests to mutual advantage in a deep and fundamentally important way, so that liberty itself serves mutual advantage, is even a mutual-advantage good, as in the argument for Austrian social theory above.

One might raise two objections to this argument. First, some might not actually value the right to free speech and might prefer to be able to block many kinds of speech rather than to protect it. Of course, that can be true; and it probably is true of most of the individual rights that are protected in any constitution that some people would rather they not be protected. It is still the

---

[36] Haakonssen, 'Hume's Political Theory,' 200.
[37] This discussion draws on Hardin, 'Democratic Aggregation.'
[38] Olson, The Logic of Collective Action.

case, however, that in defending my right to free speech I am simultaneously defending your right, whether you want to exercise that right or not.

Second, one might argue that, case by case, there will commonly be losers in any decision to protect someone's right. The reason to take one's case to court would be that someone else has blocked one's exercise of a right, and presumably that someone loses if the courts protect the right. Moreover a claim of right for one party often entails a claim that some other party has a duty, possibly a very onerous duty. Again, the issue here is not that each individual defense of a right is itself without losers—that is likely to be false. Rather, the issue is that protecting the right generally is desirable for certain citizens or even virtually all citizens ex ante, when laws are being drafted and adopted, even if not ex post when the laws are being applied to actual cases. The design of rights is ex ante, and it generally would not make sense to argue for a right exclusively in an individual context or case by case ex post. My defense of my right in a court case is, of course, ex post, but it is in defense of a right that was created ex ante and that is general and not specific to me and my present case. My successful defense helps secure that right for others ex ante.

Incidentally, although Thomas Jefferson (in the US 'Declaration of Independence') and others characterize certain rights as natural, the defense of the original Bill of Rights of the US constitution seems clearly to have been animated by the view that protection of these rights would serve the mutual advantage. Many of these rights are directed at abusive practices of the British Crown. There was possibly little chance that the new US government would ever have commandeered private homes to house its soldiers, but the English practice of doing so still rankled; and the US Congress strongly supported the adoption of an explicit constitutional prohibition of any such actions by the US government.

Today, it is probably far more common to defend rights in terms that were not those of the generation of James Madison by claiming that they contribute to Kantian or Millian autonomy. Madison's welfarist defense did not depend on such later views. In this respect, political theory is similar to legal theory. The best way to protect me legally against, say, theft is to have prohibitions on everyone, including me. I cannot expect any support for solipsistic law that prohibits all others but that allows license to me alone. Arguably, as Hobbes noted, law was brought into existence to limit the 'natural liberty' of particular individuals, the bad apples in our lot.[39] It does that by limiting all, even though some of us, perhaps even the overwhelming majority of us, might not require the constraints of law to keep us from major offenses against others.

---

[39] Hobbes, *Leviathan* 26.8 [138-9].

Interests and Consumptions

To be able to indulge my passions, I will need certain resources.[40] It is my interest to have these resources. Hume focuses on interests and utility, both at individual and collective levels, as what pleases and as what benevolence would address. Utility is treated by Jeremy Bentham as pleasure and absence of pain. This will not do for Hume. He says utility pleases, and he clearly does not mean this statement as a tautology; he means to be making a claim with bite. In many passages he seems to use the term as an alternative to interests. But then the focus on utility and interests as what motivate us and what please us is slightly odd. What directly pleases us is such things as good company, good food, and various other consumptions. Utility could be taken as a measure of the pleasure we get from our consumptions (including, for Hume, pleasure in the pleasure of others, especially those close to us). Or it could be taken as the full analog of interests, so that we can think of it as resources that will enable consumptions.[41] If I am pleased at the utility I get from a higher salary or a bountiful produce from my farm or business, I am pleased because this boon will bring additional consumptions. Somehow, we psychologically manage to take the resources as proxy for this further concern. We get indirect pleasure in some collection of as yet undefined consumptions.

Why then should we focus on interests and utility rather than on what directly pleases? In part the story is analogous to that of my taking pleasure in the pleasure of another, such as the child (mentioned in chapter 2) who enjoys peanut butter—something I would not enjoy at all. My sympathy with the child is with the more abstract pleasure as a general category rather than with the specific pleasure of the taste of peanut butter. One step removed from this, I also take pleasure in contemplating the future pleasure of my child as I arrange for some future treat for him. Similarly, I take pleasure in the opportunities that I might face for my own consumptions in the near future, opportunities for great pleasure, directly felt pleasure. What we need for Hume's kind of theory is a general category that can subsume all the details, which are not generalizable across people as the general category is. That general category is interests. Hume makes the clear distinction between resources and consumptions in a claim that a generous action is no more a losing expense than is 'the indulgence' of some personal pleasure, such as love of great wines or travel to exotic places (EPM9.20, SBN 281).

[40] See e.g. EPM App.2.12: SBN 301–2.
[41] See further, Hardin, 'The Normative Core of Rational Choice Theory.'

We could go further and say that giving someone greater resources might be more valuable to them than giving them some particular consumption, even if the latter should cost as much as the resources we might have given. (This might not be true for gifts to a child, who might not have an adequately vivid imagination of what pleasures the resources could bring.) Although I might be delighted to have a bottle of wine that costs $1,000, I would likely sooner have the money. With it I could buy a dozen or more bottles of very good wine, dinner for two or more at Jean-Georges (depending on the price of the wine), a week in the mountains or at the sea, the collected works of the Scottish Enlightenment, or—the list goes on. It is an article of faith among many contemporary economists that, keeping costs constant, welfare programs should therefore entail transfers of cash rather than of services. The services would be valued less than the money, because the money can be used in far more ways, and the particular services might not be valued by the recipient as highly as by the donor.

Against this standard policy argument, we might note that the transfer of specific goods, such as housing, medical care, or food, will also have less effect in reducing the recipients' incentives to earn money to buy other, preferred things.[42] Mill goes further with these policy issues than Hume does. He says that in all such cases of helping 'there are two sets of consequences to be considered; the consequences of the assistance itself, and the consequences of relying on the assistance. The former are generally beneficial, but the latter, for the most part, injurious; so much so, in many cases, as greatly to outweigh the value of the benefit. And this is never more likely to happen than in the very cases where the need of help is the most intense.'[43] For the second consequence, recall Hume's concern with the prospect of 'idleness and debauchery' (EPM2.18, SBN 180).

But the core problem for Hume's theory of moral approbation as the fundamental psychology of morality is merely that he needs a general category of what benefits us and of what pleases us both for ourselves and for others when we or they are benefited. Interest provides that category. Perhaps the force of our pleasure in some boon to our resources in its abstract promise of consumptions is so great that we react psychologically about as strongly as we would to the actual consumptions. In that case, by a psychological trick, we need not look beyond the resources or interests to be pleased by them. The very general and even abstract category of interests does Hume's job well enough for us to think of it as his value theory even though it is a means and

---

[42] See further, Hardin, *Morality within the Limits of Reason*, 162–5.
[43] Mill, *Principles of Political Economy* 5.11.13, 960.

not the kind of end that we normally think a value must be. Causally, it is merely one step removed from various ends, and psychologically it is often not even a step removed, at least on first apprehension of a boon to our resources. Interest is for Hume a psychological proxy for value.

Utility

Bentham defined utility ambiguously as both the value inherent in an object, as in the utility of a shovel, and as the value we get from it or from using it. The first is ostensibly objective and the latter is subjective. If I never want to dig, the shovel might be of no value to me. Bentham might readily have acknowledged the confusion in his writings of viewing utility both as objectively intrinsic to the objects we use and enjoy and as the subjective sum of our pleasures and pains. In his all too common definitional mode, he wrote: 'By utility is meant *that property in any object*, whereby it tends to produce benefit, advantage, pleasure, good, or happiness [or] to prevent the happening of mischief, pain, evil, or unhappiness to the party whose interest is considered.'[44]

In his richer explanatory mode, however, Bentham developed an account of utility as the net of pleasures and pains. Presumably, he would have expanded his conception of pleasures and pains and he would have attempted to master the much later developments in value theory—alas, mostly in economic value theory, because about a century ago philosophers abandoned the field to join Moore in contemplating the beauty and supposed utility of exquisite rocks far out in space where no sentient being would ever experience them.[45] After an arduous intellectual struggle of more than a century, economists had very nearly demolished the idea of objective value as inherent in objects, but in a few sentences Moore carried philosophy back to before Hume and Hobbes. Had the economists' ideas of the twentieth century been available in his time, Bentham surely would not have ignored them, although it might be unduly optimistic to suppose he would have got the issues entirely right.

Hume and Hobbes know better than to assign an objective value to any object even though they want to say that an object can be useful. For them, value is inherently subjective. Hence, when we read Hume today, we have to be alert to his meaning and to avoid Bentham's objective meaning. Still, for Hume it is the object or action or personal character that has or gives utility. He sometimes joins utility with usefulness, as though the two are synonymous.

---

[44] Bentham, *An Introduction to the Principles of Morals and Legislation* 1.3, 12, emphasis added.
[45] Moore, *Principia Ethica* 84.

And he applies the notion to a wide array of objects, the most important of which are virtues.

The accounts here of interests and utility help to clarify an issue in Hume's categorizations of particular virtues. Because they underlie the approbation of the institutions that benefit all citizens, he clearly holds justice and benevolence to be greater virtues than those of manners, wit, and so forth, and yet they are all virtues. Critics have remarked that we praise benevolence differently from the way we praise wit, as though perhaps to say that they must be not merely different things, but different kinds of thing. Our different attitudes toward them follow for the simple reason that benevolence is useful very generally, as when someone bestows money, so that it adds to the resources of the beneficiary. Wit has far less general value. It is a consumption good for those who observe it in another, because the wit we enjoy from another person cannot typically help us to obtain anything else that we might want or need, so that it is not 'useful' to us who enjoy it the way the person's benevolence would be useful. Wit may, however, be useful to the person who is witty, because it enables her to enjoy good company. Anyone who contributes to our interests or resources benefits us more than someone who, at similar cost, contributes a particular consumption—unless that consumption is one we would have bought at the relevant price, that is, at a price equivalent to the resources given to us.

Concluding Remarks

If individuals give heavy weight to welfare values, the Humean–Austrian vision is essentially utilitarian.[46] But even if individuals do not focus on welfare values, one can still think that a kind of Austrian laissez-faire is correct for social relations. Some society might not give heavy weight to welfare values and therefore need not be particularly utilitarian, but that would be because its citizens, as individuals, do not give heavy weight to welfare values. In the Austrian vision each citizen in such a society should be left free of constraint—subject to some variant of Mill's harm principle[47]—with the result that welfare would not be collectively very important even though it might be important to some individuals. The welfare of those to whom it is important might suffer substantially from the low level of overall productivity

---

[46] This would have to be ordinal utilitarianism, as in Hardin, *Morality within the Limits of Reason*, chap. 3.

[47] Mill, *On Liberty* 1.223−4

because, for example, my welfare is arguably more the result of the overall welfare of my own society than it is of my personal efforts. And in any case my welfare is heavily influenced by the range of opportunities provided by my society.

In our actual world, with the virtually inescapable interaction between states and peoples, it might be very difficult for any society to become autarkic in its social values and to give little weight to welfare values. It is difficult because in any society that is left very far behind in economic development, large sections of the populace are likely to want greater prosperity and to consume the kinds of things available elsewhere. Hence, we may experience what the critics of globalization bemoan, which is the seeming westernization of every society. A distressing aspect of such forces is that, although many people might wish to live in a non-westernized society, they can generally do so only at the price of suppressing the desires of their many compatriots who share many of the supposedly western values. It is not practicably possible to create genuinely autarkic societies that can survive without at least some of their citizenry succumbing to the blandishments of greater material prosperity.

It is perhaps in this Humean–Austrian vision of social order that we can see most clearly why economic and political theories are joined in the work of Hume and his heirs on into the twentieth-century rational-choice school. They are joined not because they have the same value theory, even though they generally assume, as Hume does, utilitarian individual values. The central, fundamental feature is, rather, that they are grounded in individual values, whatever those might be. Political philosophy need have no value theory at base. It can merely posit the structure of institutions that enable people to seek their own individual values.

It would be wrong, in the shibboleth of our time, to say that the institutions could be neutral, that is, that they would have no effect on what values people seek. A massively coercive religious state could have great impact on individual values, as seems to be shown by the cases of Iran under the Ayatollahs and of Afghanistan under the Taliban. But liberal economic and political institutions likely would substantially undercut such values. One individual immersed in a licentious society can find it difficult to sustain personal adherence to a rigidly religious or moralistic value system. Some value systems therefore seem likely to require specific institutional supports. In any case, it is prima facie false to suppose that any major social institution can be neutral with respect to all values or value systems.

What seems to be evident, however, is that individuals who are left to their own values commonly have strong welfarist preferences. Market economic and liberal political institutions allow them to pursue those values. In both cases, the central theoretical move is to create institutions that let individuals seek their own values, which in experienced fact generally means to seek their own welfare to a substantial extent. The institutions of market economics and of liberal politics are mutual-advantage, and in both economics and politics the underlying individual value theory is own-welfare. These two—own-welfare and mutual advantage—work very well together, the first at the individual level and the second at the aggregate level.

Critics of consumerism and welfarism (can one genuinely object to welfare?) often suppose that people are manipulated into having the strong welfarist urges that we witness. Barry Schwartz, for example, frames his criticism of contemporary welfarism as 'the battle for human nature'[48] —a battle that Hume helps to start, even declares with his *Treatise of Human Nature*. Hume, of course, supposes he is merely spelling out the human nature that is, while Schwartz thinks we are somehow choosing or at least influencing what human nature will be. The battle that Schwartz sees is carried out by academics with their variant visions of human nature. That would be merely an academic debate, perhaps even in the derogatory sense of that phrase. Sometimes, Schwartz's claim seems, however, to be that economic theory has itself reformed the values of masses of people. This seems implausible without a lot of argument to demonstrate the intervening causal connections between academic visions and popular visions. What seems far more likely is that individuals put in the way of various material and non-material pleasures find them to be very appealing and they seek them, work for them, and give over much of their lives for them.

[48] Schwartz, *The Battle for Human Nature.*

9

Retrospective

> The whole scheme ... of law and justice is advantageous to the society and
> to every individual; and 'twas with a view to this advantage, that men,
> by their voluntary conventions establish'd it. After it is once establish'd
> by these conventions, it is *naturally* attended with a strong sentiment of
> morals; which can proceed from nothing but our sympathy with the
> interests of society.[1]

Let us pull together some strands of argument that arise in scattered places
throughout this book. The main points are noted in the brief but densely packed
epigraph above. First, I will discuss Hume's sometimes explicit, sometimes
implicit views of other moral theories—as opposed to strictly political theories.
I will also compare Hume to his forerunners, Hobbes, who seems to have
set out the main initial problems for Hume's own theory of social order,
and Locke, who is one of Hume's greatest antagonists in political philosophy
even while he is an important influence in Hume's epistemology.[2] There are
others to whom one might instructively compare Hume at length, such as
Hume's friend Smith,[3] who had related views, especially on liberty and the
relation between politics and commerce, and whose economic theories were
substantially influenced by Hume; or Francis Hutcheson, who in the view of
some had extensive influence on the structure of Hume's moral theory, with
its focus on sympathy, anti-rationalism, and the roles of the passions and reason
in moral approbation;[4] or Rawls, to whom I have made some comparisons,
especially in the discussion of distributive justice in chapter 3.[5] Rawls has also

---

[1] T3.3.1.12, SBN 579–80. I read 'which can proceed from nothing but' to mean 'there can be no
other source but.'

[2] On Locke's influence in epistemology, see Owen, 'Hume's Doubts about Probable Reasoning,'
and *Hume's Reason*, 124–7; Stewart, 'Hume's Historical View of Miracles.'

[3] See e.g. Skinner, 'David Hume: Principles of Political Economy'; Árdal, *Passion and Value in
Hume's Treatise*, 133–47; Haakonssen, *The Science of a Legislator*; and Raphael, '"The True Old
Humean Philosophy" and Adam Smith.'

[4] But see Moore, 'Hume and Hutcheson.'

[5] For surveys, see contributions to Stewart and Wright, *Hume and Hume's Connexions*.

written extensively on Hume, and I have discussed his often critical views in relevant contexts.

Hobbes, Hume, and Rawls are among the greatest political philosophers. The pairs have very much in common but they also differ in significant ways that set them apart. Hobbes and Rawls both have strong rationalist tendencies, Rawls especially in verging on Kantianism; Hume is rigorously naturalistic and anti-rationalist. The other two also have tendencies to suppose there is an objective good or right, whereas Hume thinks any claim to moral goodness or rightness is merely a psychological feeling because such claims cannot be matters of truth or falsity.

Hume supposes that we are all pleased by utility, foremost our own utility. He is therefore held by some writers to be a strictly egoistic hedonist. That view is prima facie wrong because he holds that we are typically moved by benevolence, so much indeed that our concern for all others together, primarily for those nearest us, may outweigh our self-love (T3.2.2.6, SBN 487). Psychologically, therefore, we are partially egoist and partially benevolent—it seems implausible that anyone could claim otherwise but probably somewhere there is an artful philosopher—someone 'trained in a philosophical system'[6]—who does claim otherwise. If we were not partially benevolent, Hume's entire edifice of artificial virtues would collapse and be of no interest to him or us. He recognizes that it needs at least a dollop of beneficence to cement it in place. It is therefore contradictory to virtually the whole of his argument to suppose he is solely egoistic. It would perhaps be most reasonable to say that he valued only individual benefits, that he had no collective or social values other than those that are the result or aggregate of individual values. You must be pleased by the utility of social institutions, for example, because that utility consists in their service to individuals including, at least in tendency, yourself. In this vision, Hume was at one with twentieth-century economic value theory nearly two centuries ahead of that theory.

Perhaps in our time Hume would find himself most at home with the social theory of the Austrian school of economics. He argues persuasively that the economic developments of the time and political liberty are strongly associated. His central point is that the growth of economic decentralization and of the individualism of the economic changes contribute to the growth of political liberty and parliamentary government.[7] Smith thinks this is the

---

[6] This is Hume's disparaging phrase for those who ground political obligation in a promise to obey ('Of the Original Contract,' 481).

[7] Rotwein, *David Hume: Writings on Economics*, pp. ci–cii.

most important of all the effects of the growth of commerce and manufactures and, perhaps too generously, attributes the insight to Hume.[8] More generally, Hume's commitments to liberty, individualism, and mutual advantage partially depend on his recognizing that information is not available to government but is widely distributed (he also supposes that the incentives of government are often distorted) and that distributing discovery widely through the society rather than controlling it through a hierarchy is the path to rapid development and prosperity. Therefore he thinks that government should be kept small and not intrusive, as he argues in his varied essays on economics, such as his argument against mercantilism.[9]

Alternative Visions of Morality

Hume often displays strong views about moral theories of his era. He seems to object not only to the misfit of the theories with our psychology but also to the content of the theories. We might attempt to infer what Hume must think, from within his own account of moral psychology, of alternative systems or accounts of morality—not only those he addresses but also others, including others that gained greater currency after his time. For almost all of what philosophers mean when they speak of ethics, Hume is partially beside the point, because his focus is on explaining our commitments and views, not on justifying, correcting, or asserting them (except in the occasional 'sally of panegyric'). Moral theory is primarily the enterprise of justifying or criticizing the content of morality in various theories or accounts, or even in real world instantiations in popular morality (Hume's vulgar systems). Because almost all moral views until Hume's time make and seem to require claims about people or idealized versions of people, psychological issues seem likely to matter. One might claim that Kant's program, half a century after Hume, is founded on the elimination of any role for psychology in morality, particularly the elimination of many of Hume's passions, for Kant's idealized rational beings.

Alternative justifications of the state might be seen as parts of general moral theories, but these are addressed in chapter 5 and will not be taken up here. For example, we have already considered Hume's rejection of contractarian explanation and justification of the state (T3.2.2.9–10, SBN 489–90; T3.2.8.5, SBN 543–4) and need not take up contractarian or consensualist arguments here, although there is now a recent branch (with many twigs) of consensualist

---

[8] Smith, *Wealth of Nations* 3.4.412.   [9] See e.g. Hume, 'Of the Jealousy of Trade.'

moral theory, sometimes under the label of contractualism.[10] Let us address only certain tendencies that Hume objects to or clearly would: rationalist moral theory, religious ethics, and intuitionism. Also let us discuss the Socratic identification of morality and interest, about which Hume in his panegyric moments is perhaps ambivalent. We might also discuss natural law, but it has much in common with intuitionism and rationalism in some of its variants and with theological views in other variants.

Rationalist Moral Theory

A Humean writing today would immediately think of Kant and contemporary Kantian views as probably the leading example of rationalist morality, although there were others in Hume's time. Hume generally attacks merely a view, not nameable advocates of it. The view he attacks is that morality consists in acting according to a rule of right (EPM App. 1.9, SBN 288–9), as in Kantian rationalism. Kant's very clever derivation of ethics from an analysis of the kingdom of ends (that is, of fully rational beings) is beside the point on Hume's analysis. It transfers morality for an ideal world to our all-too-real and un-ideal world. Hume's empiricism and perhaps especially his discussion of the circumstances of justice say why he thinks this is a specious move.[11] Moreover, Hume attacks head on any deontological morality that stipulates rightness and wrongness of actions as its substantive core. 'Actions per se, not proceeding from any constant principle, … are never considered in morality' (T3.3.1.4, SBN 575). This should be read: Because they do not proceed from any constant principle but can follow from varied kinds of motive, actions per se can be neither right nor wrong in general. Hume is rigorously anti-deontological. Rules for action per se have no normative valence (unless the rules include normative claims, for example, about the effect of the actions on interests).

In general, all views that reach supposedly true conclusions must be wrong. Morality is not a matter of truth or falsity. What can be handled by reason is capable of being true or false; morality is not. It therefore cannot come under the purview of reason. Therefore laudable and blamable are not related to reasonable and unreasonable (T3.1.1.9, SBN 458). Although this view is sometimes assimilated to Hume's skepticism, it is not a matter of his vaunted skepticism, which is epistemological and is about our assessments of evidence.

[10] See Gauthier, *Morals by Agreement*; Scanlon, *What We Owe to Each Other*; Darwall, *Contractarianism / Contractualism*.

[11] See T3.2.5–7, T3.2.2.16–18, SBN 486–8, 494–5; and more fully in EPM3.1–13, SBN 183–8. The arguments are summarized in chapter 6.

His epistemological skepticism is not about meaning[12]—Hume can suppose a statement is meaningful but doubt any proof of its truth. Hume's skepticism about induction of causal relations from correlations of facts is epistemological. His rejection of objective truths of morality, both personal and social, turns on not accepting objective moral claims as meaningful or intelligible. This is not skepticism about evidence. It is more or less positivist and analytical. Hume thinks there are no moral facts of the relevant kind, not that we cannot be sure of them or cannot demonstrate their truth by investigation of some kind. There is no evidence whose truth or falsity we can even investigate. Hume's frontal assault on the truth of claims of substantive moral principles does not entail that he lacks the sympathy to be pleased when people's interests are well served, when they feel pleasure but not pain. Indeed, it does not entail that he cannot approve, with his own passions, all of these things.

Religious Ethics

Hume rejects religious explanations or justifications of morality and he excoriates the practice in his time of assimilating morality to religious views. In his lifetime he was reluctant to publish his fuller views on religion, which often reduce it to the ridiculous. As J. C. A. Gaskin says, Hume's views on religion have since been recognized as 'terminally destructive.'[13] His more extensive views were published in two very sharply argued books, one of them published posthumously.[14] In the *Treatise*, however, where his concern is with epistemology and therefore with the supposed truth of any religious belief that has no empirical backing, he says: 'Generally speaking, the errors of religion are dangerous; those in philosophy only ridiculous' (T1.4.7.13, SBN 272).[15] This is a statement that he could as acutely make in the context of his political philosophy, because it has been in matters of control of politics that religion has been most appallingly destructive and bloody. Philosophy may often have led particular philosophers into absurdity and absurd practices in their lives; but until roughly the twentieth century it had not gained a grip on politics. Since gaining such a grip, it may have wreaked even more destruction than religion has done.

Hume explains why philosophers in the centuries before him have given us such different theories than the ancients did: 'In later times, philosophy of all kinds, especially ethics, have been more closely united with theology than

[12] See in general, Fogelin, *Hume's Skepticism in the* Treatise of Human Nature.
[13] Gaskin, *Hume's Philosophy of Religion*, 1.
[14] Hume, *Dialogues Concerning Natural Religion* and *The Natural History of Religion*.
[15] See further, Livingston, *Hume's Philosophy of Common Life*, 311–13.

ever they were observed to be among the Heathens; and as this latter science admits of no terms of composition, but bends every branch of knowledge to its own purpose, without much regard to the phaenomena of nature, or to the unbiassed sentiments of the mind, hence reasoning, and even language, have been warped from their natural course, and distinctions have been endeavoured to be established, where the difference of the objects was, in a manner, imperceptible' (EPM App. 4.21, SBN 322).[16] Divines under the disguise of philosophers cannot be trusted to deal with morality without religious bias.

Moreover, divines disguised as philosophers tend to treat 'all morals, as on a like footing with civil laws, guarded by the sanctions of reward and punishment,' and therefore they make the distinction between *voluntary* and *involuntary* action 'the foundation of their whole theory.' Against such usage, Hume insists that we must daily blame and praise *sentiments* that 'have objects beyond the dominion of the will or choice.' It therefore 'behoves us, if not as moralists, as speculative philosophers at least, to give some satisfactory theory and explication' of these sentiments, as Hume's psychological theory does (EPM App. 4.21, SBN 322). It is Hume's misfortune to have to write against the religiosity of his day. In the beginning he has to react to Samuel Clarke and near the end he has to suffer the reactions of James Beattie, whom Hume dismisses as 'that bigoted silly fellow' and who calls Hume 'stupid' in print.[17] Religion was not a saving grace in the world of philosophy. Bigotry ran wild in the society of Hume and Beattie, and silly Beattie was received with great acclaim.

One suspects that Hume thinks religion is itself the biggest error of religion. Hume challenges those who insist that order in the universe necessarily requires a divine orderer: 'To say, that the different Ideas, which compose the Reason of the supreme Being, fall into Order, of themselves, and by their own Nature, is really to talk without any precise Meaning. If it has a Meaning, I wou'd fain know, why it is not as good Sense to say, that the Parts of the material World fall into Order, of themselves, and by their own Nature? Can the one Opinion be intelligible, while the other is not so?'[18] This is merely skepticism about the claims of truth for religious views. This is scorn: 'Survey most nations and most ages. Examine the religious principles, which have, in fact, prevailed in the world. You will scarcely be persuaded, that they are other than sick men's dreams: Or perhaps will regard them more as the playsome whimsies of

---

[16] As Schneewind ('Introduction,' 2) remarks, Hume's purpose is to explain how the world looks, including our moral beliefs, 'without any reliance on religious doctrine.'

[17] Mossner (*The Life of David Hume*, 577–8) sees that response as an ironic dismissal of the work.

[18] Hume, *Dialogues Concerning Natural Religion* 4. 185–6.

monkeys in human shape, than the serious, positive, dogmatical asseverations of a being, who dignifies himself with the name of rational.'[19]

Many people, especially religious fundamentalists, think their good is other than utility—at least in this life. The epistemology of their views is corrupted, however, by how they came to the views.[20] Indeed, we must want a sociological explanation for why people in a certain region or social group have their particular views while people in a different region or group have contrary views—even contradictory and hostile views. The views people hold cannot be explained by the truth of the views—for example, by their persuasiveness to anyone who did not grow up into the views. This is exactly the program of Hume in accounting for moral views—not surprisingly, because he says religion 'is nothing but a species of philosophy.'[21] For Hume, religious views share with substantive moral views the defect of being neither true nor false in that there is no evidence either way for them. There is, however, one perverse bit of evidence about religious views. Strictly contrary religious views cannot all be true. Therefore most religious views must be false insofar as they include different claims of fact, such as claims that some deity exists, that there will be an afterlife, or that some deity created the universe in a particular way.

Intuitionism (Innate Moral Knowledge)

Intuitionist ethics is discussed in chapter 1, and there is little to add here other than Hume's views on it and its rise partially in response to his philosophy. Thomas Reid, a major later figure in the Scottish Common Sense school of intuitionist philosophy, misunderstands Hume's central arguments from a failure to grasp just how far he was willing to go in claiming that there are no moral truths of the form of saying that action X or outcome Y is morally right or wrong, good or bad. Reid's *Inquiry into the Human Mind*, which was published in 1764 shortly after Hume saw it in manuscript, is an attack on Hume's epistemology. Hume seems to have given up on trying to correct its errors and merely gracefully commented on it, mentioning a single turn of phrase that was infelicitous English.[22] Hume almost automatically was inclined to reject Reid's work just because Reid was a parson and therefore likely to argue for a conclusion rather than reach a conclusion after argument.[23] Reid's eventual arguments that we just do know many moral things from simple

---

[19] Hume, *The Natural History of Religion* 15. 94.

[20] Hardin, 'The Economics of Religious Belief.'

[21] EHU 11. 146.   [22] Mossner, *The Life of David Hume*, 298–300.

[23] This may be unfair in Reid's case, but it seems to fit his view that Hume's skepticism is dangerous (Haakonssen, 'Introduction and Commentary,' 40).

intuition without any argument or investigation—this is supposed Common Sense—justify Hume's skepticism about him.

The more important work of Reid for our purposes of grasping moral and political theory was published long after Hume's death. In the later work Reid rejects Hume's views entirely. In Hume all we have are psychological judgments of the virtuous, very much like esthetic judgments of the beautiful. The virtuous and the beautiful cannot be subjected to tests of truth and they will not be universally seen as virtuous or beautiful. We see actions or characters as virtuous insofar as they are useful and therefore pleasing. Against these claims, Reid says, 'It is true, that every virtue is both agreeable and useful in the highest degree; and that every quality that is agreeable or useful, has a merit upon that account. But virtue has a merit peculiar to itself, a merit which does not arise from its being useful or agreeable, but from its being virtue. This merit is discerned by the same faculty by which we discern it to be virtue, and by no other.'[24] We could go on for many pages of bravado assertion that we just do know what is right and wrong, good and bad, virtue and vice. In a world of widely differing views of these beliefs, it is odd to claim that we all just do know any of this. A tiny bit of Hume's empiricism would sweep all such talk from the table.

An even stranger misreading than Reid's is that of the supposedly sympathetic J. Y. T. Grieg, who says that Hume is a moral sense theorist, holding that 'man is endowed with a special moral sense (conscience), which enables him, as soon as all the circumstances in a given case are known, to pronounce, without further processes of reasoning, whether an action or character is virtuous or vicious.'[25] That would roughly make Hume hold Reid's positions, a conclusion that would astonish both Hume and Reid. Many of Hume's critics seem simply not to believe he means what he says. Or perhaps they do not understand; after all, how can someone so cheerful be so pessimistic about knowledge, especially knowledge of the good? But Hume so thoroughly undercuts claims of moral truth that his critics have to invent new ways to find and authenticate moral truths. The main ways in his time were common sense and moral intuition, which are very close relatives. (Kant moves in the other direction, toward reason. But his appeal to transcendental reason comes after Hume's time, and I will not address it other than to suggest that Hume would reject its anti-empiricist stance.)

We can argue in several ways against the broad collection of theorists who hold that we just do happen to have moral knowledge in our heads. Obviously, Hume can argue against the crippled and inexplicable epistemology of such

---

[24] Reid, *Essays on the Active Powers of the Human Mind*, 404.   [25] Grieg, *David Hume*, 22–3.

views. But he also argues against the intellectual possibility that we could have all of the requisite knowledge to cover any reasonably complex issue of social order somehow in our heads. We have to learn other relatively complex things, such as language and the facts of how to negotiate life in our society. Unlike these wonderfully useful things that require great effort for us to master them, innate moral knowledge just happens to be already there, ready for use at a moment's notice. To see that the demands of such a view are incredible, let us argue from merely a single topic of interest to Hume: property. Here the issue is not whether we have innate ideas, but that such ideas cannot fit our moral views as established in law in the matters of justice and property. Despite the inordinate variety of them, diverse laws on property can all be right in the sense that they all serve the general interest. Innate ideas must be more specific than this. Hence, property is not an innate idea. Its morality is not grounded in intuition (EPM3.42, SBN 202).

If one notes that property is not a simple, pure thing that the individual owns, but that it virtually always has constraints placed on it by the larger society, it is not only libertarians who instantly object that then it is not really property. A few minutes' discussion convinces almost everyone of the meaningfulness of variation in laws on ownership, for example, of the mineral rights underneath a piece of privately owned land, or of restrictions on uses of property that have external effects. An extreme example is the necessity of constraints on building in Amsterdam, where the liquidity of the soil means that all building foundations are inherently tied together, so that no one can simply tear down a building without making arrangements to hold up buildings next to it. Dutch restrictions on property rights strike virtually everyone, including libertarians, as mutually advantageous and as clearly acceptable. As Hume says, property rights are de facto a bundle of vastly many conditions, laws, and so forth that cannot be contained in countless volumes. All of this could be understood as a result of efforts to address interests. It could not readily be subsumed in a catalog of reams of innate knowledge.

As an aside, note that Smith's theory of moral sentiments is often compared to Hume's moral theory. If sympathy (and sentiments) come from mirroring, then it is psychologically almost impossible that Smith's moral spectator, looking on from outside, can react the way an ordinary person can through mirroring the moral responses of others. The moral spectator might generalize from others' reactions to yours in this moment or from the mutual advantage to any individual's interests, but that gives reason a very large role, far more than Hume wishes to give it, in our moral judgments and assessments. No moral spectator can do what Hume's account requires for us to reach moral judgments. Smith therefore takes us toward moral sense theories and intuitionism and away from Hume.

Identity of Morality and Interest

There is a view, commonly identified with Socrates, that doing the good or observing the right is in our interest. In social theory, this view appears to be founded on a major logical error: a fallacy of composition. Such fallacies in the aggregation from individual to collective choice or good are a standard background problem for modern choice theory. We are guilty of a fallacy of composition when, without argument, we assume that the attributes of an entity are the attributes of its constituents. This is a form of metaphorical or analogical reasoning that might sometimes accidentally yield correct results, but it often leads us astray. For example, we argue from the premise that every individual is rational to the conclusion that a nation or a group of individuals is rational in the same sense. It is only a slight exaggeration to say that contemporary rational-choice political theory is essentially an effort to block conclusions that are fallacies of composition.[26]

Perhaps the central claim in Socrates's political philosophy is that it is in an individual's interest to act justly, to be just. This claim contradicts appearances that we, Glaucon in Plato's *Republic*, and others cannot deny. Through long bits of brilliant, diabolical, hectoring dialogue, Socrates essentially denies that there is a fallacy of composition in going from what is best for the community to what is best for the individual. It takes a great deal of devious argument and an adoring audience for him to seem convincing. Many teenage university students have since been hectored into accepting Socrates's conclusion and have therefore misconceived politics and group action from the beginnings of their supposed understanding. Perhaps it does not require more hectoring than it does merely because the fallacy is remarkably easy and seemingly natural, even for people who give the lie to its content with every second action they take.

Long after the reign of Greek philosophy, the church secured a match between individual interest and morality by inventing everlasting punishment for immorality, a move that Hume excoriates. In effect, the church established a causal motivational connection between individual and collective good to

---

[26] The three biggest bodies of work in rational-choice political theory—the aggregation of individual into collective preferences in Kenneth Arrow's impossibility theorem, the rational-choice theory of voting and democracy, and the logic of collective action—are deflations of fallacies of composition, as is the prisoner's dilemma game, which is related to the collective action and voting problems. For varied discussions of these, see Barry and Hardin, *Rational Man and Irrational Society?*

replace the failed conceptual connection. The causal connection it created makes full use of self-interest.

Eventually Hobbes and others demolish the fallacy of composition at the heart of Socrates's claims. In his allegory of the state of nature, Hobbes explicitly supposes that individuals would naturally follow their own interests and that the result would be collective misery. There is no beneficial composition. This result gives license to Hobbes's invocation of an all-powerful sovereign to bring harmony and well-being, because it can generally be my interest to act well toward others only if there is a government prepared to coerce both me and the others to behave well. In three short chapters, arguably the best such concentrated great argument in the history of political philosophy, Hobbes lays the foundations for rational choice theory and for a major branch of political philosophy thereafter.[27] A rational choice theorist might finally wish to say that Hobbes is the first modern political philosopher because he is the first to recognize and be persistent in avoiding fallacies of composition inherent in much of political philosophy before him (and, alas, since).[28] Hume continues the assault on claims from the fallacy of composition. He also brings self-love and benevolence into the complexly broad tent of our values while recognizing that they inherently conflict in many contexts. Sidgwick makes this split the main divide in his survey of systems of ethics from egoism to utilitarianism. Almost no theorist now holds Socrates's view.[29]

Yet, Hume famously asks, 'what theory of morals can ever serve any useful purpose, unless it can show, by a particular detail, that all the duties which it recommends, are also the true interest of each individual?' (EPM9.16, SBN 280) Doing what is right is in one's interest. That sounds Socratic. In some ways and contexts, it is not Socratic because Hume's system accomplishes this matching of individual and collective interests through all of the devices of his artificial virtues, many of which entail the creation of *institutions to make it our interest* to do what is in the mutual advantage. Mutual-advantage political institutions are organized to achieve their outcomes through the ordinary choices and actions of individuals who act from their own pragmatic incentives. These institutions do not require extensive individual commitment to values other than their own interest. This works because the mutual advantage of all is de facto the

---

[27] Hobbes, *Leviathan* chaps. 13–15.

[28] For example, after Socrates, Aristotle begins his *Politics* with his own variant fallacy of composition. He supposes that, because every man acts with the intention of producing something that is a good, the polis, the most sovereign association of men, must pursue the most sovereign of goods. Aristotle's views have often been taught less with hectoring than with the weight of authority, but they too have set beginners on the path of confusion.

[29] But see Raz, *The Morality of Freedom*, chap. 12.

collective implication of self-interest. Moreover, because mutual advantage is a collective principle, not an individual principle, and is therefore normatively different from own-welfare, the theory that recommends such institutions is inherently both normative and pragmatic in its implications.

In the passage that includes this query of Hume's, he goes on to claim that it is clearly in our interest to comply with the ordinary personal virtues, so much so that it would be superfluous to prove the claim. Moralists should therefore spare their pains in advocating these virtues. 'To what purpose collect arguments to evince that temperance is advantageous, and the excesses of pleasure hurtful. When it appears that these excesses are only denominated such, because they are hurtful' (EPM9.17, SBN 280). Anyone with a hangover knows the virtue of moderation in drinking. The real issues are the 'enlarged virtues of humanity, generosity, beneficence' (EPM9.19, SBN 281). Hume praises these here in a way that he earlier calls a 'sally of panegyric' (EPM2.5, SBN 177). His panegyrics, however, *are the kind of thing that his psychological theory explains*; they are not part of the content of a substantive moral theory that he is proposing.

The main addition here is the important observation, in keeping with the discussion of interests versus consumptions in chapter 8, that my generosity to others is just another way of consuming something that I enjoy, as much as I might enjoy spending an outrageous sum to have very good seats at an opera. It is therefore a misconception to think of acting on such virtues as somehow especially contrary to our interests. It is as contrary to our interests as is doing anything else that might please us. But in the final section of the *Enquiry* Hume seems to be saying not that such enjoyments are merely that—particular enjoyments among many others—but that they are somehow superior for the peace of mind and other benefits they bring to the virtuous person. In its relation to virtually all of the rest of his discussions of moral and political theory, this claim is panegyric. It may well have been true for him as he lived his life. Unless vast numbers of people are mistaken in their assessments of their own interests, however, the claim is false for them and therefore irrelevant to Hume's moral theory in general. It is an idiosyncratic personal fact, not a moral-theoretic truth.

Hume's Forerunners in Political Philosophy

Although the explication of various political theories other than that of Hume is not the focus here, it might be instructive to consider the political theories of Hobbes and Locke, as Hume's two great Anglo-Saxon forerunners. In the case of Hobbes, Hume essentially offers corrections to his political sociology. These corrections help to keep his own theory clear for us. In the case of Locke, he rejects the theory outright, sometimes with seeming contempt. Hence, Hume corrects Hobbes but dismisses Locke, and his grounds for rejecting the latter seem to play a role in political criticisms of Hume after his time. Locke's political theory became the background philosophy of Whig politics, so that rejection of Locke's social science was apparently taken as rejection of the Whig program and, by implication, support for Tory policies.

We could draw Hume into the future by comparing him with Mill and Rawls. I have made some remarks on these two along the way, but they are not as systematically parallel in their interests as Hobbes and Locke. Indeed, they take for granted what the three earlier philosophers see as the central issue to be understood: social order. Also, of course, Hume is not responding to them, so that comparisons would tell us less about his views. The one big area in which he differs from Rawls and very modern sensibilities more generally is in his dismissal of concern with distributive justice (as discussed in chapter 3).

Locke

Central moves in Locke involve moralizing particular actions, and his political theory is founded on two instances of deducing an ought from an is. As C. B. Macpherson says, Locke, 'the acknowledged proponent of the bourgeois state from the Whig revolution on, was the confused man's Hobbes.'[30] A major confusion is his moralizing of actions, a violation of Hume's dictum against deriving ought from is (or, more accurately in this case, founding ought in is). Locke does this in at least two very important parts of his theory: his labor theory of property and his contractarian justification of political obligation. Consider these in turn.

Locke argues that the mixing of one's labor with a piece of land makes the land one's private property.[31] In Tolstoy's 'How Much Land Does a Man Need?' Pahom is allowed to make as much land his own as he can walk around before the sun sets; he has only to mark its corners and to pay a small fee (forfeited if he does not get back to his starting point before sunset). He attempts to acquire an excessively large farm by running the whole day.[32] His action, of course, is a legal action taken under the perhaps loose auspices of a state. Locke's action is in a state of nature without backing from a state. Hobbes had long before sensibly declared that the idea of property is a legal

---

[30] Macpherson, 'Introduction: Hobbes, Analyst of Power and Peace,' 25.
[31] Locke, *Two Treatises of Government*, 2.5, §27, 288.
[32] Tolstoy, 'How Much Land Does a Man Need?'

idea, that notions of right and wrong, justice and injustice, and property have no place in the state of nature before government. They are qualities that relate to men in society.[33] Property has no meaning in a state of nature because it has no legal backing by a state there. Locke's labor theory of property is supposed to give it a moral meaning before it gets a legal meaning—and eventually to determine its legal meaning.

For Hume, there can be notions of possession in a stable small society without government, but the conventions of possession do not make it property, which is a legal matter; they certainly do not make possession or property a morally prior principle; and they cannot elevate Locke's labor theory of property. Hume casually and easily demolishes the claim that mixing one's labor with anything makes that thing one's property. Hume says there are things that clearly cannot work that way, such as grazing one's cattle on the commons. And the idea of mixing labor with property is at best a figurative notion. Moreover, there are other principles that seem clearly to trump Locke's mixing of labor (T3.2.3.6 n, SBN 505–6 n). Indeed, there is no simple principle to determine ownership in all cases.

Locke's contractarianism similarly moralizes an action, the action of agreeing.[34] How does the act of agreement make moral? Clearly it does not do so per se, not even in ostensibly contractarian agreement. There are two trivially obvious limits on the right-making power of agreement. We can agree on some future action now and then come to realize at the relevant moment that fulfilling our agreement would be harmful or bad in some way that would trump the good of fulfilling the agreement, as Nekhlyudov came to believe that his growing religious commitments trump his presumed engagement to Missy. Moreover, we can even agree to do some reprehensible thing, such as murdering someone. Mere agreement does not then make our actions in fulfilling our promise right. Even Locke's consent to form a government has to reduce to majority consent thereafter. Majority consent cannot generally be expected to lead to results that we would think good or right, unless we merely define majority consent as right per se independently of the majority's decisions. One might well suppose that procedurally we cannot do better than this, but that is a claim for compromise, not for inherent morality.

Because agreement per se is inadequate to make the objects of our agreements moral, many contemporary contractarians call themselves contractualists and they add the qualification 'reasonable,' so that it is only reasonable agreement that successfully moralizes our agreeing. Unfortunately, that word then carries all of the normative burden, virtually leaving agreement out of

---

[33] Hobbes, *Leviathan* 13.13 [63].   [34] Locke, *Two Treatises of Government*, 2.8.

discussion.[35] The qualification 'reasonable' must apply both to the object of the agreement and to the form or method of reaching agreement. The term essentially covers, with a seemingly persuasive definition, for lack of a genuine theory. Vagueness does not, however, salvage the case for the morality of agreement.

Hume and Hobbes know better than to moralize a mere action as such, to infer an ought from an is, and Hume writes the formula that makes the point clear for all of us since. Neither Hobbes nor Hume would countenance such moves as entailed in Locke's labor theory of property, and at least Hume would reject Locke's contractarian justification of political obligation; Hume says 'nothing can be more absurd than this position' (EPM App. 3.7, SBN 306). Unfortunately, without those two moves, Locke's political theory collapses. In Bertram Laing's summary, 'The theory of a contract stresses the idea of right and holds that government is, and must be, founded on right. There are rights antecedent to government and even society; and the latter are created to guarantee these rights, which set limits to them. The rights possessed by a government must be considered by reference to these antecedent rights.'[36] For Hume, this is all wrong. Against Locke's theory, Hume agrees with Hobbes that there is scarce any government in the world 'whose beginnings can in conscience be justified.'[37]

Unfortunately for Hume, Locke's views were those of the Whigs, for whom the finer philosophical points were likely irrelevant but for whom the moral appeals, however fictional, of the Lockean vision of government by the consent of the people were seized vigorously. Whigs also argued from supposedly pure reason and abstract principles, against Hume's strong rejection of founding morals and politics in such reason. The Whig party got its odd name in 1680,[38] at about the time that Locke was writing his *Two Treatises of Government*.[39] Locke, the Whig philosopher,[40] was involved in English politics through Shaftesbury and others. His rationalism and his idea of consent in the social contract were Whig doctrines, although his theory of property may have played no role outside his own philosophy. To criticize Locke's views, as Hume did very forcefully, was to criticize Whig views, and that was seen as a political action.[41]

Hobbes

Parallel readings of the two suggest that Hobbes is Hume's closest theorist of political order, but Hume's strategic analysis far outruns Hobbes's. Because of

---

[35] Hardin, 'Reasonable Agreement: Political Not Normative.'   [36] Laing, *David Hume*, 210.

[37] Hobbes, *Leviathan*, 'A Review and Conclusion,' ¶8 [392].

[38] Hume, *History of England* 6. 381.

[39] Laslett, 'Introduction,' 67. Laslett speculates on various dates, generally around 1680.

[40] Ibid. 53.   [41] See Laing, *David Hume*, 202–10.

the similarity of vocabulary and the issues in their focus, it appears that Hume is often responding to Hobbes, although he rejects much of what Hobbes says, especially his social scientific and contractarian claims. Hume has many often striking affinities to Hobbes, so that one suspects Hume knew Hobbes's writings very well or that he immediately found much of Hobbes's argument intellectually congenial. Dugald Stewart was convinced that Hume studied at least some of Hobbes's writings with utmost care.[42] Even a prima facie reading of the two suggests that Hume knew the arguments of Hobbes's *Leviathan* very well. The central problem for both is social order.

Hobbes uses the device of a social compact or contract as one of two possible ways to get a state established, but any obligation that you or I have to that state follows from its capacity to enforce its will once it is in place, not from the way it has come into being. Indeed, Hobbes does not think we are morally bound, and *obligation* is therefore the wrong term here unless its meaning is that we are merely coercively obliged to be obedient, so that it is in our interest. Hobbes seems to be ambivalent or confused on this issue. He struggles with arguments that we are obligated by our contract with our fellow citizens even though he generally insists that contracts have value only if they will be enforced by a greater power. Without that threat, they are worthless.[43] He similarly says the 'artificial chains, called *civil laws*' that we have created by mutual contract, although in their nature weak, 'may nevertheless be made to hold, by the danger (though not by the difficulty) of breaking them.'[44] Even then, he says that there probably never was a state that arose from compact. Rather, all extant governments evidently arose from conquest, internal or external, at some stage.[45] As morally compromised as that might seem to make a government, we are nevertheless obliged to obey the government because it has the power to coerce us. Hume openly and cogently ridicules the idea of the social contract.[46]

Before we turn to affinities, note that there are two very general contexts in which they seem not to agree. First, Hobbes lived in a time when the evidence of the day suggested that anarchy and lack of a powerful government must be disastrous. In the final paragraph of *Leviathan*, he says that his work is 'occasioned by the disorders of the present time.'[47] Hume lived in one of the most pleasing eras of human history and his evidence said that people can be sweet and cooperative without the threat of the sovereign's sword hanging over them. They are both empiricists—Hobbes less than Hume—and their different views

---

[42] Stewart, *Collected Works* I. 84.   [43] Hobbes, *Leviathan* 14.7   [44] Ibid. 21.5.
[45] Ibid., 'A Review and Conclusion,' ¶8 [392].   [46] Hume, 'Of the Original Contract.'
[47] Hobbes, *Leviathan*, 'A Review and Conclusion,' ¶17 [395].

of the world are well grounded. It would be perverse to say that either of them gets it wrong, unless one wishes to say that in their assessments they do not consider the possibilities of the alternative state of affairs.

A second and far more significant point is that Hobbes lacks understanding of one of Hume's most important theoretical innovations: the analysis of conventions and of their force in getting us to behave in ways that are socially beneficial (or harmful). Hobbes sees the nature of coordination interactions that can be resolved simply by having all of us choose the 'same' strategy, as in the initial choice of a sovereign. He does not see how the iteration of this kind of interaction could lead to very stable, compelling incentives for continuing coordination that is spontaneous and that is not deliberately organized through an explicit agreement or overseen by any manager to keep us in line. Hume recognizes that such situations can produce conventions to govern behavior thereafter.

Hobbes similarly does not see the force of iterated exchange at the small or dyadic level, as in ongoing exchange relations in which each of us has incentive to behave well because both of us want to continue the relationship and the future exchanges it might enable us to enjoy. Again, Hume sees this strategic possibility and he therefore concludes that the incentive for keeping promises is the interest one has in such future possibilities as well as in the future possibilities that a reputation for reliability might lead us to. Hobbes therefore, in both these contexts, overestimates the need for an especially powerful state to regulate behavior.

The most important way in which Hume's insights here resolve problems for Hobbes is that they enable government to enforce its will, both at the outset and thereafter. In his social-compact argument Hobbes lacks a credible account of the initial empowerment of government. Hobbes implicitly recognizes that explaining the power of the sovereign through the citizens' transfer of their power poses a very difficult question to which he has no answer. He acknowledges the problem in *De Cive*, where he notes that 'no man can transferre his power in a naturall manner.'[48] Hume sees that the power of government arises from conventions. Even today, many social theorists lack the answer that Hume poses with convention and slow evolution, and they assume that social order is principally built on a normative consensus, often supposedly in a social contract. Hume's solution, which seems elegant and straightforward, somehow fails to convince many people, in many cases perhaps because they have not understood the analysis of convention, which he does not explain very clearly beyond illustrating it with numerous examples, so that for more than two centuries essentially no one seems to have got the argument.

---

[48] Hobbes, *De Cive* 2.5.11, p. 90.

Let us spell out Hobbes's failure on this issue. Hobbes describes as a covenant the consensual creation of a sovereign from the state of nature in which, we may recall, all are effectively more or less equal in power of coercion. I lay down my arms if you and all others lay down yours and we individually transfer our power to a sovereign. Hobbes has forcefully argued (and even convinced us) that a covenant in the state of nature where it cannot be enforced is invalid, and should not compel us.[49] What will make this one valid, after it is entered, is the coercive power of the sovereign, either an individual or some collective body, that the social compact establishes. It becomes valid only ex post. It is still, even ex post, a contract between us, the citizens, and not with the sovereign, who is merely the enforcer of our agreement with each other.[50]

Hobbes recognizes great difficulties in this transition and he wavers between saying we transfer rights to the sovereign and saying we transfer power. The latter is clearly what matters for Hobbes's analysis of political order. What is the form of that power? In the English edition of De Cive (1651),[51] which is a more or less literal translation of the Latin edition (1642), Hobbes writes of the power of a newly elected sovereign, 'which power and Right of commanding, consists in this, that each Citizen hath conveighed all his strength and power to that man, or Counsell; which to have done (because no man can transferre his power in a naturall manner) is nothing else then to have parted with his Right of resisting.'[52]

Here Hobbes falters. We can consent all we want to but, as a matter of actual fact we cannot simply hand our power over to anyone if that power is constituted primarily of our human capacities, as in the account of coordination power in chapter 5. I consent to the movement of the mountain before us out of our path, but it will not happen therefore. And our new sovereign cannot enter office with any power worth having for the awesome tasks ahead.[53] In

---

[49] Hobbes, *Leviathan* 14.18 [68].   [50] Ibid. 17.13 [88].

[51] The English title was *Philosophicall Rudiments Concerning Government and Society.*

[52] Hobbes, *De Cive* 2.5.11, p. 90.

[53] Jean Hampton supposes that power can be more or less instantly created because the newly elected sovereign can call on a small number of citizens to capture any law breaker, say, a contract breaker. This small group, or posse, faces, she says, not a prisoner's dilemma but rather a step good problem in which everyone must cooperate or the endeavor fails. But each member of the posse would rather bear the expected cost of her participation in the posse than have the sovereign falter and return everyone to the state of nature. Hence, each will cooperate and the law breaker will be captured and brought for punishment. (Hampton, *Hobbes and the Social Contract Tradition*, 176–86.) This is a much too labored story that, like Hobbes's very problem of creating a sovereign out of the state of nature, sounds more like a story than a real problem or prospect. Gregory Kavka seems only somewhat less confident of a resolution of Hobbes's problem of the transfer of power to the newly created sovereign (Kavka, *Hobbesian Moral and Political Theory*, 243–4, 254–66). But see Braybrooke, 'The Insoluble Problem of the Social Contract.'

Leviathan, published the same year as the English *De Cive*, the parallel passage dodges the difficulty by omitting it from discussion. Hobbes here says of the sovereign upon election that, 'by this authority, given him by every particular man in the commonwealth, he hath the use of so much power and strength conferred on him that by terror thereof he is enabled to conform the wills of them all to peace at home and mutual aid against their enemies abroad.'[54] The problem of how individuals' powers get aggregated and transferred to the sovereign has magically dropped out of discussion. Yet, only a paragraph earlier, Hobbes says of the inhabitants of the state of nature that 'it is no wonder if there be somewhat else required (besides covenant) to make their agreement constant and lasting...'[55]

In sum, Hobbes knows that power is necessary for order and he knows that power cannot be conjured up by mere consent. But he does not know how to resolve this dilemma to get a state in place through agreement. His problem is an artifact of his argument from contract, which he himself thinks largely irrelevant to the actual histories of states. Hobbes recognizes that empowerment of the newly chosen sovereign is a logical problem, but he says it is not really a practical problem because there has likely been no actual case of creation of government by social compact. As he says, 'there is scarce a commonwealth in the world whose beginnings can in conscience be justified.'[56] In his account, the only role of the social compact in any case is the selection of a government, after which it is the supposed power of the government, once established, that keeps us orderly.

The second problem, maintenance of order once it has been established, is also resolved by convention, indeed, by dual convention. Conventions keep both the people and the governors in line, so that the governor need not be an all-powerful sovereign in Hobbes's sense. This means, of course, that there is no sovereign in that sense—neither the citizens as a group nor the government—because no absolute coercive sovereign is required for order. Many positive law theorists make the definitional move of asserting that there must be a final locus of power to define the law and to enforce it. The convention theory of order does not require such a final locus. It is openly circular in a way that is valid. It fits the functional explanation of chapter 4. The positive law theorists seem to think something like Aristotle's claim that

---

[54] Hobbes, *Leviathan* 17.13 [87–8]. For further discussion, see Hardin, 'Hobbesian Political Order,' 168–71. Locke blithely supposed that his social contractors 'must be understood to give up all the power, necessary to the ends for which they unite into Society, to the *majority* of the Community' (Locke, *Two Treatises of Government* 2.99, p. 333). He has no better sense of how this is to be done than Hobbes has and, unlike Hobbes, he does not appear to realize that he has a problem here.

[55] Hobbes, *Leviathan* 17.12 [87].   [56] Ibid., 'A Review and Conclusion' 8 [392].

there must be a first mover is a matter of causal logic. It is not. Social causation can be far more complex than this. Moreover, it is virtually impossible to say how the Hobbesian all-powerful sovereign could be all powerful. Even that sovereign must rely on the convention of acquiescence by various officers of the law—what Hume calls opinion.[57]

Hume's fuller grasp of strategic structures also allows him to reject Hobbes's analysis of the so-called state of nature, the significance of which Hobbes himself clearly doubts. As does Hume, Hobbes starts from two assumptions: about human nature and about the conditions of the world in which we find ourselves. Both Hume and Hobbes think we have near enough equality of bodily force to steal from each other or even to kill each other.[58] For Hobbes, this means the state of nature, which faces two central problems. First there are the many potential prisoner's dilemma interactions with others that cannot be regulated to prevent theft from wrecking exchange. The state of nature or its resolution is not itself a prisoner's dilemma; and contract cannot resolve it because there is no sovereign to enforce the contract. Rather, the collective or social problem is to coordinate on a sovereign. The second problem is that everyone in that state is self-seeking and unconstrained, so that there is a de facto state of war, with uncertain payoff from investment, and no security.

The problem Hobbes wants to resolve is how to bring order to a world of violent anarchy. Our quotidian problem in the state of nature is therefore to protect ourselves against theft and even worse violence, while also providing ourselves with sustenance and comfort. This will be difficult. In Michael Oakeshott's quick assessment, 'he who is most successful will have the most enemies and be in the greatest danger. To have built a house and cultivated a garden is to have issued an invitation to all others to take it by force, for it is against the common view of felicity to weary oneself with making what can be acquired by less arduous means.'[59] What makes sense in general for maintaining individual interests is peace, which would serve mutual advantage.[60] Theft is not a moral issue in the conditions of violent anarchy, in which Hobbes supposes that everyone is licensed to do whatever contributes to his or her well-being. There being no law, there is no property, so what we call theft here is not criminal.

Hobbes's solution of the problem of social order is characterized as a social compact or contract to establish de novo a government that can enforce laws against theft and that can enable us all to enter into daily exchanges.

---

[57] Hume, 'Of the First Principles of Government,' 32–3.
[58] Hume, 'Of the Original Contract,' 467–8; Hobbes, *Leviathan* 13.1 [60].
[59] Oakeshott, 'Introduction to *Leviathan*,' 37; Hobbes, *Leviathan* 13.3 [61].
[60] Hobbes, *Leviathan* 13.14 [63]; see also 30.1 [175].

Despite calling the resolution a contract, which implies that it is a large-number problem of exchange or collective action, Hobbes actually supposes we simply select a sovereign or form of government to rule over us. This implies that he sees the problem of creating government as strategically a problem of simple coordination, not of exchange. Hobbes sees this clearly enough even though he misdescribes it with the language of contract. Hume sees the correct strategic structure of a contract relation; and both for this analytical reason and for historical reasons, he argues against the contractarian metaphor.[61] With Hume's strategic understanding, Hobbes would presumably delete his brief discussion of the social contract and would stick with his more extensive and far more compelling arguments about acquisition of government by power.

Hobbes says that notions of right and wrong, justice and injustice have no place in the state of nature; these are qualities that relate to men in society; also property exists only under government and makes no sense prior to government.[62] The contrary view of Locke and Nozick, among many others, is that there is not merely an idea of property prior to any government but that it is a moral idea.[63] For them the morality of property is prior to any more general political or moral principle. Their view is a violation of Hume's principle that we cannot deduce an ought from an is, because they suppose that the mere act of mixing one's labor with a bit of land makes it morally one's property. Hume supposes merely that possession can be stable—for strategic reasons—in a small primitive society that has no government (T3.2.2.10–11, SBN 490–1).

Hume agrees that there would be no justice or property in a Hobbesian state of nature, but he supposes this is a fictional state (T3.2.2.28, SBN 501). He has the benefit of a far better theoretical grasp of the strategic structure of small-scale social relations. He also sensibly supposes that the origins of human society are in familial groups, who are unlikely to have been as vicious to each other as Hobbes assumes the occupants of his state of nature to be. Indeed, there could be no humans today if we had not cared for those close to us most of the time before there was a state. The very young have never met Hobbes's condition of equality of physical ability to kill others, and they would have been killed or left to starve without the generosity of their elders. We do have problems in cooperating for joint benefit, although Hume tends to frame the issue as one of the short-term influence of our passions, which are often

---

[61] See Hardin, *Liberalism, Constitutionalism, and Democracy*, 145–52.
[62] Hobbes, *Leviathan* 13.13 [63].
[63] Locke, *Two Treatises of Government*; Nozick, *Anarchy, the State, and Utopia*.

contrary to our long-term interests and sometimes contrary to order in that they often work against established order.

Hume says that an established government has an infinite advantage over any alternative.[64] That is a big advantage. Hobbes assumes similarly that any extant government is overwhelmingly to be preferred to any alternative if we consider the costs of moving from the present government to the alternative.[65] They are both exceedingly risk averse.[66]

They both assume two parts to their theoretical analyses: the need for the regulation of competition and exchange (prisoner's dilemma interactions) in daily life; and recognition that this can basically be done by coordinating on a sovereign or a government or, in Hume, through the force of norms secured by iterated interactions in small societies.

Hobbes cannot handle two problems: religious commitments and glory-seeking. Hume also cannot handle these two because his theory similarly turns on the supposition that we all primarily seek our own interests. Religious fanatics might have beliefs about their future lives that make it their interest to behave as they do, but Hume and Hobbes are concerned with this world and are concerned in particular with social order in this world. As noted in the discussion of political parties in chapter 6, Hume thinks the best political world is one in which our only conflicts are conflicts of interest. The worst is one in which, with little prospect of compromise, parties vie over principles, including 'utterly absurd' religious principles.[67] The arguments of Hume and Hobbes must be anathema to many religious believers, such as many Catholics at the height of the church's suzerainty and during the era of the Inquisition; many Protestants during Hobbes's lifetime and soon thereafter in Salem, Massachusetts; and many Islamists such as Sayyid Qutb in our time.[68] Similarly, if I am so interested in glory as to sacrifice all other interests in its quest, wreaking havoc for everyone else, then I do not fit their accounts.

Hobbes's laws of nature are theorems, not commands of a sovereign.[69] Similarly, what Hume calls laws of nature (T3.2.1.19, SBN 484) are sociological, not normative, laws. They are necessary but artificial (T3.2.6.1, SBN 526).

---

[64] Hume, 'Idea of a Perfect Commonwealth,' 512.   [65] Hobbes, *Leviathan* 30.7 [177].

[66] As is Rawls. It is a remarkable fact, worthy of some investigation, that these three men are so risk averse.

[67] Hume, 'Of Parties in General,' 59.

[68] Qutb, *Milestones*. See also Berman, 'Sayyid Qutb: The Philosopher of Militant Islam.' Qutb says that the only system that can provide mankind with the high ideals and values of Islam requires that the Muslim community be restored to its original form to provide the leadership of all mankind (in Qutb's 'Introduction'). He was executed in Egypt in 1966.

[69] Hobbes, *Leviathan* 15.41 [80].

They include such duties as to honor conventions of property and to perform covenants made, etc.[70] How do these bind either in Hobbes's state of nature or in civil society? Hobbes answers these questions by taking over a traditional Catholic doctrine and naturalizing it. In the traditional doctrine, I am bound in my own heart—in *foro interno*—to be moral even if there are no laws—in *foro externo*—to force me to be. When Hobbes says that I am bound in *foro interno* he is saying that I can deduce what principles (or laws of nature) I should obey *if* I were bound in *foro externo* by actual law, by a sovereign.[71] He turns the traditional concern into a sociological claim, not a moral claim. As a result, and this is his major claim, I am not bound unless there is a powerful sovereign in *foro externo* to force me to follow the laws that can be deduced in *foro interno*. Whether the laws of nature are seen as sociological or moral, they do not bind internally and rationally, as David Gauthier, Alan Gewirth, John Searle, and many others suppose in their own rationalist ways,[72] but only when enforced externally. We can deduce the content of laws of nature but not any motivation to follow them. They become compelling for us only when we have government to enforce and define them and to motivate us to adhere to them.

Hume largely agrees with Hobbes on this set of claims, except that he imagines that even without government, *people within a small society could develop a sense of justice and could succeed* in maintaining reciprocity, keeping promises, recognizing a crude sort of possession, and so forth. People in such a society can keep each other in line through the force of conventions, or norms. This is a mutual monitoring device that lacks sufficient reach once the society grows substantially larger. Indeed, a suggestion of the truth of this view can be seen in the wide range of activities that small groups and communities can regulate among themselves without much backing by the state. State regulation of promise-keeping of the ordinary kind that does not include legal contract would be very cumbersome and costly, so that we would not even think to use the state to keep us cooperative in minor matters. Our concern for our reputations, which Hume values very highly, can be adequate to make us reciprocate favors and cooperative actions at the small scale.[73]

---

[70] Hobbes, *Leviathan* 15.1 [71].

[71] Ibid. 15.36 [79]. He says, 'The laws of nature oblige *in foro interno*, that is to say, they bind to a desire they should take place; but *in foro externo*, that is, to the putting them in act, not always. For he that should be modest and tractable, and perform all he promises, in such time and place where no man else should do so, should but make himself a prey to others, and procure his own certain ruin, contrary to the ground of all laws of nature, which tend to nature's preservation.'

[72] Gauthier, *Morals by Agreement*; Gewirth, *Reason and Morality* (a title and project that Hume would reject); Searle, 'How to Derive "Ought" from "Is."'

[73] Hume, 'Of the Independency of Parliament,' 43.

There is debate over whether or how much Hobbes is a rationalist. Oakeshott and Hayek, for example, suppose he is.[74] Others insist that Hobbes is an empiricist. Unfortunately, Hobbes gives license to both claims, so that taking one view rather than the other likely turns on seeing the fit of the whole set of his political views with rationalism or empiricism. Hume clearly takes up Hobbes's empiricism and essentially ignores rationalist claims such as Hobbes's sometime claim that his laws of nature are deduced from pure reason. One can sensibly suppose that Hobbes is not particularly alert to the issue and that he holds both rationalist and empiricist views. One suspects that, if he could have read Hume on the circumstances of justice, Hobbes would have agreed with Hume's empiricist claims against deducing moral principles from pure reason.

Both suppose that they need different accounts of the creation of government and the maintenance of government. Hume tells a just-so story of the rise of government and the increasing scale of society. Hobbes refers to creation of government by imposition or, in his own just-so story, by contract. In Hume, however, both accounts derive from interests or utility of the relevant individuals and these accounts depend on contingent facts (as in the discussion of treaties in international relations versus promises between individuals, in chapter 5). In Hobbes, maintenance is motivated by draconian force.

Both have vexed discussions of how to think about the knave (Hume) or the fool (Hobbes) who, once laws of justice are in place, insists that it would be reasonable to cheat under those laws so long as there is very little chance of being caught. Their theories do not have answers for such people, other than the contingent answer that their knavery might be caught and their lives might then be ruined or severely damaged. That is not the strong answer that Hobbes and Hume seem to want, but the contrived answers they give are not clearly derived from their theories.[75] Hume admits as much and then resorts to panegyric (EPM9.22–4, SBN 282–3). He thus shows that his theory has nothing constructive to say on the issue—and this is the correct response for him.

Hart says that Hume and Hobbes see 'in the modest aim of survival the central indisputable element which gives empirical good sense to the terminology of Natural Law.'[76] This is a distortion; mere survival is not the whole issue. Hume says that under institutions of justice, 'men acquire a security against each other's weakness and passion, as well as against their own, and under

---

[74] Oakeshott, 'Introduction to *Leviathan*,' 27; Hayek, 'The Legal and Political Philosophy of David Hume,' 336. Hayek refers to Hobbes's constructivist views.

[75] Hobbes, *Leviathan* 15.4–7 [72–3].   [76] Hart, *The Concept of Law*, 187.

the shelter of their governors, begin to taste at ease the sweets of society and mutual assistance. But government extends farther its beneficial influence; and not contented to protect men in those conventions they make for their mutual interest, it often obliges them to make such conventions, and forces them to seek their own advantage, by a concurrence in some common end or purpose' (T3.2.7.8, SBN 538). Hart seems to be relying on distant memory of what Hume might have said. No one who has recently read Hume could narrow Hume's concern in this way. Hart is also wrong on Hobbes, although Hobbes is often represented as having the view Hart attributes to him as though he were a frightened little man. Instead, what he actually says is that 'by safety is not meant a bare preservation, but also all other contentments of life, which every man by lawful industry, without danger or hurt to the commonwealth, shall acquire to himself.'[77] Neither of these great theorists has even a small fraction of the pettiness that is often attributed to them, even by so great a scholar as Hart. Both of these theorists make their views clear more than once, and they are very assertive in doing so. It is cavalier to read them in so limited a way.

Hobbes is perhaps the original discoverer of the fact that ordinary exchange relations are a Prisoner's Dilemma problem unless there is some coercive power to back them up—although he obviously did not have the vocabulary of game theory to state the issue this way. He is sometimes read as though he thinks the state of nature itself is a Prisoner's Dilemma that can be resolved only by contracting out.[78] His most cogent arguments, however, imply that the creation of a sovereign to resolve quotidian Prisoner's Dilemma interactions is itself a coordination problem rather than a contractual or exchange problem. His view that political order is merely a problem of coordinating on one out of many possible governments explains his conservative commitment to any extant government and opposition to revolution, views that sit uncomfortably with his supposed contractarianism.

Contra Hobbes, Hume supposes that government can be quite stable even if it does not have absolute power. One could reach this conclusion by commonsense political sociology. But the argument is reinforced by analyzing the problem as de facto a large-number coordination interaction. In such an interaction, you have an interest in going along with the coordination that others have established once it has, through iteration, become a convention. That is to say, you are compelled by an established convention to obey the government or at least to acquiesce in its rule. The established convention is that almost everyone does obey so that you benefit best if you also acquiesce in

---

[77] Hobbes, *Leviathan* 30.1 [175].   [78] See e.g. Mackie, *Hume's Moral Theory*, 9–10.

the government's policies. Some of us might prefer to have other conventions. Indeed, after a long time, virtually all of us might prefer to have a different convention to govern our behavior. But we might be stuck with our current convention, which is then the residue of a past pattern of interests. This is only a sketch of Hume's position, which is an analysis with extensive and deep implications.

Arguably, in their views of human nature, the main differences between Hume and Hobbes are in the empirical understandings available to them in their different times and circumstances. For example, in Hobbes's sociological view small societies without all-powerful government must be violent and destructive. One could correct this view by glancing at the seemingly well-ordered societies of the Indians of North America, as Hume might have done in his time, when accounts were beginning to be numerous, but as Hobbes could not have done so readily in his time. Even Hobbes's much reviled view of the selfishness of individuals was arguably compelling in his time, when he absented himself from Great Britain for a decade out of fear for his life during political turmoil in what was likely the most violent century of British domestic history. Hume lived in the relatively benign society of literary Scotland at the peak of the Scottish Enlightenment, in many ways one of the great eras of civilization. Indeed, it is often noted that he is a rare case among major political philosophers in that he was not writing against a backdrop of urgent political concern. He was not hoping to resolve a real political problem but only to understand the nature of political order. (After publication of his *Treatise* he was away during the Jacobite Rising of 1745 in Scotland, which he seems to have treated as a farce.)[79]

In the massive literature on Hume in the twentieth century, there is remarkably little discussion of his relationship to Hobbes, perhaps largely because that literature has focused more on Hume's epistemology than on his moral and political theory.[80] It is often pointed out that Hume had a more sanguine view of the possibilities of a good life in an anarchic small society, as noted above. And there is frequent reference to Hume's own remarks on Hobbes. For example, in his *History of England*, he writes that 'Hobbes's politics are fitted only to promote tyranny, and his ethics to encourage licentiousness. Though an enemy to religion, he partakes nothing of the spirit of skepticism;

---

[79] Mossner, *The Life of David Hume*, 177–86.
[80] But see Allen, 'Scarcity and Order: The Hobbesian Problem and the Humean Resolution'; Moore, 'Hume and Hutcheson'; Moss, 'Thomas Hobbes's Influence on David Hume: The Emergence of a Public Choice Tradition'; and Russell, 'Hume's *Treatise* and Hobbes's *The Elements of Law*.'

but is as positive and dogmatical as if human reason, and his reason in particular, could attain a thorough conviction in these subjects.'[81]

Despite this judgment, Hume's theory of politics seems to have more in common with that of Hobbes than with any other. Mossner reports that, when book 3 of Hume's *Treatise* was published, there was only one contemporary review of it.[82] The reviewer rightly asserts that, in his discussion of the origin of justice and of property rights, Hume presents 'the system of Hobbes dressed up in a new taste.'[83] Apart from the differences in arguments or assumptions that fit the differences in their own sociological experiences, their accounts are remarkably similar. And that similarity is remarkably overlooked.

In summary, the biggest theoretical difference between Hobbes and Hume is in Hume's richer strategic understanding, especially of convention, which arises from and is reinforced by iterated coordination of large numbers of people. From his strategic grasp, Hume has a solution to Hobbes's central problem, a solution that did not occur to Hobbes, who was therefore conspicuously bothered by the seeming flaw in his argument for the transfer of power from the citizenry to the sovereign. Hume's resolution of Hobbes's problem is coordination for order, not draconian enforcement. The incentives that back conventions can partially control even political office holders, who can be constrained in ways that Hobbes did not grasp. Moreover, on Hume's account from convention, it is not necessary to 'create' a government or to turn power over to it. Government just happens, as a convention, by evolutionary development from one state of affairs to another.

Major Arguments of Hume

We can list a surprising number of fundamentally important contributions of Hume, some of which are apparently original to him and some of which are ideas he emphasizes in new ways and thereby helps to establish. These could include contributions beyond moral and political theory, but I will leave such contributions aside here. They could also include his remarkable insights in economics throughout his work but especially in many of his short essays.[84] I will also leave these aside.

[81] Hume, *History of England*, 6. 412. Hobbes would presumably object that his theory and his views could not 'promote' any kind of government but could only support whatever government was actually in place. Hume's own views are not far different.

[82] That review appeared in the spring 1741 issue of the *Bibliothèque raisonnée*.

[83] Mossner, *The Life of David Hume*, 138–9.

[84] See Rotwein, *David Hume: Writings on Economics*; Sturn, 'The Sceptic as an Economist's Philosopher?'

First in order must come his overall program of explaining moral ideas, rather than demonstrating the truth of them, because he essentially holds that moral views have no truth value. The explanatory program is grounded in Hume's naturalism—his focus on the way people are and the world in which they live. Stroud thinks that this insistence on naturalism is perhaps Hume's greatest contribution, except that if his naturalism is in service of the science of man, especially the social science of man, then Stroud supposes Hume's contributions are 'ludicrously inadequate.'[85] That is a fairly full spread of the possibilities. Hume says his is an inquiry into the 'true *origins* of morals' (EPM1.9, SNB 173; emphasis added)—*not into true morals*. Except during his sallies of panegyric, he is firm in this enterprise. But even his panegyrics are often merely about the psychological appeal of various virtues or characters (e.g., EPM2.5, SBN 177–8), while his more frequent claims about *what pleases us* are about happiness, satisfaction, utility, usefulness, pleasure (pain), benefit, and other terms of welfare. What we can often say is true is that you or I just do have a moral view about something.

At the center of Hume's program is his theory of our psychology. At the time of writing the *Treatise*, Hume himself would likely have ranked his theory of moral psychology—an amalgam of sympathy and moral sentiments—as his most important innovation. We may finally today, in the past two decades only, be coming to an understanding of how his notions of sympathy and moral sentiments might work neurologically, an understanding that fits remarkably well with Hume's account, although we may now incline to run sympathy and moral sentiments into a single joint neural phenomenon if we rely on recent work on mirroring (as discussed in chapter 2). The neurological phenomenon of mirroring also seems to support Hume's view that utility pleases.

Perhaps second in Hume's own list would have been his theory of artificial virtues, which resolved a major problem left over from Hutcheson's explanation of morality from sympathy. That problem was how to explain our approbation for actions taken under the aegis or in support of institutions of justice.[86]

A social theorist must reckon Hume's analysis of convention and his use of it to explain social order the greatest contribution of all of Hume's work in social and political theory. Hume continues Hobbes's concern with social order but he presents a richer theory of it, a theory that is essentially complete

[85] Stroud, *Hume*, 222–3. On the evidence of Hume's increasingly plausible moral psychology and of his strategic analysis, Stroud appears to be wrong on this final judgment. Hume's views from more than two centuries ago are still live issues that could provoke extensive research.

[86] The distinction between justice and the so-called natural virtues reputedly goes back at least to Epicurus. For some of the history, see Moore, 'Hume and Hutcheson.'

and that includes substantial elements of spontaneity. It is a theory that is compelling still today. An understanding of it should lead us to retire all the other proposed theories, from shared values (religious or otherwise) to draconian enforcement as the grounds of social order—at least in modern liberal states.

Hume couples the analysis of convention with frequent invocation of unintended consequences; together these lead to stable social institutions and practices that no one intended and that are therefore accidental. Such consequences also lurk behind evolutionary social developments and, in what are read by some scholars as remarkably original insights, behind human and animal evolution as well.[87] Christian Bay says that 'Hume may be called a precursor of Darwin in the field of ethics. In effect, he proclaimed a doctrine of the survival of the fittest among human conventions—fittest not in terms of good teeth but in terms of maximum social utility.'[88] Hence, we do not need to have an account of origins as of some moment but can nevertheless understand the existence now of various institutions and practices, such as the variously detailed institutions of property that different polities have and the disparate collection of languages that different peoples speak. ''Tis interest which gives the general instinct; but 'tis custom which gives the particular direction' (T3.2.10.4, SBN 556). In contemporary vocabulary, Hume gives us functional accounts of many social institutions. We can see such an institution (for example, government) to be self-reinforcing because it serves a function (such as maintaining social order) for its clientele or citizenry, whose incentives (to be orderly because virtually everyone else is orderly) feed back to support the institution.

Related to the grasp of coordination problems and of unintended consequences is Hume's frequent invocation of indeterminacy of actions and outcomes. To say that there is a coordination problem is to say that there is more than one appealing outcome on which to coordinate. If it were determinate which outcome to choose, in the sense of its being obviously the best for all of us, there would be no problem. Hume sees problems of indeterminacy in many contexts. As usual, he does not step back and state the general rule or pattern but merely notes it in context when it matters. Indeterminacy is pervasive in social choice contexts, in which it is generally impossible for me to choose well without knowing how you will choose, but you may wish to choose in a way that outsmarts my choice.[89]

---

[87] See Hayek, 'The Legal and Political Philosophy of David Hume,' 356–7.

[88] Bay, *The Structure of Freedom*, 33; Penelhum, 'Hume's Moral Psychology,' 124. Bay's 'maximum' would not be Hume's term.

[89] Hardin, *Indeterminacy and Society*.

Moral theorists should be impressed with Hume's analysis of promise-keeping, but many moral theorists today continue to attack his account as specious. A possible reason for this stance is that Hume's account contributes to his claim that moral views are contingent on circumstances in a deep way that rules out any claim that a particular moral virtue is right per se and that says that many of our moral virtues are socially constructed (that is to say, they are artificial in Hume's sense and therefore potentially variable according to circumstances). This can be a devastating conclusion for a rigid deontologist or an assertive intuitionist. Some critics simply misread Hume's analysis to claim, for example, that iterated interaction leads us to be altruistic rather than to see that it gives us a strong interest in maintaining an iterated promising relationship by fulfilling the promises we make in that relationship.[90]

Hume analyzes the variety of strategic structures of social interaction to give a quasi game theoretic explanation of many phenomena. He represents three strategic forms, each with examples: conflict, coordination, and cooperation (or exchange). He also recognizes the differences between small-number and large-number interactions.

Finally, Hume recognizes the effects of repeated interaction in changing the incentives individuals have in these interactions. This insight has deep and pervasive implications.

I have called Hume a late twentieth-century political philosopher. The sense in which I mean that is that he uses all of these contributions of his own to theorize about politics. Yet many of these contributions are only recently available to political philosophers in general. Others, including Hobbes a century before Hume, have used game theoretic claims to analyze political and moral problems, but until very recently only Hume had laid out virtually a complete map of the most important interactions for us. Only over the past few decades have social theorists and political philosophers had available to them the strategic analysis that Hume used. Schelling contributes a rich understanding of coordination interactions only in the 1950s. And Lewis presents a solid account of Hume's convention only in 1969.[91] Before those dates, it would have taken someone with very nearly Hume's intellect even to read Hume with adequate understanding on these issues. Now a well-tutored undergraduate can read him clearly.[92]

---

[90] Hiskes, 'Has Hume a Theory of Social Justice?' 89.

[91] Schelling, *The Strategy of Conflict*; Lewis, *Convention*.

[92] Recall Hume's remark at the opening of book 3: 'There is an inconvenience which attends all abstruse reasoning, that it ... requires the same intense study to make us sensible of its force, that was at first requisite for its invention' (T3.1.1.1, SBN 455). No wonder the *Treatise* fell dead-born from the press.

Concluding Remarks

As noted by Hume, the Greeks have been very important in philosophical ethics in part because they needed a voluntarist reason for doing or being good, because they did not have punishment in an afterlife to motivate them.[93] For the past few centuries, after an oppressively long theological hegemony over thought, this is again the position in the west. Hobbes is intermediate between religious theorists and secular theorists. With the Christian theorists, he supposes that we need to have a sword, a harshly menacing external force, hanging over us to motivate us to behave well in lieu of the theologian's threat of punishment in an afterlife.[94] He attempts to supply this need with a sword that is held by a human sovereign, not a full deity but only a man-god. Greek philosophers attempted to ground morality directly in the individual, making morality one of the goods of the individual, as though virtue were its own reward (a view sometimes also expressed in Hume's panegyrics).

Neither of these strategies is credible for the generality of humankind and societies. Hume shows us a world in which it is we who push all of us to behave well and in which institutions make it easier. If good behavior is defined somehow as acting in ways that entail mutually advantageous support of the interests of all, then *the incentive to good behavior is endogenous to human society*; it is not simply grounded in the individual even though it is voluntarist in at least the way ordinary exchange relations and ordinary coordinations in conventions are voluntarist (T3.2.2.4, SBN 486). But even this is saying too much. If Hume's psychology of moral approbation is correct, then our sentiments are not voluntary in the usual sense of moral theorists, because 'they have objects beyond the domain of the will or choice' (EPM App.4.21, SBN 322). Hence, our morality is about how to deal with our social interactions and it is derived from them and it is driven by our uncontrollable psychology. Hume socializes and psychologizes morality. He thus does not take us back to the Greeks, who sought a way to make morality our individual personal interest, but he escapes theology and its 'utmost Licence of Fancy and Hypothesis.'[95] He makes the analysis of morality and political philosophy a distinctively modern problem. If we just happen to take personal pleasure in some moral actions (altruism toward those near to us), we might internalize morality, but otherwise not.

John Passmore speculates that, in the end Hume 'is prepared to abandon ethics and aesthetics to the realm of taste, if only he can preserve the status

---

[93] As quoted above (EPM App. 4.21, SBN 322).
[94] Hume, *Dialogues Concerning Natural Religion* 12.251. See also, Butler, *The Analogy of Religion*, 136.
[95] Hume, *Dialogues Concerning Natural Religion* 5.194.

of politics, as a science at least as securely founded as physics.'[96] Duncan Forbes speculates that Hume is, 'for a number of reasons, especially attracted to the study of politics, in which, he thinks, the regularity of human nature is strikingly obvious.'[97] One might suppose he would also wish to be credited with the beginnings of a science of human nature. In both cases, of course, if we speak in today's vocabulary, it is as a scientist that he would want to be seen. In either case, it is in the realm of social and political life that his most insightful inventions play their grandest roles. Among these are a rich and original theory of the psychology of sympathy and accounts of unintended consequences, virtues as functional, convention, strategic structures, the strategic effects of repeated interactions, artificial virtues, ordinal value, and the spontaneous rise of institutions, norms, and practices. This is an astonishing list. We could add to the list Haakonssen's sharp methodological claim that Hume's political theory is an explanation of why abstract theorizing about politics and political order is futile and even dangerous.[98]

Hume himself lacked a vocabulary for some of these insights and claims, and subsequent generations have not generally taken on much of the vocabulary he uses, such as his fundamentally important category of 'artificial' duties or virtues. In many ways Hume was too early to get his labels right. Now those who read him may often fail to grasp that he has cogently analyzed problems with theories and concepts that have since come to bear other labels. As with other great philosophers of earlier times, the peculiar vocabulary makes it hard to get through to the core of his arguments, many of which still sound novel today.

In addition to having a vocabulary different from ours, Hume omits doing something that might be taken for granted now but was not taken for granted by him. Perhaps because his explanatory focus is entirely on the psychology of moral views, he does not give summary accounts of theories of other things that he discusses and even uses. Most obviously, he gives us no summary account of game theory or strategic analysis, of convention, or of the theory of the state. These are all there only when necessary for the discussion of the moment. The game theoretic or strategic analysis is used very systematically in his canvassing of major problems of moral and political theory and of convention. And the theory of the state shows up in passing in the *Treatise* and sometimes more deliberately in later short essays. I have attempted to construct both of these in the spirit of Hume's own remarks. These lacks are not uniquely a problem for

---

[96] Passmore, *Hume's Intentions*, 11.
[97] Forbes, *Hume's Philosophical Politics*, 120; see also 224–30.
[98] Haakonssen, 'Hume's Political Theory,' 196.

Hume. Early contributors to mathematical decision theory and the theory of games resolved specific problems, such as how best to play a particular game (therefore, the unfortunate and trivializing name: theory of games). They did not generalize their conclusions into abstract theories or categories, and their findings were commonly neglected.[99]

Hume is a proto-social scientist. Many of his arguments have been advanced by sociologists, political scientists, psychologists, and economists far more than by philosophers, although philosophers have also subjected his views to intensive, clarifying scrutiny. He is a forerunner of Smith in economics; John von Neumann, Oskar Morgenstern, and Thomas Schelling in game theory; Robert Merton in sociology; Friedrich Hayek and the Austrians in political and social theory; David Lewis in philosophy; and vast numbers of psychologists. A price he pays for his precocious originality is that many of these people do their work as though Hume had not been a predecessor to stimulate them. The difficulty of his ideas is massively exacerbated by the vocabulary in which they are presented. Today, many of these ideas sound like second nature to us. It has taken more than two centuries of work by uncounted thinkers to bring them down to that accessible level.

One might question just how much we have grasped a complex issue if we have not come to label it analytically. In general, however, it is clear that we can act from motives that fit a theory we do not know and might not even understand. The transcendent move of Hume is to see many actions so clearly as to see the similarities in the structures of the motivations that lie behind them. He could consistently apply a theory that he never stated. This capacity is most strikingly clear in his rich grasp of what is now called game theory.

For Hume, political philosophy derives substantially from social science and is empirical. Similarly, his moral philosophy is fundamentally empirical, as he insists it should be, because it is about the psychology of our moral beliefs. His moral and political philosophy are essentially one. This unity is arguably truer of his work than of the work of any other major philosopher other than the subsequent utilitarians. Kant's moral philosophy, for example, is seldom articulated into political understanding and is therefore seldom made relevant to political life. His discussions of law and international relations seem largely independent of his moral theory. The union of these in Hume partially follows merely from structural considerations. In many contexts the personal and the political interact strategically so that we cannot separate them. The issue for Hume is less that *morality* is grounded in the nature of the individual than that

---

[99] See e.g. Dimand and Dimand, 'The Early History of the Theory of Strategic Games from Waldegrave to Borel.'

moral problems are grounded in the nature of the individual *in social interaction.* Morality therefore is inescapably almost political.

Hume wrote at an unusual time, when a long dominant moral tradition was tipping into steep decline. Virtue theory was almost the whole of ethics in several traditions, especially including Catholic and Protestant religious traditions, but it could not survive the Scottish intellectual assault of Hume and Smith, who simply focused elsewhere and restored—all too briefly—the unified approach to moral and political philosophy while also bringing social science to both of them. James Fieser says that Hume is the first purely secular moral thinker in the modern era,[100] but secular thought becomes a flood soon after his time.

As noted in chapter 8, Hume is also the first major thinker to rely on utility as the standard ground for action and for justifying actions. For him this is largely a psychological claim, because utility is pleasing, as a work of art might be. One might suppose that it is pleasing because it is good for people, which comes close to being a moral-theoretic rather than merely a psychological or esthetic claim. Indeed, Hume supposes that concern for utility substantially accounts for the origin of morality (EPM5.17, SBN 219). Laying aside panegyric and declamation, Hume can find no substantive moral content in our claims or behavior. All he can find is the psychology that leads us to assert moral claims. Much of that psychology is to approve happiness, pleasure, and beneficial things of various kinds. By focusing on utility and putting moral and political theory into a single coherent frame, he opens the door for the grand entry of utilitarianism.

---

[100] Fieser, 'David Hume: Moral Theory,' 1.

Bibliography

ACKERMAN, BRUCE A. 1980. *Social Justice in a Liberal State*. New Haven, Conn.: Yale University Press.

AIKEN, HENRY. 1948. 'Introduction.' In Aiken, ed., *Hume's Moral and Political Philosophy*. New York: ix–li.

AINSLIE, GEORGE. 1992. *Picoeconomics: The Strategic Interaction of Successive Motivational States within the Person*. New York: Cambridge University Press.

ALLEN, WILLIAM R. 1976. 'Scarcity and Order: The Hobbesian Problem and the Humean Resolution.' *Social Science Quarterly* 57 (Sept.): 263–75.

ALMOND, GABRIEL, and VERBA, SIDNEY. 1963. *The Civic Culture: Political Attitudes and Democracy in Five Nations*. Princeton, NJ: Princeton University Press.

ANSCOMBE, G. E. M. 1958. 'Modern Moral Philosophy.' *Philosophy* 33 (124): 1–19. (Reprinted in Anscombe, *Ethics, Religion, and Politics*, vol. 3 of *Collected Philosophical Papers*. Minneapolis: University of Minnesota Press, 1981: 26–42.)

ÁRDAL, PÁLL. 1966. *Passion and Value in Hume's* Treatise. Edinburgh: Edinburgh University Press.

ARISTOTLE. [4th century BCE] 1998. *Politics*, trans. C. D. C. Reeve. Indianapolis: Hackett.

ASHCROFT, JOHN. 1997. 'Keep Big Brother's Hands off the Internet.' *USIA Electronic Journal*, 2 (Oct.).

AUSTEN, JANE. [1813] 1952. *Pride and Prejudice*. London: Collins.

———— [1816] 1985. *Emma*. London: Penguin.

AUSTIN, JOHN. [1832] 1954. *The Province of Jurisprudence Determined*. New York: Noonday.

BAIER, ANNETTE C. 1991. *A Progress of Sentiments: Reflections on Hume's* Treatise. Cambridge, Mass.: Harvard University Press.

BARRY, BRIAN. 1989. *Theories of Justice*. Berkeley, Calif.: University of California Press.

———— and HARDIN, RUSSELL. 1982. *Rational Man and Irrational Society?* Beverly Hills, Calif.: Sage Publications.

BARTKY, IAN R., and HARRISON, ELIZABETH. 1979. 'Standard and Daylight Saving Time.' *Scientific American* 240 (May): 46–53.

BAY, CHRISTIAN. 1970. *The Structure of Freedom*, rev. edn. Stanford, Calif.: Stanford University Press.

BENTHAM, JEREMY. [1787] 1952. 'Defense of Usury.' In W. Stark, ed., *Jeremy Bentham's Economic Writings*. London: George Allen & Unwin, 1.121–207.

———— [1789] 1970. *An Introduction to the Principles of Morals and Legislation*, ed. J. H. Burns and H. L. A. Hart. London: Methuen.

BERKELEY, GEORGE. [1712] 1891. 'Passive Obedience: or, The Christian Doctrine of not resisting the Supreme Power, proved and vindicated, upon the Principles of the

Law of Nature.' In Alexander Campbell Fraser, ed., *The Works of George Berkeley*. Oxford: Oxford University Press, 4.95–135.

BERMAN, PAUL. 2003. 'Sayyid Qutb: The Philosopher of Militant Islam.' *New York Times Magazine* (22 Mar.): 24 ff.

BOSWELL, JAMES. [1791] 1976. *Life of Johnson*. London: Oxford University Press.

BOWER, BRUCE. 2003. 'Repeat after Me: Imitation is the Sincerest Form of Perception.' *Science News* 163 (24 May): 330–2.

—— 2006. 'Copycat Monkeys: Macaque Babies Ape Adults' Facial Feats.' *Science News* 170 (9 Sept.): 163.

BRAITHWAITE, R. B. 1955. *Theory of Games as a Tool for the Moral Philosopher*. Cambridge: Cambridge University Press.

BRAYBROOKE, DAVID. 1976. 'The Insoluble Problem of the Social Contract.' *Dialogue* 15 (Mar.): 3–37.

BROAD, C. D. 1914. 'The Doctrine of Consequences in Ethics.' *International Journal of Ethics* [now *Ethics*] 24 (3): 293–320.

BRONTË, EMILY. 1981. *Wuthering Heights*. London: Oxford University Press World's Classics.

BURKE, EDMUND. [1774] 1969. 'Speech to the Electors of Bristol.' In Burke, *Speeches and Letters on American Affairs*. London: Everyman: 68–75.

BUTLER, JOSEPH. 1736. *The Analogy of Religion*. London.

CAPALDI, NICHOLAS. 1975. *David Hume*. Boston: Twayne.

—— 1992. 'The Dogmatic Slumber of Hume Scholarship.' *Hume Studies* (Nov.) 18: 117–35.

CARNAP, RUDOLF. 1962. *Logical Foundations of Probability*, 2nd edn. Chicago: University of Chicago Press.

CHEKHOV, ANTON. 1984. 'The Duel.' In *The Duel and Other Stories*, trans. Constance Garnet. New York: Ecco Press.

CLARKE, SAMUEL. 1706. *A Discourse concerning the Unchangeable Obligations of Natural Religion, and the Truth and Certainty of the Christian Revelation*. London: James Knapton.

COOK, KAREN S., and HARDIN, RUSSELL. 2001. 'Norms of Cooperativeness and Networks of Trust.' In Michael Hechter and Karl-Dieter Opp, eds., *Social Norms*. New York: Russell Sage Foundation: 327–47.

CORN, DAVID. 2002. 'The Fundamental John Ashcroft.' *Mother Jones* (Mar./Apr.).

DARWALL, STEPHEN, ed. 2003. *Contractarianism/Contractualism*. Oxford: Blackwell.

DAWSON, JOHN P. *Gifts and Promises: Continental and American Law Compared*. New Haven, Conn.: Yale University Press.

DENDLE, PETER. 1994. 'A Note on Hume's Letter to Gilbert Elliot.' *Hume Studies* 20 (Nov.): 289–91.

DEWEY, JOHN. [1929] 1960. *The Quest for Certainty: A Study of the Relation of Knowledge and Action*. New York: Putnam.

DIMAND, ROBERT W., and DIMAND, MARY ANN. 1992. 'The Early History of the Theory of Strategic Games from Waldegrave to Borel.' In Roy Weintraub, ed., *Toward a History of Game Theory*. Durham, NC: Duke University Press.

DURKHEIM, ÉMILE. [1893] 1933. *The Division of Labor in Society*. New York: Macmillan.

EDGEWORTH, F. Y. 1881. *Mathematical Psychics: An Essay on the Application of Mathematics to the Moral Sciences*. London: C. Kegan Paul.

ELSTER, JON. 1979. *Ulysses and the Sirens: Studies in Rationality and Irrationality*. Cambridge: Cambridge University Press.

EMERSON, ROGER L. 1995. 'The "Affair" at Edinburgh and the "Project" at Glasgow: The Politics of Hume's Attempts to Become a Professor.' In M. A. Stewart and John P. Wright, eds., *Hume and Hume's Connexions*. University Park, Penn.: Penn State University Press: 1–22.

FERGUSON, ADAM. [1767] 1980. *An Essay on the History of Civil Society*. New Brunswick, NJ: Transaction.

FIESER, JAMES. 2001. 'David Hume: Moral Theory.' *Internet Encyclopedia of Philosophy*.

FOGELIN, ROBERT J. 1985. *Hume's Skepticism in the* Treatise of Human Nature. London: Routledge & Kegan Paul.

FORBES, DUNCAN. 1975. *Hume's Philosophical Politics*. Cambridge: Cambridge University Press.

FULLER, LON L. 1978. 'Law and Human Interaction.' In H. M. Johnson, ed., *Social System and Legal Process*. San Francisco, Calif.: Jossey-Bass: 59–89.

GADDIS, WILLIAM. 1985. *Carpenter's Gothic*. New York: Viking.

GARRETT, DON. 1997. *Cognition and Commitment in Hume's Philosophy*. Oxford: Oxford University Press.

GASKIN, J. C. A. [1978] 1988. *Hume's Philosophy of Religion*, 2nd edn. Atlantic Highlands, NJ: Humanities Press.

GAUTHIER, DAVID. 1986. *Morals by Agreement*. Oxford: Oxford University Press.

GEWIRTH, ALAN. 1978. *Reason and Morality*. Chicago: University of Chicago Press.

GODWIN, WILLIAM. [1793] 1985. *Enquiry Concerning Political Justice*. Harmondsworth: Penguin.

GOMBROWICZ, WITOLD. 1961. *Ferdydurke*. New York: Harcourt Brace, Jovanovich.

GOODMAN, NELSON. 1955. *Fact, Fiction, and Forecast*. Cambridge, Mass.: Harvard University Press.

GRIEG, J. Y. T. 1931. *David Hume*. New York: Oxford University Press.

HAAKONSSEN, KNUD. 1981. *The Science of a Legislator: The Natural Jurisprudence of David Hume and Adam Smith*. Cambridge: Cambridge University Press.

—— 1990. 'Introduction and Commentary.' In Thomas Reid, *Practical Ethics*, ed. Knud Haakonssen. Princeton: Princeton University Press: 1–99, 301–445.

—— 1993. 'Hume's Political Theory.' In David Fate Norton, ed., *The Cambridge Companion to Hume*. Cambridge: Cambridge University Press: 182–221.

HAMPTON, JEAN. 1986. *Hobbes and the Social Contract Tradition*. Cambridge: Cambridge University Press.

HARDIN, RUSSELL. 1971. 'Collective Action as an Agreeable n-Prisoners' Dilemma.' *Behavioral Science*, 16 (Sept.): 472–81.

—— 1980. 'Rationality, Irrationality, and Functionalist Explanation.' *Social Science Information* 19 (Sept.): 755–72.

———— 1982. *Collective Action*. Baltimore: Johns Hopkins University Press for Resources for the Future.

———— 1982. 'Exchange Theory on Strategic Bases.' *Social Science Information* 21 (2): 251–72.

———— 1988. *Morality within the Limits of Reason*. Chicago: University of Chicago Press.

———— 1990. 'Contractarianism: Wistful Thinking.' *Constitutional Political Economy*, 1: 35–52.

———— 1991. 'Hobbesian Political Order.' *Political Theory* 19 (May): 156–80.

———— 1993. 'Altruism and Mutual Advantage.' *Social Service Review* 67 (Sept.): 358–73.

———— 1993. 'From Power to Order, from Hobbes to Hume.' *Journal of Political Philosophy*, 1 (Mar.): 195–207.

———— 1995. *One for All: The Logic of Group Conflict*. Princeton: Princeton University Press.

———— 1997. 'The Economics of Religious Belief.' *Journal of Institutional and Theoretical Economics* 153 (Mar.): 259–78.

———— 1997. 'Economic Theories of the State.' In Dennis C. Mueller, ed., *Perspectives on Public Choice: A Handbook*. New York: Cambridge University Press: 21–34.

———— 1998. 'Reasonable Agreement: Political Not Normative.' In Paul J. Kelly, ed., *Impartiality, Neutrality and Justice: Re-Reading Brian Barry's Justice as Impartiality*. Edinburgh: Edinburgh University Press: 137–53.

———— 1999. *Liberalism, Constitutionalism, and Democracy*. Oxford: Oxford University Press.

———— 2001. 'The Normative Core of Rational Choice Theory.' In Uskali Maki, ed., *The Economic World View: Studies in the Ontology of Economics*. Cambridge: Cambridge University Press: 57–74.

———— 2001. 'Democratic Aggregation.' In Yung-ming Hsu and Chi Huang, eds., *Level-of-Analysis Effects on Political Research*. Taipei: Weber Publication: 7–33.

———— 2002. *Trust and Trustworthiness*. New York: Russell Sage Foundation.

———— 2002. 'Liberal Distrust.' *European Review* 10 (1): 73–89.

———— 2003. *Indeterminacy and Society*. Princeton: Princeton University Press.

———— 2005. 'From Order to Justice,' *Politics, Philosophy and Economics* 4(2):175–94.

———— 2006. *Trust*. Cambridge: Polity Press.

HARRISON, JONATHAN. 1981. *Hume's Theory of Justice*. Oxford: Oxford University Press.

HARSANYI, JOHN C. 1953. 'Cardinal Utility in Welfare Economics and in the Theory of Risk-Taking.' *Journal of Political Economy* 61 (5): 434–5.

HART, H. L. A. 1955. 'Are There Any Natural Rights?' *Philosophical Review* 64 (Apr.): 175–91.

———— 1961. *The Concept of Law*. Oxford: Oxford University Press.

———— 1983. *Essays in Jurisprudence and Philosophy*. Oxford: Oxford University Press.

HAYEK, F. A. [1944] 1994. *The Road to Serfdom*. Chicago: University of Chicago Press.

———— 1952. *The Counter-Revolution of Science: Studies on the Abuse of Reason*. Glencoe, Ill.: Free Press.

HAYEK, F. A. 1967. 'The Results of Human Action but not of Human Design.' In Hayek, *Studies in Philosophy, Politics, and Economics*. Chicago: University of Chicago Press: 96–105.

_____ 1967. 'The Legal and Political Philosophy of David Hume.' In Hayek, *Studies in Philosophy, Politics, and Economics*. Chicago: University of Chicago Press: 106–21.

HIRSCHMAN, ALBERT O. 1977. *The Passions and the Interests: Political Arguments for Capitalism before Its Triumph*. Princeton: Princeton University Press.

HISKES, RICHARD. 1977. 'Has Hume a Theory of Social Justice?' *Hume Studies* 3 (Nov.): 72–93.

HOBBES, THOMAS. [1651] 1983. *De Cive*, ed. Howard Warrender. Oxford: Oxford University Press; originally published in Latin, 1642.

_____ [1651] 1994. *Leviathan*, ed. by Edwin Curley. Indianapolis: Hackett. Cited in the text as *Leviathan* followed by chapter and paragraph numbers with pages numbers for the original edition in [square brackets].

HODGSON, D. H. 1967. *Consequences of Utilitarianism*. Oxford: Oxford University Press.

HOME, HENRY (Lord Kames). [1751] 1983. *Essays on the Principles of Morality and Natural Religion*. New York: Garland (facsimile reprint).

HUMBOLDT, WILHELM VON. [1854] 1969. *The Limits of State Action*, ed. J. W. Burrow. Cambridge: Cambridge University Press. Reprinted Indianapolis: Liberty Press, 1993.

HUME, DAVID. [1739–40] 1978. *A Treatise of Human Nature*, ed. L. A. Selby-Bigge and P. H. Nidditch, 2nd edn. Oxford: Oxford University Press. Cited in the text as T followed by SBN and book, part, section, and page numbers.

_____ [1739–40] 2000. *A Treatise of Human Nature*, ed. David Fate Norton and Mary J. Norton. Oxford: Oxford University Press. Cited in the text as T followed by book, part, section, and paragraph numbers.

_____ [1741] 1985. 'Of the Dignity or Meanness of Human Nature.' In Eugene F. Miller, ed., *David Hume: Essays Moral, Political and Literary*. Indianapolis: Liberty Classics: 80–6.

_____ [1741] 1985. 'Of the First Principles of Government.' In Eugene F. Miller, ed., *David Hume: Essays Moral, Political, and Literary*. Indianapolis: Liberty Classics: 32–6.

_____ [1741] 1985. 'Of the Independency of Parliament.' In Eugene F. Miller, ed., *David Hume: Essays Moral, Political, and Literary*. Indianapolis: Liberty Classics: 42–6.

_____ [1741] 1985. 'Of Parties in General.' In Eugene F. Miller, ed., *David Hume: Essays Moral, Political, and Literary*. Indianapolis: Liberty Classics: 54–63.

_____ [1741] 1985. 'Of Superstition and Enthusiasm.' In Eugene F. Miller, ed., *David Hume: Essays Moral, Political, and Literary*. Indianapolis: Liberty Classics: 73–9.

_____ [1742] 1985. 'Of the Rise and Progress of the Arts and Sciences.' In Eugene F. Miller, ed., *David Hume: Essays Moral, Political, and Literary*. Indianapolis: Liberty Classics: 111–37.

_____ [1748] 1975. *An Enquiry Concerning Human Understanding*. In Hume, *Enquiries*, ed. L. A. Selby-Bigge and P. H. Nidditch, 3rd edn. Oxford: Oxford

University Press: 1–165. Cited in the text as EHU followed by SBN and page numbers.

—— [1748] 1985. 'Of the Original Contract.' In Eugene F. Miller, ed., *David Hume: Essays Moral, Political, and Literary*. Indianapolis: Liberty Classics: 465–87.

—— [1748] 2000. *An Enquiry Concerning Human Understanding*. ed. Tom L. Beauchamp. Oxford: Oxford University Press. Cited in the text as EHU followed by section and paragraph numbers.

—— [1751] 1975. *An Enquiry Concerning the Principles of Morals*. In Hume, *Enquiries*, ed. L. A. Selby-Bigge and P. H. Nidditch, 3rd edn. Oxford: Oxford University Press: 167–323. Cited in the text as EPM followed by SBN and page numbers.

—— [1751] 1998. *An Enquiry Concerning the Principles of Morals*, ed. Tom L. Beauchamp. Oxford: Oxford University Press. Cited in the text as EPM followed by section and paragraph numbers.

—— [1752] 1985. 'Of Commerce.' In Eugene F. Miller, ed., *David Hume: Essays Moral, Political, and Literary*. Indianapolis: Liberty Classics: 253–67.

—— [1752] 1985. 'Of Interest.' In Eugene F. Miller, ed., *David Hume: Essays Moral, Political, and Literary*. Indianapolis: Liberty Classics: 295–307.

—— [1752] 1985. 'Of the Protestant Succession.' In Eugene F. Miller, ed., *David Hume: Essays Moral, Political, and Literary*. Indianapolis: Liberty Classics: 502–11.

—— [1752] 1985. 'Of Money.' In Eugene F. Miller, ed., David Hume: *Essays Moral, Political and Literary*. Indianapolis: Liberty Classics: 281–94.

—— [1752] 1985. 'Of Public Credit.' In Eugene F. Miller, ed., *David Hume: Essays Moral, Political, and Literary*. Indianapolis: Liberty Classics: 349–65.

—— [1752] 1985. 'Of Refinement in the Arts.' In Eugene F. Miller, ed., *David Hume: Essays Moral, Political, and Literary*. Indianapolis: Liberty Classics: 268–80.

—— [1752] 1985. 'Idea of a Perfect Commonwealth.' In Eugene F. Miller, ed., *David Hume: Essays Moral, Political, and Literary*. Indianapolis: Liberty Classics: 512–29.

—— [1754–62] 1983–5. *History of England: From the Invasion of Julius Caesar to the Revolution in 1688*, 6 vols. Indianapolis: Liberty Classics.

—— [1757] 1976. *The Natural History of Religion*. In *David Hume on Religion*, ed. A. Wayne Colver and John Vladimir Price. Oxford: Oxford University Press: 23–95.

—— [1758] 1985. 'Of the Jealousy of Trade.' In Eugene F. Miller, ed., *David Hume: Essays Moral, Political, and Literary*. Indianapolis: Liberty Classics: 327–31.

—— [1977] 1985. 'My Own Life.' In Eugene F. Miller, ed., *David Hume: Essays Moral, Political, and Literary*. Indianapolis: Liberty Classics: pp. xxxi–xli.

—— [1777] 1985. 'Of the Origin of Government.' In Eugene F. Miller, ed., *David Hume: Essays Moral, Political, and Literary*. Indianapolis: Liberty Classics: 37–41.

—— [1779] 1976. *Dialogues Concerning Natural Religion*. In *David Hume on Religion*, ed. A. Wayne Colver and John Vladimir Price. Oxford: Oxford University Press: 99–261.

—— 1932. *The Letters of David Hume*, 2 vol., ed. J. Y. T. Grieg. Oxford: Oxford University Press.

HUME, DAVID. 1954. *New Letters of David Hume*, ed. Raymond Klibansky and Ernest C. Mossner. Oxford: Oxford University Press.

HUTCHESON, FRANCIS. [1728] 2002. *An Essay on the Nature and Conduct of the Passions and Affections, with Illustrations on the Moral Sense* [cited as *Essay with Illustrations*], ed. Aaron Garrett. Indianapolis: Liberty Fund.

HUTCHISON, TERENCE W. 1988. *Before Adam Smith: The Emergence of Political Economy, 1622–1776*. Oxford: Oxford University Press.

JOHNSON, ALLEN W., and EARLE, TIMOTHY. 2000. *The Evolution of Human Societies: From Foraging Group to Agrarian State*, 2nd edn. Stanford, Calif.: Stanford University Press.

JONES, PETER. 1982. *Hume's Sentiments: Their Ciceronian and French Context*. Edinburgh: Edinburgh University Press.

KAFKA, FRANZ. 1967. *Tagebücher 1910–1923*, ed. Max Brod. Frankfurt: S. Fischer.

KANT, IMMANUEL. 1902. *Prolegomena to Any Future Metaphysics*, trans. Paul Carus. La Salle, Ill.: Open Court.

KAVKA, GREGORY. 1986. *Hobbesian Moral and Political Theory*. Princeton: Princeton University Press.

KEMP SMITH, NORMAN. 1941. *The Philosophy of David Hume: A Critical Study of its Origins and Central Doctrines*. London: Macmillan.

KIERNAN, V. G. 1986. *The Duel in European History*. Oxford: Oxford University Press.

KNIGHT, FRANK H. 1956. *On the History and Method of Economics*. Chicago: University of Chicago Press.

LAING, BERTRAM M. 1932. *David Hume*. London: Ernest Benn.

LASLETT, PETER. 1988. 'Introduction.' In John Locke, *Two Treatises of Government*. Cambridge: Cambridge University Press: 3–126.

LEWIS, DAVID K. 1969. *Convention*. Cambridge, Mass.: Harvard University Press.

LIVINGSTON, DONALD W. 1984. *Hume's Philosophy of Common Life*. Chicago: University of Chicago Press.

LOCKE, JOHN. [1689] 1950. *A Letter Concerning Toleration*. Indianapolis: Bobbs-Merrill.

_____ [1690] 1988. *Two Treatises of Government*. Cambridge: Cambridge University Press.

MACKIE, GERALD. 1966. 'Ending Foot-Binding and Infibulation: A Convention Account.' *American Sociological Review* 61 (Dec.): 999–1017.

MACKIE, J. L. 1977. *Inventing Right and Wrong*. Harmondsworth Penguin.

_____ 1980. *Hume's Moral Theory*. London: Routledge & Kegan Paul.

MACPHERSON, C. B. 1968. 'Introduction: Hobbes, Analyst of Power and Peace.' In Thomas Hobbes, *Leviathan*. London: Penguin, 9–63.

MADISON, JAMES. [1788] 2001. *Federalist* numbers 10 and 51. In Alexander Hamilton, John Jay, and James Madison, *The Federalist Papers*, ed. George W. Carey and James McClellan: 42–9 and 267–72. Indianapolis: Liberty Fund.

MANDEVILLE, BERNARD. [1714] 1924. *The Fable of the Bees: Private Vices, Publick Benefits*, ed. F. B. Kaye. Oxford: Oxford University Press; reprinted by Liberty Press, 1988.

MANENT, PIERRE. 1995. 'Aurel Kolnai: A Political Philosopher Confronts the Scourge of Our Epoch.' In Kolnai, *The Utopian Mind and Other Essays*, ed. Francis Dunlop. Atlantic Highlands, NJ: Athlone, pp. xiii–xxvi.

MELTZHOFF, A. N., and PRINZ, W. eds. 2002. *The Imitative Mind*. Cambridge: Cambridge University Press.

MERTON, ROBERT K. [1949] 1968. *Social Theory and Social Structure*, enlarged edn. New York: Free Press

MILL, JOHN STUART. [1848] 1965. *Principles of Political Economy*. 7th edn. In J. M. Robson, ed., *Collected Works of John Stuart Mill*, vols. 2 and 3. Toronto: University of Toronto Press.

―――― [1859] 1977. *On Liberty*. In J. M. Robson (ed.), *Collected Works of John Stuart Mill*, vol. 18. Toronto: University of Toronto Press; 213–310.

―――― [1861] 1977. *Considerations on Representative Government*, in Mill, *Essays on Politics and Society*, vol. 19 of *Collected Works of John Stuart Mill*, ed. J. M. Robson. Toronto: University of Toronto Press: 371–613.

―――― [1861] 1969. *Utilitarianism*. In *Collected Works of John Stuart Mill*, vol. 10, ed. J. M. Robson. Toronto: University of Toronto Press; 203–59.

MILLER, GREG. 2005. 'Reflecting on Another's Mind.' *Science* (13 May): 945–7.

MOORE, G. E. 1903. *Principia Ethica*. Cambridge: Cambridge University Press.

MOORE, JAMES. 1995. 'Hume and Hutcheson.' In M. A. Stewart and John P. Wright, eds., *Hume and Hume's Connexions*. University Park, Penn.: Penn State University Press: 23–57.

MOSS, LAWRENCE S. 1991. 'Thomas Hobbes's Influence on David Hume: The Emergence of a Public Choice Tradition.' *History of Political Economy* 23 (4): 587–612.

MOSSNER, ERNEST CAMPBELL. [1954] 1980. *The Life of David Hume*. Oxford: Oxford University Press, 2nd edition.

NEDELSKY, JENNIFER. 1990. *Private Property and the Limits of American Constitutionalism: The Madisonian Framework and Its Legacy*. Chicago: University of Chicago Press.

NORTON, DAVID FATE. 1982. *David Hume: Common-Sense Moralist, Sceptical Metaphysician*. Princeton: Princeton University Press.

―――― 1993. 'Hume, Human Nature, and the Foundations of Morality.' In David Fate Norton, ed., *The Cambridge Companion to Hume*. Cambridge: Cambridge University Press: 148–81.

NOXON, JAMES. 1975. *Hume's Philosophical Development: A Study of His Methods*. Oxford: Oxford University Press.

NOZICK, ROBERT. 1974. *Anarchy, the State, and Utopia*. New York: Basic Books.

OAKESHOTT, MICHAEL. [1937] 1975. 'Introduction to *Leviathan*.' In Oakeshott, *Hobbes on Civil Association*. Indianapolis: Liberty Fund: 1–79.

OKUN, ARTHUR M. 1975. *Equality and Efficiency: The Big Tradeoff*. Washington: Brookings Institution.

OLSON, MANCUR, Jr. 1965. *The Logic of Collective Action*. Cambridge, Mass.: Harvard University Press.

OSBORNE, DOROTHY. [1653] 1987. 'Letter 24 [Thursday 2–Saturday 4 June 1653],' in *Letters to Sir William Temple*, ed. Kenneth Parker. New York: Penguin: pp. 88–91.

OWEN, DAVID. 1994. 'Reason, Reflection, and *Reductios*.' *Hume Studies* 20(2): 195–210.

―――― 1995. 'Hume's Doubts about Probable Reasoning: Was Locke the Target?' In M. A. Stewart and John P. Wright, eds., *Hume and Hume's Connexions*. University Park, Penn.: Penn State University Press: 140–59.

OWEN, DAVID. 1999. *Hume's Reason*. Oxford: Oxford University Press.

PALEY, WILLIAM. [1785] 2002. *The Principles of Moral and Political Philosophy*. Indianapolis: Liberty Fund.

PARETO, VILFREDO. 1935. *The Mind and Society*, ed. Arthur Livingston. New York: Harcourt, Brace.

—— [1927] 1971. *Manual of Political Economy*. New York: Kelley, trans. from French edition.

PARSONS, TALCOTT. [1937] 1968. *The Structure of Social Action*. New York: Free Press.

PASSMORE, JOHN. [1968] 1980. *Hume's Intentions*, 3rd edn. London: Duckworth.

PENELHUM, TERENCE. 1975. *Hume*. New York: St Martin's.

—— 1993. 'Hume's Moral Psychology.' In David Fate Norton, ed., *The Cambridge Companion to Hume*. Cambridge: Cambridge University Press: 117–47.

PLATO. [4th century BCE] 1974. *The Republic*, trans. G. M. A. Grube. Indianapolis: Hackett.

PRETZ, VERA. 1977. 'Promises and Threats.' *Mind* 86 (Oct.): 578–81.

PRICHARD, H. A. [1912] 1968. 'Does Moral Philosophy Rest on a Mistake?' In Prichard, *Moral Obligation and Duty and Interest*. Oxford: Oxford University Press.

QUTB, SAYYID. 1990. *Milestones*, trans. Ahmad Zaki Hammad. Indianapolis: American Trust Publications.

RAPHAEL, D. D. 1977. ' "The True Old Humean Philosophy" and Adam Smith.' In G. P. Morice, ed., *David Hume: Bicentenary Papers*. Austin, Tex.: University of Texas Press: 23–38.

RAWLS, JOHN. 1955. 'Two Concepts of Rules.' *Philosophical Review* 64 (Apr.): 3–32.

—— 1958. 'Justice as Fairness.' *Philosophical Review* 67 (Apr.): 164–94.

—— [1971] 1999. *A Theory of Justice*, rev. edn. Cambridge, Mass.: Harvard University Press.

—— [1987] 1999. 'The Idea of an Overlapping Consensus.' In *John Rawls: Collected Papers*, ed. Samuel Freeman. Cambridge, Mass.: Harvard University Press.

—— 2000. *Lectures on the History of Moral Philosophy*, ed. Barbara Herman. Cambridge, Mass.: Harvard.

RAZ, JOSEPH. 1986. *The Morality of Freedom*. Oxford: Oxford University Press.

REID, THOMAS. [1764] 1970. *An Inquiry into the Human Mind*, ed. Timothy J. Duggan. Chicago: University of Chicago Press.

—— [1788] 1969. *Essays on the Active Powers of the Human Mind*. Cambridge, Mass.: MIT Press.

ROTWEIN, EUGENE, ed. 1970. *David Hume: Writings on Economics*. Madison: University of Wisconsin Press.

RUSSELL, PAUL. 1985. 'Hume's *Treatise* and Hobbes's *The Elements of Law*.' *Journal of the History of Ideas* (Jan.): 51–63.

SACKS, OLIVER. 1993/1994. 'An Anthropologist on Mars.' *New Yorker* (27 Dec./3 Jan.): 106–25.

SAMUELSON, PAUL. 1974. 'Complementarity: An Essay on the 40th Anniversary of the Hicks-Allen Revolution in Demand Theory.' *Journal of Economic Literature* 12: 1255–89.

SCANLON, THOMAS M. 1999. *What We Owe to Each Other*. Cambridge, Mass.: Harvard University Press.

SCHELLING, THOMAS C. 1960. *The Strategy of Conflict*. Cambridge, Mass.: Harvard University Press.

SCHNEEWIND, J. B. 1983. 'Introduction,' to David Hume, *An Enquiry Concerning the Principles of Morals*. Indianapolis: Hackett: 1–10.

_____ 1990. 'The Misfortunes of Virtue.' *Ethics* 101: 42–63.

SCHULTZ, BRUNO. 1977. *The Street of Crocodiles*, trans. Celina Wieniewska. New York: Penguin Books.

SCHWARTZ, BARRY. 1986. *The Battle for Human Nature*. New York: Norton.

SCITOVSKY, TIBOR. 1952. *Welfare and Competition*. London: George Allen & Unwin.

SCOTT, WALTER. 1831. *Count Robert of Paris*. Edinburgh.

SEARLE, JOHN R. 1964. 'How to Derive "Ought" from "Is."' *Philosophical Review* 73 (1): 43–58.

SHAFTESBURY, (Third) Earl of (Anthony Ashley Cooper). [1711] 2001. *Characteristics of Men, Manners, Opinions, Times*, 3 vols., ed. J. M. Robertson. Indianapolis: Liberty Fund.

SIDGWICK, HENRY. 1907. *The Methods of Ethics*. London: Macmillan, seventh edition.

SKINNER, ANDREW S. 1993. 'David Hume: Principles of Political Economy.' In David Fate Norton, ed., *The Cambridge Companion to Hume*. Cambridge: Cambridge University Press: 222–54.

SMITH, ADAM. [1776] 1976. *An Inquiry into the Nature and Causes of the Wealth of Nations*. Oxford: Oxford University Press; Indianapolis: Liberty Classics, 1981, reprint.

STEWART, DUGALD. [1855] 1968. *Lectures on Political Economy*. New York: Augustus M. Kelley, reprint of original edition, in 2 volumes.

_____ 1877. *Collected Works*, ed. William Hamilton, vol. 1. Edinburgh. T. T. Clark.

STEWART, M. A. 1995. 'Hume's Historical View of Miracles.' In M. A. Stewart and John P. Wright, eds., *Hume and Hume's Connexions*. University Park, Penn.: Penn State University Press: 171–200.

_____ and Wright, John P., eds. 1995. *Hume and Hume's Connexions*. University Park, Penn.: Penn State University Press.

STINCHCOMBE, ARTHUR L. 1968. *Constructing Social Theories*. New York: Harcourt, Brace & World.

STROUD, BARRY. 1977. *Hume*. London: Routledge & Kegan Paul.

STURGEON, NICHOLAS L. 2001. 'Moral Skepticism and Moral Naturalism in Hume's *Treatise*.' *Hume Studies* 27 (1): 3–83.

STURN, RICHARD. 2004. 'The Sceptic as an Economist's Philosopher? Humean Utility as a Positive Principle.' *European Journal of Economic Thought* 11 (Autumn): 345–75.

SUPPES, PATRICK. 2003. 'Rationality, Habits and Freedom.' In N. Dimitri, M. Basili, and I. Gilboa, eds., *Cognitive Processes and Economic Behavior*. New York: Routledge: 137–67.

TAYLOR, A. J. P. 1965. *English History 1914–1945*. Oxford: Oxford University Press.

TOCQUEVILLE, ALEXIS DE. [1835] 1968.'Memoir on Pauperism.' In Seymour Drescher, *Tocqueville and Beaumont on Social Reform*. New York: Harper: 1–2.

TOLSTOY, LEO. [1899] 1966. *Resurrection*, trans. Rosemary Edmonds. London: Penguin.

—— 2001. 'How Much Land Does a Man Need?' In Tolstoy, *Collected Shorter Fiction*, vol. 2, trans. Louise and Aylmer Maude and Nigel J. Cooper. London: Everyman: 191–207.

TOWNSEND, JOSEPH. [1786] 1971. *A Dissertation on the Poor Laws, By a Well-Wisher to Mankind*. Berkeley, Calif.: University of California Press.

TREFUSIS, VIOLET. [1935] 1985. *Broderie Anglaise*. New York: Harcourt Brace Jovanovich.

TUFTE, EDWARD. 2001. *The Visual Display of Quantitative Information*. Cheshire, Conn.: Graphics Press, 2nd edition.

URMSON, J. O. 1953. 'The Interpretation of the Moral Philosophy of J. S. Mill.' *Philosophical Quarterly* 3: 33–9.

VENNING, COREY. 1976. 'Hume on Property, Commerce, and Empire in the Good Society: The Role of Historical Necessity.' *Journal of the History of Ideas* 37 (1): 79–92.

WARNOCK, G. J. 1971. *The Object of Morality*. London: Methuen.

WEINGAST, BARRY R. 1997. 'The Political Foundations of Democracy and the Rule of Law.' *American Political Science Review* 91 (2): 245–63.

—— 1997. 'The Political Foundations of Limited Government: Parliament and Sovereign Debt in 17th and 18th Century England.' In John V. C. Nye and John N. Drobak, eds., *Frontiers of the New Institutional Economics*. New York: Academic Press.

WIKAN, UNNI. 1994. 'Deadly Distrust: Honor Killings and Swedish Multiculturalism.' In Russell Hardin, ed., *Distrust*. New York: Russell Sage Foundation: 192–204.

WINSTANLEY, GERRARD. [1652] 1973. *The Law of Freedom in a Platform or, True Magistracy Restored*, ed. Robert W. Kenny. New York: Schocken Books.

WOLIN, SHELDON S. 1954. 'Hume and Conservatism.' *American Political Science Review* 48: 999–1016.

WOOLF, VIRGINIA. [1929] 1945. *A Room of One's Own*. New York: Harcourt Brace & Jovanovich.

WRONG, DENNIS. 1994. *The Problem of Order: What Unites and Divides Society*. New York: Free Press.

XENOPHON. [4th century BCE] 2001. *Education of Cyrus*. Ithaca, NY: Cornell University Press, trans. Wayne Ambler.

YEGHIAYAN, EDDIE. 1981. 'Promises: A Bibliography.' *Philosophy Research Archives* 7: 1055–1092.

Index

and prosperity, 151
as beneficial and not merely desirable in its
  own right, 185
as deontological matter, 185
as enhancing creativity, 185
as essentially utilitarian for Hume, 185
as multilevel principle, 130
defense of, for causal, not conceptual or
  moral reasons, 185
economic, 187
for mutual advantage, 185
Hume on value of, 169
political, as product of economic
  decentralization, 199
protected by property, 147
Livingston, Donald, on Hume's supposed
  conservatism, 25
Locke,
and contractarian justification of political
  obligation, 210
as confused man's Hobbes, 210
as deducing ought from is, 210
as influence in Hume's epistemology, 198
as Hume's antagonist in political
  philosophy, 198
as proponent of bourgeois state, 210
as Whig philosopher, 212
contractarianism of, 211
Hume contra labor-theory of property
  of, 211
Hume's criticism of views of, seen as
  criticism of Whigs, 212
Hume's rejection of social science of,
  mistakenly taken as support for Tory
  policies, 210
John (1632–1704), in British tradition, 2
labor theory of property of, 210–12
on contracting transfer of power to
  government, 217
on natural law of property, 145
on politics of interest, 153
on property as prior to government, 219
on taxation without consent, 96
on treaty abrogation, 131
political theory of, rejected by Hume, 210
*An Essay Concerning Human
Understanding*, 2
Locke's political theory, as misfit with those
  of Hobbes and Hume, 6
Lockean libertarians, 61n, 138
v. Hobbes on property, 61n
logic of collective action, Plato's Glaucon
  on, 79

logic of collective action, Olson's, 79, 121
logical positivism, 29
logical positivists, Hume as forerunner of,
  12
Louisiana, Napoleonic Code in, 144

Machiavelli, Nicolo, on property, 147
Mackie, J.L.,
  contra Hume's dictum, 10
  on Hume's account of property, 144–5
  on Hume's rejection of egalitarianism, 69
  on inventing right and wrong, 28
  on redistribution, 70
  on treaties and promises, 130
  on two men rowing a boat, 79
Macpherson, C. B., on Locke, 210
Madison, James,
  on ambition to counter ambition, 116
  on factions, 117, 151
  on politics of interest, 153
  on weak government, 101
  welfarist defense of rights of, 191
Magna Carta of 1215, 147
maintenance vs. origins of government, 87
Mandeville, Bernard,
  and individualist economic theory, 175
  on artificial virtue, 145
  on public benefits of greed, 22
  praised by Hume, 21
  value theory of, 176
  wrecker of traditional virtue theory, 21
Manent, Pierre, contra keeping value
  judgments out of social science, 2
manifest and latent functions, 50
marginalism, in value theory, 178
market leaders, in altering convention, 94
marriage, 54
maximin, defined, 161
maximin, Rawls's, 161
merchants, Aristotle's hostility to, 150
merchants, usefulness of, 150
Merton, Robert,
  Hume as forerunner to, 231
  on manifest and latent functions, 50
Mill, J.S.,
  in British tradition, 2
  as libertarian, 118
  and libertarian focus on autonomy, 185
  and utilitarianism, 156
  as not deontologist, 166
  as taking social order for granted, 210
  on destitute criticisms of utilitarianism, 73,
    162